D0569331

Children Taken Seriously

Children in Charge
Editor: Mary John

This series concentrates on the theme of children's rights, reflecting the increasing knowledge in the area. The perspectives of empowerment and of 'voice' run through the series and the United Nations' Convention on the Rights of the Child is used as a benchmark. The editor, Mary John, is a developmental psychologist and Professor Emeritus at the University of Exeter. She has worked in the field of disability rehabilitation and independent living and has researched with minority rights groups.

Children's Rights and Power
Charging Up for a New Century
Mary John
ISBN 1 85302 659 X pb
ISBN 1 85302 658 1 hb
Children in Charge 9

Children's Rights in Education
*Edited by Stuart Hart, Cynthia Price Cohen, Martha Farrell Erickson
and Målfrid Flekkøy*
ISBN 1 85302 977 7
Children in Charge 11

Young Children's Rights
Exploring Beliefs, Principles and Practice
Priscilla Alderson
Forewords by Save the Children and Mary John
ISBN 1 85302 880 0
Children in Charge 10

Traveller Children
A Voice for Themselves
Cathy Kiddle
ISBN 1 85302 684 0
Children in Charge 8

Children as Citizens
Education for Participation
Edited by Cathie Holden and Nick Clough
ISBN 1 85302 566 6
Children in Charge 5

A Charge Against Society
The Child's Right to Protection
Edited by Mary John
ISBN 1 85302 411 2
Children in Charge 3

Children in Charge 12

Children Taken Seriously
In Theory, Policy and Practice

Edited by
Jan Mason and Toby Fattore

Foreword by Mary John

Jessica Kingsley Publishers
London and Philadelphia

First published in 2005
by Jessica Kingsley Publishers Ltd
116 Pentonville Road
London N1 9JB, UK
and
400 Market Street, Suite 400
Philadelphia, PA 19106, USA
www.jkp.com

Copyright © Jessica Kingsley Publishers 2005
Foreword copyright © Mary John 2005

Library of Congress Cataloging in Publication Data

Children taken seriously : in theory, policy and practice / edited by Jan Mason and Toby Fattore.
        p. cm. -- (Children in charge ; 12)
Includes bibliographical references and index.
Revised versions of papers originally presented at a national workshop held in 1999 in Sydney, Australia.
        ISBN 1-84310-250-1 (pbk.)
        1. Children's rights--Australia--Congresses. 2. Children--Australia--Congresses. 3. Child welfare--Australia--Congresses. 4. Children and adults--Australia--Congresses. I. Mason, Jan. II. Fattore, Toby. III. Children in charge series ; 12.
        HQ792.A85C49 2005
        305.23'0994--dc22

                                                                2004022161

British Library Cataloguing in Publication Data

A CIP catalogue record for this book is available from the British Library

ISBN-13: 978 1 84310 250 2
ISBN-10: 1 84310 250 1

Printed and Bound in Great Britain by
Athenaeum Press, Gateshead, Tyne and Wear

This book is dedicated to Marie Wilkinson, whose academic career tragically ended with her death in 2003. Marie's contribution to 'children being taken seriously' is evident to some extent in this book. First, in the chapter authored by her, but additionally and importantly in the fact that this book exists. Marie was a founding and most active member of the University of Western Sydney's Childhood and Youth Policy Research Unit (CYPRU), which hosted the workshop of which this book is ultimately a product. She also co-edited the proceedings from the workshop on which this book is based. Her death was a very sad loss for those of us in Australia who are concerned about taking children seriously and about making changes in the way children's welfare is promoted.

Acknowledgements

This book had its genesis in a national workshop for which the University of Western Sydney provided valuable financial assistance. Financial support was also provided for the workshop by New South Wales Department of Community Services and by Campbelltown City Council. The workshop proceedings were published in a University of Western Sydney publication *Taking Children Seriously, Proceedings of a National Workshop* (Mason and Wilkinson 1999). A number of persons were identified in that publication for their contributions to its production and the organization of the workshop. These were Hilary Weatherburn, Bronwyn Steadman, Christine Baxter and Shalmalee Palekar. Toni Downes and Jan Falloon, as members of the editorial committee with Marie Wilkinson and Jan Mason, provided help with the initial publication. Here, as editors of this book, we repeat our acknowledgement of the value of the work of this team of people, and in particular highlight the work of Marie Wilkinson, the co-editor of the earlier publication. Their work made our role in preparing the current book a much easier one than would otherwise have been the case.

In editing this book, we have been lucky as editors to have had the assistance of Samia Michail, whose considerable expertise in a multiplicity of editorial tasks has been invaluable. The quality and commitment with which she carried out these tasks has been much appreciated. We have also appreciated Jason White's willingness to apply his computer skills to problems we met along the way.

We are grateful to all the contributors to this book for their work in updating and considerably revising their contributions. Special thanks are due to Marie Wilkinson's partner Tom Kelly for his help in making Marie's chapter available for this book and to her friend Jan Larbelestier for assistance with editing this chapter.

Finally, a sincere thank you to George for his support, emotionally and domestically, to Jan during a time when the colliding of a number of deadlines meant that life and completion of the production of this book, without this support, would have been much more difficult. Also to Sonia, Emilie and Linden, whose patience and care made it possible for Toby to work on this book.

Contents

Part 2 Policy

Part 3 Practice

Foreword

Children Taken Seriously signifies the coming of age of a movement to recognize young people's realities in new partnerships. This volume is therefore particularly timely and welcome in the *Children in Charge* series. The most challenging aspect of the realization of the United Nations Convention on the Rights of the Child for governments, policy makers, researchers and practitioners alike, has been how to honour and facilitate participation by children. The work reported in this book subtly charts, from many perspectives and angles, the way in which thinking with children about their lives has developed in different epistemologies, disciplines, research practices, and policy developments. Looking at the theoretical underpinnings of thinking about the human rights of this group to be acknowledged as having rights, usefully locates developments in a historical cross-cultural trajectory.

The early volumes in this series were concerned with the exploration of 'voicing' in a variety of contexts. We cumulatively examined how to liberate our adult senses in order to hear and respond to children's realities, recognizing that young people's self-defined aspirations and priorities are very different from the needs defined for them by adults. Resonances were identified with the oppression of other minority rights groups in the struggle against the power implicit in imposing a particular version of the world. The early days of the *Children in Charge* series included inspirational examples of Australian work. In Volume 3 (Cousens and Stevens 1997) a paediatric oncology unit explored the rights of a dying child to decide to cease treatment. Creative work was being undertaken with often very young children to establish *their* understanding of what was happening. In that same volume, Judy Cashmore took the reader through the ways in which policies and provision for children could themselves be a source of oppression and abuse, drawing on earlier work with the Systems Abuse Inquiry commissioned in Australia by the New South Wales Child Protection Council (Cashmore 1997). That fearless interrogation of systems of provision drew me to Australia on the final

11

trawl for data for the analysis of children and power (Volume 9, John 2003). The Childhood and Youth Policy Research Unit at the University of Western Sydney has over many years addressed the ways in which child-sensitive policies can be developed, and how practice can be imaginative and responsive in honouring children's views of the world they inhabit. This unit has recently been incorporated into the Social Justice and Social Change Research Centre.

Research and practice that brings about social change lies at the heart of the *Children in Charge* series. The 1992 World Conference on "Research and Practice in Children's Rights: A matter of Empowerment?" that gave birth to the series raised the question as to whether the United Nations Convention on the Rights of the Child had in any way empowered children themselves.

Throughout this series there has been an attempt to present the ways in which research, professional practice and engagement in various contexts throughout the world have moved on to new ways of working together with children. Working in such partnerships can be fraught. The challenge is to take account of theory, policy frameworks, financial constraints and accountability while still remaining true to the young people themselves. Evidence of new and brave ways of striking that balance is provided in this new collection, *Children Taken Seriously*.

This volume is not simply a portfolio of Australian work. The international contributors share common concerns about central issues. It is refreshing, nevertheless, to have perspectives here on power sharing drawn together by thinkers located in a culture which has had to face up resolutely to the responsibilities of its own history and development as a nation, with all the accompanying complexities, contradictions and dashed hopes. The film 'Rabbit Proof Fence' powerfully portrayed the plight for Aboriginal children under early policy interventions. This struggle over indigenous rights goes on. Who among us who were there in 1998 can forget the sight of Bondi Beach planted with the Sea of Hands organized by Australians for Native Title and Reconciliation? These visual vignettes encode two issues crucial to the series and the chapters here: whose realities count in exclusion, inclusion, or token participation; and more subtly, the issue of consent. The reader is challenged to think further about whether it is possible to develop a form of democracy based on intersubjectivities understood and negotiated between adult and child, researcher and researched. Sadly, the thrilling moments of insight arising from consciousness raising are countered or followed by blundering indifference and worse. How seriously are children and young people's views ever taken and do they really serve those children's best interests or are there other sinister motivations?

As I write, children en masse have indeed been taken very seriously at the fulcrum of power as potent 'ammunition' in political bargaining for Chechen independence resulting in the Beslan school massacre. The slaughter of these children in cold blood and on an unprecedented scale shocked a world which, it seems, has become increasingly inured to terrorist outrage, by breaking one of the last taboos – children's right to protection from adults. This formed a titillating part of the 'pornography of war' added to which, some analyses claim, are the voyeuristic thrills of watching the drama unfold from the safety of our own living room in what has been dubbed the age of 'Reality Terrorvision'.

Using children in this way repositions them in new constructions of their power and powerlessness. Throughout the series such constructions have been analysed in terms of their roots in theories and the history of other minority rights groups where the climate of the times has been crucial. Social structures are not the only way to challenge the usefulness of theoretical analyses and throw into question prevailing myths. The analysis of trauma, for example, in child warriors on the front line of various battlefields around the world, has caused us to re-examine the inherent vulnerability and dependence of children. Again, the issue of consent, social pressures in extreme circumstances and assumptions about children's realities are all prefigured here and further developed within this volume.

I noted in Volume 9 of the series (John 2003) the claims that at the beginning of the twenty-first century there should be a re-engagement with the promise of qualitative research as a form of radical democratic practice. In enabling such democracies between children and adults, Jan Mason, Toby Fattore and their colleagues have a shared vision, commitment, and determination to practise what they preach. The recent report of a project undertaken by researchers of the Social Justice and Social Change Research Centre and their partners at UnitingCare Burnside on the *Needs of Children in Care* (Mason and Gibson 2004) provides proof that it can be done and that practice, guided by experienced practitioners, can go a long way towards making perfect.

Mary John,
Professor Emeritus, University of Exeter

Working Seriously Towards New Partnerships

An Introduction

Toby Fattore and Jan Mason with Chris Sidoti

> Good research, improved knowledge and understanding are essential if children are to be taken seriously within our community. But, I must say that just as important as good research and good knowledge, equally essential, is communicating that knowledge and understanding to the general community, including political leaders. (Sidoti 1999, p.7)

This book is an attempt to broadly communicate knowledge about children and childhood. The following introduction is divided into three sections. The first section provides a general context for the book, the second section a specific context (the legal framework for children being 'taken seriously') and the third section describes the themes that emerge as dominant in the book. The contributors to this book, who are academics, policy makers and practitioners based for the most part in Australia, have a common interest in applying in their work and contributing to developments in 'the new sociology of childhood' or the 'new childhood studies'. They are concerned with the relevance and applications of research that positions children centrally, as social actors, in theory, policy and practice relating to children.

The context: Theory, policy and practice

The organization of the book is designed within a framework that recognizes the emphasis placed by the contributors in their chapters on theory, policy or practice. That this has been no easy task highlights the extent to which if children are indeed taken seriously, the compartmentalization of knowledge that has characterized the positivist, developmental approach to childhood is undermined. The approach to knowledge taken by those working within the new childhood studies paradigm, challenges both disciplinary and theory–practice boundaries. This collection, therefore, also reflects how the new childhood studies have become an organizing approach that has influenced a range of disciplinary areas. This is illustrated in the diversity of topics covered in this book.

Further, through the range of ways in which childhood and children are studied, this collection challenges the idea that there are 'traditional' areas in which the study of children should be circumscribed. For example, in this book some chapters study childhood within specific systems; in others, children are studied negotiating across systems, while in still others, the focus is on the role and impact of the ways in which specific systems construct childhood. Beyond this, some chapters consider childhood more broadly, outside and across specific systems. This broad focus is also achieved in the book as a whole, as a consequence of taking the chapters cumulatively.

In particular, the contributions to the book are valuable in that they illustrate the importance of moving between children's experiences and adult analyses of broader social structures, processes and ideologies of childhood and society. They also illustrate the importance of taking into account learnings gained from observations of children grounded in the new paradigm.

The contributions in the policy section utilize particular theoretical orientations to inform on how policy should be constructed for, and with, children. At the practice level, theory contributes both to ways in which practitioners can effectively relate with children at the point of service delivery and to how practice is entrenched within a particular context or understanding of childhood – a context that either reinforces certain constructions of children or challenges them. The theoretical papers take into account the nexus between theory and practice. This is the case where theory is used as critique to illuminate the way in which existing policy and practice constructs children, and where theory is used in a reconstructive way, outlining how policy and practice can be renewed to be child-oriented. In both cases theory is grounded, driven by experience and practice. These ideas, of course, are not new, but are important in that, as embedded in the contributions in this book, they illustrate that learning and doing are an integrated process. When taken as a whole, the book reminds us of the necessity of thinking from children's experience and including children's knowledge.

In the following section, Chris Sidoti, former Human Rights Commissioner in Australia, contributes the legal framework for children being 'taken seriously' in the various chapters in this book.

The law and taking children seriously *by Chris Sidoti*

Changing legal perceptions of children

The law has changed a great deal over the past two centuries in the ways in which childhood is conceptualized and the ways in which the role of children within a community is seen. Only two centuries ago, the law – at least the English Common Law that we in Australia inherited – did not recognize children as separate legal persons. Rather, children were seen simply as the property of their fathers. In this, their status was somewhat similar to the status of a married woman, who was regarded as the property of her husband. There was very little, if any, legal recognition of individual status, of autonomous legal rights vested in children themselves. Children could not sue or be sued in their own name. There was no legal interference in the rights of a father over a child, except in the case of the most serious criminal offences, such as murder. The position of the state and the position of the law started to change during the course of the nineteenth century. This reflected changes in the approach of the broader community to the needs and welfare of children. Children were seen as having welfare needs. They were obvious in their poverty on the streets of England's major cities. They were exploited in mines and factories. The campaign for children's protection became associated with an acknowledgment of the role of the state as *parens patriae*, parent of the nation. As the ultimate parent the state assumed responsibility first for orphans and foundlings and then started to take on increasing responsibility in relation to juvenile offenders and the neglect and abuse of children.

The nineteenth-century legal approach towards children, which arose from the role of the state as *parens patriae*, placed its emphasis on the conceptualization of children as humans in the making: junior adults who required protection. Elements of that approach are still very much evident in the law today. Child-protection laws are the most obvious example. But during the past fifty years the law has also started to recognize the child as distinct from father or parent in many areas of life. So the law has come to accord rights to children that did not exist previously, including the right to leave home and to establish his or her own form of housing, rights to health and medical care, to employment and to enter into certain forms of contract. Because two centuries ago children had no legal personality, they could not enter contracts even for the necessities of life. Now we accord at least that degree of contracting capacity to children.

The law today then reflects a tension between two different approaches to the nature of childhood and the responsibilities and rights of children. The protective approach deriving very much from the nineteenth century persists. Right alongside it is a rights-based approach that recognizes the child as a separate legal actor. In stating that, however, I should emphasize that I am not saying that the law recognizes the child as autonomous. Indeed, particularly so far as human rights law is concerned, I do not see any room for any human beings being established as fully autonomous persons. Rather, human-rights law always locates the individual within the community in which he or she lives, moves and has his or her being. In the rights-based approach to children, therefore, the recognition of a child as a separate legal actor is not the same as recognition of the child in law as autonomous.

The Convention on the Rights of the Child

This movement towards a rights-based approach to childhood and children has taken on new meaning and has acquired new strength through the Convention on the Rights of the Child. This important human-rights treaty was adopted within a legal environment that is seeking to identify children as separate from their parents and as more than just in need of protection from the state.

The development of the Convention on the Rights of the Child was a very long and tortuous process. The proposal was first put forward in 1979 during the International Year of the Child but it was a full ten years before the international community could agree what the contents of the Convention should be. There was a great deal of debate among representatives from nations with very different legal, political, economic, social, religious and cultural traditions that make up the international community today. The fact that the international community was able to agree upon a Convention on the Rights of the Child, setting out a common understanding of the nature of children and childhood, is an achievement in itself.

That Convention now stands as a definitive statement of a universal understanding of the rights of children and of what children are entitled to expect from the rest of the community. It recognizes, of course, children's rights to care and protection. The protective approach to childhood therefore remains a key part of law. There are express provisions in the Convention dealing with the abuse and neglect of children and the entitlement of children to be protected by their parents and families and by the state from both. Perhaps this protective approach is best expressed in one of the two fundamental principles in the Convention found in Article 3. It says,

> In all actions concerning children, whether undertaken by public or private social welfare institutions, courts of law, administrative authorities or legislative bodies, the best interests of the child shall be a primary consideration.

The Convention, however, also expresses a broader human-rights approach to participation of children as legal persons. This was already present in other human-rights law but here was applied for the first time specifically for the benefit of children. So children are recognized as having civil and political rights, including rights to speech, to movement, to assembly, to religion and belief. They are recognized as having economic, social and cultural rights, including rights to education, to health-care, to cultural identity and language, to housing and to social security. This area of the Convention's activity is also expressed in a fundamental principle contained within Article 12:

> State parties [that is, those governments and nations that have ratified the Convention] shall assure to the child who is capable of forming his or her own views the right to express those views freely in all matters affecting the child, the views of the child being given due weight in accordance with the age and maturity of the child.

The Convention on the Rights of the Child also recognizes and supports the role of parents, in its words,

> to provide, in a manner consistent with the evolving capacities of the child, appropriate direction and guidance in the exercise by the child of the rights recognized in the present Convention. (Article 5)

Many have presented the Convention as setting up conflict between children and parents, between children and teachers and between children and community. Yet, in fact, the Convention tries to strike a delicate balance between, on the one hand, the evolving capacity of the child to exercise his or her rights on his or her own account and, on the other, the guidance to be provided by parents and the ultimate protection to be provided by the community or the government. In this way the Convention seeks to recognize the interests of all those involved in the care and development of children. But it places the individual child in his or her community as the central point, the focus of legal and political activity so far as children are concerned.

In May 2002 a Special Session of the United Nations General Assembly on Children took a further step in promoting children's rights. It not only placed children centrally, but also allowed the voices of children to be presented *by* children. The Special Session for the first time included children as official delegates. Four hundred and four children between the ages of 7 and 18, from around the world, were given a three-day global platform to address decision makers. This special session culminated in the official adoption, by around 180 nations, of its outcome document, *A World Fit for Children* (UNICEF 2004). The document is significant in that it reaffirms the obligations of world leaders to promote and protect the rights of each child and accepts the legal benchmarks that were put in place by the Convention on the Rights of the Child (UNICEF 2002). The Special Session was significant in that while the Convention sought to make children the centre of their communities, the Special Session asked adults to change existing adult–child relationships and recognize children's abilities and rights to be active in their communities.

Taking children seriously

The Convention then, to summarize, persists in recognizing the protective approach to children but also requires that children be accepted as participants in their own right. That obligation extends to participation in every area of activity that concerns them, whether it is the legal system, social welfare organization, education or health-care or other forms of institution or politics. The Convention requires that children, their views, their wishes and their needs are heard and taken into account. This means they must be included as participants, not just consumers. The Special Session was an important example of progress in applying this participatory approach to children. It was an historic event that began to take children seriously.

This approach means that in legal processes, for example, a court should not simply decide what is in a child's best interests. Rather, it should acknowledge the child's right to express his or her own views and to have those views taken into account. Yet so often children are silent in courts, or rather are treated simply as the victims from whom information is to be extracted with the maximum degree of pain.

Children are also entitled to be participants, not just consumers, in education. Yet so often they have no real role to play in educational decisions concerning them and their lives. That is particularly so in disciplinary procedures within schools, where the children who are to be disciplined are often not even asked for their views on the nature of the offence, or the nature of the punishment to be imposed. Particularly at the most serious end of the disciplining spectrum – long-term suspension or even expulsion – children are entitled to be full participants in the process, with all the requirements of natural justice applying to them as much as to anybody else who is subject to a disciplinary system.

And, indeed, children are entitled to be participants, not just consumers, in politics, even though they are not yet entitled to vote. Voting is only one form of public participation in the political life of the community. Children are entitled to have their views heard in all the other ways in which our political system works.

Most fundamentally, recognizing the entitlements of children as participants means seeing them as important now and not just in the future: for who they are and not only for who they might be. There is far too much talk in our community about children as 'the future' or 'our future' or 'Australia's future' or 'the world's future'. It is also true that this is little more than a cliché now. The more important issue for me is that children are entitled to be taken seriously *now*. They are entitled to be seen and to be responded to as important players now, in their own right as children and not just as prospective adults.

The book: *Children Taken Seriously*

Children taken seriously as participants

The common thread running through the chapters in this book is that emphasized by Chris Sidoti: taking children seriously as 'participants', in the present. This has a number of dimensions, evident in the various chapters. Pertinent, however, to the more specific themes that emerge in the book is the definition of participation by Roche (1999). He states that participation is 'about being counted as a member of the community, it is about governing and being governed' (p.484). When this definition is taken in conjunction with the emphasis in many of the chapters – on critiquing the traditional, developmental construction of childhood – it provides a foundation for the specific themes that track through this book. These themes have to do with the importance of children being counted and included, so that they are not just governed by adults in terms of re-producing their society in the future, but are also contributing to governing in the present. The themes also have to do with the obstacles to, and strategies for, progressing the goal of children being taken seriously.

Including children

The issue of visibility of children is a focus of most of the chapters in this book. It is articulated particularly strongly in some of the chapters in the theory and policy sections. In her chapter, Leena Alanen highlights the way in which, prior to the 1980s, sociological research had rendered children invisible, even when the issue being studied was an aspect of children's lives. Her chapter is important in the way it articulates the theoretical developments contributing to, and necessary for, ensuring the visibility and inclusion of children. It does so by 'reaching beyond the liberal and humanist attitude of respecting children's voice and vision' and taking them seriously 'as competent actors and knowers' and, indeed, 'as partners'.

While Alanen's focus is on sociology's role in the invisibilization/visibility of children, Berry Mayall's chapter (on the status of children in the United Kingdom) draws attention to how psychological knowledge has contributed to children's invisibility, except where they come into attention as victims or threats. Berry Mayall and Jan Mason both point to the way in which social policy has rendered children invisible by only recognizing them within family relations as dependents, not as individuals with rights. Mayall discusses how the move to residual models of social welfare has shifted financial and social responsibility for children away from the state and onto parents.

Even where attention is directed at children as victims or threats (as in the focus of the child-welfare system) children may, as Marie Wilkinson demonstrates in her chapter, still remain invisible – a 'virtual reality' only, as clients of the child-welfare system. She illustrates how the strength of mythologies about children's needs and interests have ensured the continued 'virtualization' of children over time, in spite of information challenging these myths.

In her chapter, Natalie Bolzan demonstrates the importance of children's visibility in countering mythologies about them as villains and victims. Bolzan explores what impact discourses of young people presented in the media have on the everyday social practices and perceptions of young people by adults. She highlights that adult attitudes to children differ according to whether or not they have had contact with young people. Her research indicates that those adults who have had contact with young people construct them more positively than those who have not had such contact. In promoting a positive attitude to young people, the discourse of adults with personal knowledge of children provides a challenge to the dominance of the negative construction of young people as problematic, conveyed by the media and reflected in part by the broader community. Bolzan also points out that young people are generally excluded from the mechanisms of discourse production. As such, they have only limited means to create their own discourse in the public sphere.

Children as 'becomings' vulnerable to abuse

The construction of children as 'becomings' (in contrast with adults as 'beings') has been argued as being central to the developmental paradigm's construction of children as lesser than adults. The way in which the construction of children as 'becoming' reinforces children's vulnerability to abuse is discussed in several chapters. In their chapter, Saunders and Goddard identify the way the subordination of children to adults as 'becomings' makes possible the trivialization of violence against children. They point out that this is reproduced and reinforced by public media that create a discourse of childhood that undermines children's right to physical integrity. Acceptance of this violence, as defined by euphemisms such as 'physical discipline', justifies treatment of children in a way that would be condemned if it were directed at adults.

Jan Mason, in her historical analysis of child-protection policy, illustrates how treating children as 'becomings' and dependent has contributed to their objectification, including denying them as 'knowers'. A consequence has frequently been their continued vulnerability to further abuse within the very system designed to protect them. The chapters by Mason and by Saunders and

Goddard, in which children's voices are included, make clear children's sense of marginalization by adults.

In her chapter, Kerry Robinson points out how the 'othering' of children by adults denies sexuality as an integral part of children's identities, except where children are part of adult contexts that deviate from the heterosexual norm. Of particular salience is the construction of childhood (in contrast with adulthood) as a period of 'innocence' – a construction strong amongst those childhood educators who participated in her research. Robinson describes the way this construction, and the associated adult strategy of denying children the language and knowledge of sexuality issues, contributes to children's increased vulnerability to sexual abuse.

Children and competence

Fundamental to children being taken seriously is acknowledging their competence as social agents. Mayall concludes from her research outlined in her chapter that 'children are indeed social actors…social agents, in the sense of making a difference'. They are, within the constraints of child–adult relations, participants in constructing their childhoods and lives with orientations to both the present and future. This conclusion is supported by research described in the chapter by Toni Downes. In this research, children were positioned as 'key informants of their experiences with computers in their daily lives'. The research demonstrated that children in their daily interactions with computers are actors who construct both childhood and computing within the context of a social environment influenced by dominant discourses around these concepts.

The importance of social environments as contexts for children's competence is emphasized by Hutchby and Moran Ellis (1998b) in their book on that topic. They note that children's social competence 'is bounded by structural features of the milieux in which children live their lives' (p.1). Several chapters in our book also illustrate how particular versions of competence are produced and reproduced by institutional and interpersonal arrangements that establish a framework within which children can deploy their competence or, alternatively, not have their specific competencies recognized.

In particular, the significance of schools as a milieu for children being taken seriously is attested to by the number of chapters in this book that concern children within school and preschool settings. Schools play an important role in the construction of children's competence and as contexts in which their competencies are enacted. Structurally, it can be argued that schools have been part of a process in Western industrialized countries for reinforcing adult–child relations, locating children at the bottom of the knowledge hierarchy. This thereby excludes them from adult forums, on the basis of their knowledge deficits or lack of competence.

Structural inequalities in the classroom are central to Donna Berthelsen's findings. She describes how in the early-childhood classrooms where she undertook her research, 'the teacher remains at the centre, the single individual in every classroom whose beliefs, decisions and outlook count most in giving shape to what happens in that environment'. Berthelsen highlighted the way in which teachers' failure to take into account their use of authority to instil values of responsibility and attentiveness in children, within a milieu in which there was a diversity in children's experiences, acted as a barrier to children's participation. This failure was highlighted by a context in which teachers espoused child-centred, constructivist ideology, which allows for negotiation between children and teachers in the construction of personal moralities. Berthelsen raises important issues about the connections between children's relational morality and the organizational morality of schooling, and how schooling can be made more democratic by giving greater recognition to children's relational morality – especially given the role that education plays in meeting community expectations for moral education.

The authority of teachers is a powerful factor in defining inequalities between teachers and students in Neriman Osman's chapter. She reports on her study of children's experiences in a Sydney primary school. The children described unjust and devaluing behaviour by teachers and indicated that a lack of opportunities for them to assert control and negotiate with teachers was central to their feelings of powerlessness. As in Berthelsen's study, the failure of teachers to take children seriously had the effect of circumscribing their agency and competence.

Roger Holdsworth discusses the alienation of young people in schools, where the focus is on preparing them for competency in the future. He describes the way this approach devalues young people by not taking seriously their knowledge and competencies in the present. Holdsworth's chapter focuses on ways in which children and young people in schools can be taken seriously. He points out the importance in taking children seriously, of children in schools having serious things to do and of productive outcomes in the present. This may mean going beyond a focus on young people 'speaking out' to acknowledging them as actors, by giving them serious and important things to do – things that draw on their competencies in the present and enable them to be involved in governance within their community.

Significant in this context is Per Miljeteig's chapter, where he describes how attempts to locate working children in schools by excluding them from work are challenged by these children. By organizing themselves collectively and engaging in serious dialogue with each other and with adults, these working children have been able to assert their needs in the contested debates on child labour about alleviating their experiences of poverty and improving their working conditions in the present. Miljeteig underlines their competence and agency in governance, as partners with adults at the local, regional and international levels and in influencing legislative and organizational changes towards children's well-being. In doing so, Miljeteig asks 'whether we are willing to revise (or even change) our understandings of democracy' and extend children's citizenship rights.

By positioning children as informants (although within very different methodologies), Downes' and Danby's chapters both provide additional challenges to adult constructions of children's activities. In Downes' research, children emphasized their use of computers as being for work (as well as for the future). This contrasted with adults' emphasis on children's use of computers as tools in learning for the future.

In identifying the ways in which three preschool-aged girls organized their everyday preschool activities in building social orders, Susan Danby highlights how this reflects the seriousness of the children's activities and interactions. Danby describes children as competent interpreters of the world. While teachers may provide a moral discourse, children utilize or adapt this discourse to find solutions to their own issues. Danby also discusses the power of adults to define important social categories of children's activities. She concludes that play is a concept constructed by adults for children and that work and play are not dichotomous. Her findings on the way children actively build and maintain their social orders challenges constructions of children that place them at the bottom of a hierarchy of knowledge.

Another challenge to constructions of child incompetence is evident in Michelle Leiminer and Carolyn Baker's chapter. They demonstrate how, given an enabling context, a preschool child can negotiate his way effectively through conflicting constructions of him as a child by a parent and a preschool teacher. By his competent participation in the adult social world of parent–teacher talk, he not only negotiates the conflict but also asserts his own construction of himself as a child, in a way that influences adults in their understanding of their world.

These chapters illustrate an interplay between children exercising their competence (including negotiating and subverting the expectations adults have of them) and children being bounded by their social environment. Hence, the chapters raise issues around how the process of interaction and engagement effects the expectations of children themselves.

Strategies for engaging children as participants

Toby Fattore and Nick Turnbull highlight the way in which organizational practice can facilitate or impede children expressing their competence as participants. In their chapter they directly confront the political processes around children and seek ways of making these processes inclusive of them. They do this by discussing ways that children can be engaged in conventional political processes and be sincerely represented as a social group in these processes. Drawing on Habermas' theory of communicative action, they provide a framework to facilitate inclusive practice with children by enabling them to be informants on their issues. They show how child-oriented discourse, in which adult–child inequalities are in focus, can be translated into administrative practice. It is through processes of dialogue under certain conditions between children and adults that political action with and for children can be achieved.

Focusing on ways of engaging children as participants and establishing adult responsibility for bridging barriers between children and adults is an essential step to taking children seriously. Other chapters, such as those by Berthelsen and Leiminer and Baker, emphasize how particular processes of communication (in which children are taken seriously as participants) are a means of sharing power between adults and children. Miljeteig highlights the importance children and young people place on access to information in facilitating their participation in adult processes. That these young people are not calling for existing processes to be altered, but, rather, are requesting resources to help them engage with these processes, raises important issues about the extent to which children and young people are excluded from 'adult structures' with which they should have the opportunity to engage. He also points to the importance in hearing children and understanding them, in spite of the fact that they may present opinions different from those of adults with whom they are in partnership. This, he notes, requires that rights claims made by children and groups of children be dealt with genuinely and authentically, through understanding participation rights as *democratic* rights.

Helen Woodward and Patricia Kiely in their chapters discuss specific methods for involving children and parents/families as experts in partnership around decision-making, in areas typically seen as the province of professionals. Woodward outlines three key strategies that can be used to engage children as active partners in assessment. She identifies the contribution children can make towards assessment of their performance in school that is accurate, just and complete.

Similarly, Kiely describes how child-inclusive practice that allows for children's competencies provides an opportunity for improved decision-making in child welfare. She identifies the importance of establishing environments conducive to children being both heard and responded to as actors. Kiely identifies a number of the questions and dilemmas that remain if children are to participate effectively in such decision-making forums with professionals and with other adults with whom they may have fraught relationships.

These two chapters, as well as others in the book, illustrate that characteristics of engagement and communication have political implications. The processes of engagement and communication between adults and children need to be understood within the institutional arrangements that value and encourage the sharing of power between children and adults.

Fundamental to creating institutional arrangements that promote the sharing of power between children and adults, is the process referred to by Sidoti in the opening quote of this chapter, whereby knowledge and understanding of children and childhood is effectively transmitted to 'the general community, including politicians'. We hope that this publication will accelerate this process, by making available the research and knowledge brought together within it, to those who have the desire and the power to promote children being taken seriously individually and as a group.

PART 1

Theory

CHAPTER ONE

Women's Studies/Childhood Studies
Parallels, Links and Perspectives

Leena Alanen

Introduction

The ongoing project of constructing a sociology of childhood may be seen to have started more or less in the 1980s, and concurrently in several countries. It first appeared in the form of a few isolated voices drawing critical attention to the ways in which children were (re)presented in the empirical and theoretical knowledge of the discipline: hardly at all, marginally at best, and when treated then merely as an 'afterthought and as a support for the main construction' (Jenks 1982, p. 13), and in any case not taken seriously and studied 'in their own right' (Hardman, as early as 1973, p.85). The worlds that sociologists studied were seemingly populated by adults only.

As such messages were carried forward they grew into critical self-reflection, leading first to a closer inspection of sociologists' research practices, in order to find out how this 'invisibilization' of children was, in fact, produced.

The most obvious practice is, of course, the plain explicit exclusion of children as the empirical objects of study even when the issue was one or another aspect of children's lives. Pseudo-inclusion was another common practice. Here children are, or at least seem to be, a genuine concern, but in the end they disappear from view. This occurs by way of treating children as 'dependent variables' of, or appendages to, some category of adults (such as parents). Pseudo-inclusion occurs also by way of focusing merely on those who 'have' children, take care of or work with them, or in some other way participate in the organizing of children's everyday life conditions. Pseudo- inclusion is the case also when the focus is on the institutional regimes (family, school, child-work professions) under or within which children are subsumed, instead of focusing on children living and acting within these regimes.

On these grounds it is now possible to call sociology's conceptual practices to account for these faults. The notion that was held particularly responsible for them was 'socialization' – perhaps naturally, for the simple reason that 'socialization' had long been foundational to sociological understandings of what children and childhood are. From the classical texts of the discipline to the latest textbooks, children were (and continue to be) depicted as non-social, not-yet-social or in the process of becoming social and therefore outside the province of sociology (see Ambert 1986). The perspective on children provided by 'socialization' was now seen to be, first, inherently adult-centred, or 'adultist', because children came into view only from the viewpoint of adults and their specific concerns; and, second, it was an inherently 'forward-looking', or anticipatory, perspective in its interest in what children were going to be, and not in what they currently were: social becomings, not social beings.[1] Sociology, in summary, was in a number of ways and for several reasons, massively adult-centred – adultist – and therefore partial and even biased (e.g. Goode 1986; Waksler 1986).

The project now became one of bringing children and their perspectives into sociology. Turning away from the adultist and forward-looking perspective suggested that the new approaches now needed to be 'child-centred': they would focus directly on children, as speaking, acting and experiencing subjects with their own perspectives to the world in which they – and we – live.

This launching stage in the field of Childhood Studies bears comparison with the beginnings of Women's Studies. Some 15 to 20 years earlier, another wave of critique and subsequent corrective refocusing of research had appeared in social science (as in science in general). Then, feminists had observed the remarkable and parallel absence of women and women's issues in both the theoretical and the empirical subject matter of science, despite its prevailing beliefs and pretensions to scientific truth and objectivity – this was, of course, a clear inconsistency. By bringing this to general awareness and by demanding that it be redressed, feminists posed 'the "woman question" in science' (Harding 1986 p.29; 1991, p.49).

As a *public* issue, the 'woman question' was not a new one: it already had a history. But it was only in the 1970s that the issue was brought inside academic institutions, by the force of the second wave of the women's movement, with a new social consciousness and a new political analysis of women's oppression as a sex. With this analysis in mind it soon became obvious that equality did not prevail in academia either, in its institutions and in the knowledge produced in them. 'Sexism' – the unequal treatment of people based on their sex – existed even here. The posing of the 'woman question in science' marked the political identification and the opposition to this situation, and the emerging scholarship of Women's Studies was the practical response, aimed at reconstructing both the institution and the knowledge.

Critiques of old scholarship and attempts at reconstruction have appeared in the history of social sciences even before this,[2] and since the emergence of Women's Studies the critical tradition has only continued. After feminists, other social movements, such as those of people of colour, sexual minorities, ethnic minorities, postcolonial and native peoples, and others, have each in turn criticized science for gaps in its knowledge and for distorted understandings of 'race', ethnicity, sexuality, postcolonial relations, and so on (e.g. Albrow 1990; Krüger 1987; Nicholson 1990). As in the case of the feminist challenge, these critiques have been followed by new fields of critical investigation: witness Black Studies, Gay and Lesbian Studies, Race and Ethnicity Studies, Postcolonial Studies, Native Studies – all with the aim of intervening within the existing knowledge in the interests of their own particular constituency.

Placing the critique of adultism in science within this tradition of critical interventions means arguing that children now also constitute a social category that has been 'done wrong' – with similar consequences of absenting them and distorting their social place and contributions. It also means that for the new Childhood Studies, parallels and even models exist that suggest possible routes to proceed along, and conceptual tools to try out in developing a sociology that this time will take children seriously.

In everyday social life, women and children are, of course, socially linked in many ways, and they share a number a social characteristics (see e.g. Alanen 1992; 1994; Oakley 1994). This alliance of women and children already suggests possibilities for using the achievements of feminist scholarship as a resource for developing the new field of Childhood Studies. A closer examination of the stages through which Women's Studies have gone reveals that even more is to be gained from reading Women's Studies and Childhood Studies in parallel, and looking for links and perspectives for developing the latter. To me, the concept of gender is one powerful resource to be borrowed from Women's Studies and made useful for Childhood Studies. Children, too, are gendered, of course, but the usefulness of the notion of gender lies beyond this. For gender is essentially a relational concept, as is childhood. In a sociological sense, 'children' and 'adults' name two social categories that are positioned within a generational relation to each other. So here elaborations on the relational logic of gender, as it has been developed within Women's Studies, provides inspiration also for rethinking childhood relationally.

The main part of the following chapter consists of a rather compact analysis of the development of feminist scholarship. I organize this development into stages, and then read the achievements of each stage in relation to Childhood Studies. Based on this, three succeeding stages leading from one to another can also be recognized for Childhood Studies:

1. The stage of critique and child-centred research.

2. The stage of developing generational concepts specific to a sociology of childhood.

3. The stage of theoretical reconstruction by means of developing a children's standpoint.

The chapter ends with the suggestion that constructing a 'children's standpoint' opens up issues of generational power to consider, not only by researchers in their research contexts, but also in the everyday practical politics of childhood, where it may provide a more comprehensive and effective instrument than respecting 'children's own perspectives'.

Women's Studies/Childhood Studies: Parallel departures and developments

There exists, then, a clear parallel between Women's Studies and Childhood Studies already in the beginning stage of each. Just as feminism had entered the field of science with the criticism that a 'sexual politics' reigns in its institutions, causing a systematic male-centredness in its knowledge, sociologists of childhood have presented a parallel critique of adultism in social-science knowledge. Critique called for 'better' science, in both cases.

In the case of Women's Studies, the new research began with the twin task of (1) filling the gaps observed in existing knowledge, and (2) revising it for its biases and distortions. Also, completely new issues needed to be studied reflecting a range of women's long neglected concerns, such as housework, childbirth, mothering, incest, abortion, rape, domestic violence, heterosexuality, sexual harassment, pornography and equal rights. Also a number of mainstream topics, such as (paid) work, power, political participation, modernization or class structure, were in need of re-examination because women's part in them had been missing; re-examinations, in turn, lead to reinterpretations, especially when new empirical findings could not be fitted into existing analytical frames and theories.

Observations of children's marginal place, if not absence, in social science was a similar point of departure for organizing Childhood Studies. The critique of adultist bias and partiality, and the claim that childhood is a social phenomenon deserving to be studied in its own right, parallels with the feminist challenge, as does the recent upsurge of new research with its direct focusing on children. Here we can see the logic of the first stage of academic feminism – adding of women into science – repeated. Now children, too, were 'added' to existing accounts of social life where previously only adults has been identified as actors.

From critique to child-centred research

The first researchers within social science to take children seriously – as 'persons in their own right' and as the sociological equals of adults – often shared a background in ethnography, symbolic interactionism or phenomenological analysis (e.g. Mayall 1996; Prout and James 1990). Actors' involvement in the construction of their own lives is foundational to such approaches. Therefore, the study of children's work, cultures and social relationships has been 'natural' within them, as also has been the practice of suspending (as far as it goes) researchers' own perspectives. Beginning from critique, then, a space was opened for investigations that start with the assumption that children are actively present in social life, and then goes on to explore their daily lives, relationships, experiences, identities, knowledges and cultures. Many new topics and issues have become researchable, and new interpretations on children and their lives have been added to existing knowledge.

The shift in the approaches and contents of the study of children has been remarkable enough to deserve the name of a completely new paradigm. Since the new paradigm was introduced, as in the book edited by Allison James and Alan Prout (1990), some of its 'tenets' have cohered so much as to rename it the 'competence paradigm' (Hutchby and Moran-Ellis 1998b). This is the methodology for child-centred research that seeks

- to take children seriously as social agents in their own right;

- to examine how social constructions of childhood not only structure their lives but also are structured by the activities of children themselves; and

- to explicate the social competencies which children manifest in the course of their everyday lives as children, with other children and with adults, in peer groups and in families, as well as the manifold other arenas of social action. (Hutchby and Moran-Ellis 1998a, p.8)

One significant feature, recurrently appearing in and strengthened through this child-centred research, is its tendency to play down many presumed differences between children and adults. Children, in and through this research, appear as 'ordinary social beings', in contrast to their previously assumed difference as social 'becomings' (Qvortrup 1985; Waksler 1991). Children are now seen to move and act in the very same world as other people do, and not only within these limited worlds of play, care and learning that have been especially 'appointed' for them. Their ordinariness is even more manifest in the range of capacities that this research demonstrates as theirs: interpretative skills, social and interactional competences, sophisticated knowledges and strategic thinking (e.g. Fine and Sandstrom 1988; Hutchby and Moran-Ellis 1998b; James 1993).

Evidence of children's social ordinariness helps to de-emphasize the dissimilarities of children in comparison with adults, and highlights their similarities. Consequently, the completely separate study of children or childhood, with separate sets of methods, concepts and theories, begins to lose its justification and we are left with no clear reason for why the 'normal' conceptual apparatus of the discipline should also be inappropriate or unworkable in the case of children. This suggests a novel strategy – of 'stretching' – as a useful one for expanding the field of childhood research.

The sociology of work provides an example. By choosing to look at a number of children's activities as work (instead of learning, play, or development), the range of meanings that normally, or conventionally, are attached to the activities in question is also 'stretched' to include even other meanings – in this case, social meanings of work. Stretching the notion of work does even more: by assuming and elaborating on specific activities as children's work, new issues come into view for consideration, such as the social valuation of children's activities, benefits and profits that accrue from their work, the distribution of these benefits, children's relative positioning in the actual organization of work, as well as the consequences of their positioning for their own experiences and knowledge.

A stretching practice is, of course, open for extension to any of the sociological subfields: family sociology, sociology of knowledge, political sociology, sociology of social change. Also, any of the available theoretical framings in the subfield in question may be tried out, on the crucial condition that children are brought on stage and focused on as actors.

There are yet few examples of such conceptual practice in the sociology of childhood. The fact that the first cases have been in the sociology of work is hardly accidental: for if one chooses to signify particular activities as 'work', automatically a sense of 'agency' is attributed to the subjects performing those activities. Work, moreover, is immediately also a social activity, performed under particular social conditions. Signifying an activity expressly as work helps (perhaps more easily than any other signification) to preserve within the analytic frame the agency of those doing the work – in this case, children – and confines the research to the new 'competence paradigm'.

We are reminded that conceptual stretching was frequently practised also during the first 'add-on' stage of feminist scholarship – as, for instance, in the conceptual move from 'motherhood' as a given, passive, perhaps 'natural' condition of being a woman to 'mothering' as a social activity or socially necessary work that is differentially, and unequally, divided between women and men and also economically and culturally devalued (Alanen 1992, pp.30–31).

Through stretching, what earlier appeared more as the effect of the work performed by other actors on or with children (such as parents, teachers, caretakers, or agents of socialization), now comes into view as children's work on themselves, and even on others. This, of course, does not in any way invalidate or devalue the work of those others involved; rather, the investments of work in the activities in question have increased, as also has the number of 'workers' who interact and cooperatively produce a concerted work achievement – including the relationships within the work organization. As members of specific work organizations, children also connect to the productive organization of society at large.

The methodological point in employing the stretching strategy is to assume that however different from adults children in the end (or 'ontologically') might be – and that is an open question – a sociology of childhood *need not accept any difference as a starting point* (Qvortrup 1985, p.135). Consequently, whatever marks children as different in our everyday understandings and observations – and it may be a specific status, their vulnerability, or a specific value attached to the condition of childhood – it is to be taken as a social construction!

Such a position begs a number of questions, such as: how are the observed differences then (socially) generated? by which (social) processes? on what (social) conditions? with whose participation? and so on. The point to underline is that however the particularity of children and childhood is taken to be in a particular society – their difference from adults and adulthood, their differential ways of being and acting in the world – this particularity (or 'difference') is to be conceived of, and analysed, as a fully social phenomenon, or a social construction. And in doing this, new generational concepts will be need to be developed.

Generational analytics

A parallel problem of difference was faced, and worked on, by feminist scholars. In both society and science, the feminist equality project was founded on the idea that any socially significant differences between men and women – and especially those linked to observed social inequalities – are by their nature social, therefore also they could be changed.

This idea was then fixed into the now well-known distinction between *sex* and *gender*. Since then, the distinction has served feminist analysis well. Essentially all the analytical categories of academic feminism and its contributions to science have sprung from working on this distinction and, later, also on the problems caused by this very same distinction.

In the first uses of the sex/gender-couple, 'sex' referred to any 'natural', biological or physiological difference that there might be between female and male, whereas the differentiations between women and men in social life were assembled under 'gender'. Thus 'gender', and not 'sex', was the central tool and target in feminist analysis.

Sex was also held to be more fixed than 'gender', first, because of its linking to a less malleable 'nature' and, second, because of the cross-cultural evidence that testified the rich variability of gender organization across cultures. Gender, then, was a *cultural* construction that was individually adopted through the intertwined processes of cultural attribution and individual learning. Gender also was the changing, and changeable, element of the two, and therefore also the target of feminist politics. This essentially culturalist notion was the first, and transitional mode in the chain of feminist elaborations of gender.

In childhood research, there is already a rich historical and cross-cultural literature to document a similarly large variation in the cultural models, ideas, concepts and other definitions of childhood (e.g. Cooter 1992; Hendrick 1990; Jordanova 1989; Schnell 1979). In a culturalist frame, these definitions of childhood are interpreted as historically and socially bounded constructions of perceived conditions or features in human offspring, attributed to the 'natural' child.

Children's bodily difference is one obvious 'natural' feature that may function as the foundation for such cultural definitions of 'the child'. Other possible foundations might have been derived from adults' experiences of difference when interacting with human children in comparison with interacting with adults. Cultural definitions of childhood might then be constructed in terms of children's dependency, immaturity, ways of communicating, or perceived vulnerability. In any case, the culturalist would assume that it is adults, and not children, who are the culture builders, and that the characteristics and conditions in human offspring that get selected for interpretation are bound to historical, social forms of adult–child interaction.

Evidence from the Minority (Western) world is converging to show how the contemporary 'modern' (that is, Western) constructions of childhood have evolved from an idea that was fragmented by both geography (urban–rural) and social class, then domesticated within the middle-class family and tied to a compulsory relationship between the State, the family and welfare services, and, finally, universalized more or less through all social classes. When not only the constructions themselves but also the constructors (builders) are drawn into focus, the contemporary 'paradigmatic childhood' can be seen to be centrally linked to the larger project of modernity. Thus cultural definitions of childhood have had an important role in defining appropriate forms for adult–child interaction – contributing to the professionalization of teachers, caretakers, public-health and social workers and other experts of childhood, on the one hand, and the familialization and scholarization of child populations, on the other. The cultural construction of childhood has thereby effected the normalization and institutionalization of the social settings and practices within which children in 'modern' societies are taken care of, raised, looked after, instructed, supervised and controlled.

Feminist understandings of gender began to move away from the culturalist frame when evidence from research, particularly in cross-cultural contexts (Moore 1994), suggested that the cultural variation was too large and arbitrary to justify the linking of sex and gender though culture. Therefore, it was not useful to understand gender as following from (biological) sex as if it were its causal effect.

This insight, when thought through to its logical limit, suggested for feminist scholars a radical discontinuity between sex and gender, and this, in turn, opened an autonomous space for rethinking the working of gender in social life. Again, with the help of some conceptual 'stretching', the idea of the historicity and social constructedness of gender proposed that gender could be understood as a social, structural formation, much like social class, and similarly it could be understood to function relatively autonomously of the everyday acts and consciousness of individual actors, while structuring them (see, e.g., Davis, Leijenaar and Oldersma 1992). This new understanding suggests that:

- gender, as a structural formation, is a power structure, or perhaps even several structures (cf. Connell 1987; Matthews 1984), that exists beyond the face-to-face, situated interactions of individual people; moreover

- the operation of such a system of power implies structuring processes – that is, social processes that effect the regulating, organizing and positioning of people into different social locations, which in turn provide them with differential access to participation in social life. Observable gender divisions and inequalities would therefore result from ongoing gendering in *all* social relations (Marshall 1994); and finally,

- 'gender' also names the existing systems of symbols, meanings or significations that constitute the 'cultural' dimension inherent in the gendering of social relations.

There appear to be no easy terminological equivalents to sex/gender in the languages of European origin that could be used for distinguishing terminologically the 'social' from the 'natural' in childhood.[3] Speaking straightforwardly in terms of a 'natural childhood' and 'natural children' (offspring?) on the one hand and a 'social childhood' and 'social children' on the other at least expresses the fact that childhood, for the sociologist, is *not* a natural phenomenon and that human offspring are *not* automatically children; instead, they would need to be seen to become children, and always in a particular time, in particular locations, by force of particular processes. A distance created between the two allows us to think of childhood and its sociality autonomously from the other side, and not as a societal response to the foundation that is the 'natural child'.

The immense theoretical productivity of the sex/gender distinction for elaborating the sociality of gender suggests also that childhood, as a social phenomenon, could be theorized by taking into use parallel terms. The observable, experienced childhoods – the focus of child-centred research – would then be linked to ongoing generational ordering in social life, and this would mean to explore:

- the generational structures composed of generational categories (positions) of childhood (or perhaps 'childness') and adulthood, linking them into a reciprocal interdependency, and relationships of power

- social, economical, political and cultural processes in which children and adults, as both individual and collective actors, are involved, and in which their everyday activities are embedded so that generational (re)structuring is recurrently effected

- systems of signification as the cultural dimension of generational structures; these provide the meanings, symbols and semantics through which the generational categories and their interrelationships are rendered culturally meaningful.

One instance of a generational ordering can be detected already in the institutionalized division of social spheres into 'public' and 'private' in that 'childhood' seems to order children into the 'private' world of home, family and care and out of the world of (for instance) economy and politics. It also orders a child's place within the family, in relation to and in difference from its adult members. The working of such a generational order usually becomes apparent first when its rules are violated, when for example, children work for wages instead of going to school or when they disregard their obligations to their parents as a dependent being by taking to autonomous living. Such instances begin to make visible a generational system: a social order composed of, but also constraining and coordinating children's relations in the social world in a pervasive and systematic way.

The public/private divide, of course, has been central for feminist social science, but only in some rare cases have feminist inquiries moved also on generational lines.[4] For analytical purposes the two structures of gender and generation can (and should) be kept apart, but not so when exploring everyday life. Women and children are positioned within *both* structures and the generational and the gendered organizations of social life intersect – women's and children's lives are both gendered and 'generationed'.[5] Research with comprehensive designs would be needed to account for the gendering and generationing processes as they take place in children's worlds.

However, we may already conclude that by elaborating on the notion of a generational structure (or generational order) children become designated as social actors with their own social contributions within the various social practices intersecting their daily lives. The social positions that such structures order for children to take not only allow, but in fact *constrain* children to actively participate in on-going social life. Children's participation may well differ from that of other social categories, for instance, it may be safely assumed that the practices through which their participation is organized significantly limit their agency, compared with adults. The freedoms and limitations, options and constraints, that are inherent in 'modern' childhood are, however, social issues to explore, and not simply to assume. Moreover, children's constrained 'membership' in society as 'children' also affects their self-construction (Wartofsky 1983). The studies that have turned to children themselves and asked them about their experiences are beginning to document the 'inside' dimensions of childhood, or 'childness' (Cook-Gumperz 1991). More often than not, they are, perhaps understandably, limited to descriptive accounting of the 'child's-eye view' on the world around them (e.g. Goodnow and Burns 1985). It is, however, worth pointing out that the visual fiction of 'the child's perspective' may include more than just accumulated descriptions of the world as it is seen, literally, through children's eyes. The notion of a generational system suggests that children are also 'knowers' – that is, they gain practical knowledge of what it is to be a 'child' in the kind of society in which they are positioned as 'children'. They have, in other words, an *understanding* – their own, based on their social location – of the very same world that sociologists have so far described and explained from their conventional adult viewpoints, and feminists from adult women's perspectives. This hints at the possibility of 'opening' the social world from a children's position, and beginning to theorize the social from a children's standpoint.

Children's standpoint

'Standpoint' as an issue has been extensively discussed in recent years within feminist philosophy, and much less put into use in empirical studies. Among sociologists particularly, Dorothy Smith (e.g. Smith 1988) has developed the idea of standpoint as a method for writing a specifically feminist sociology.

The feminist interest in standpoint grew out of the need to theorize women's participation in ongoing social life. After the stage of borrowing concepts and categories from mainstream ('malestream') science and reinterpreting ('stretching') them to include women and gender relations, the focus moved on to question their original hidden (gendered) meanings. 'Stretching', then, could not provide the only way forward. In order to find out what lies behind, and at the origin of, our conceptual knowledge – what its terms refer to, how they were originally generated, in response to what problems and issues, and to whose interests in and needs to knowing they actually respond – their 'deconstruction' was brought on to the feminist agenda.

Deconstruction is the activity that exposes knowledge as being ideological or discursively constructed rather than a natural or simple reflection of reality. It shows all knowledge to be contextual and 'political', and commits scholarship to 'perspectivism', or the view that the world is 'known' *always* from a particular – spatial, temporal, political, gendered, generational – position; knowledge therefore contains a perspective from one or another location.

In this sense, knowledge is always 'situated'. Therefore, social scientists should take it as its starting point and build it into their methodological and theoretical strategies (Smith 1990b). This is all the more important for sociology, which has (in Dorothy Smith's words) 'objectified a consciousness of society and social relations that "knows" them from a standpoint of their ruling and from the standpoint of men who do that ruling'[6] – and has thereby written patriarchy into sociology (Smith 1989). When we learn how to do sociology we learn how to look at society from such a standpoint. The sociology we have, then, is a sociology that has responded to questions that 'men have wanted answered' and that 'all too often have arisen from desires to pacify, control, exploit or manipulate women and to glorify forms of masculinity by understanding women as different from, less than, or a deviant form of men' (Harding 1987). It is, moreover, sociology that has frequently provided welfare departments, manufacturers, advertisers, psychiatrists, the medical establishment and the judicial system with answers to questions that puzzle the ruling gender in these institutions. Sociology, therefore, serves the 'apparatus of ruling', and people within the relations of ruling, by transforming the actualities of everyday life into the conceptual forms ('facts') necessary for administrative and managerial forms of ruling (Smith 1988; 1990a; 1990b).

An alternative feminist sociology – or a sociology for women – would address society and social relations from the standpoint of those who are situated *outside*, rather than within, the relations of ruling. Dorothy Smith has made the most fundamental critique so far of conventional sociology from a women's standpoint and is working for an alternative sociology, a sociology for women. In working for such a reconstruction, she calls for beginning from the everyday lives and experiences of actual women. But then the analysis has to be carried on beyond listening to what women are able to tell about their lives: their everyday knowledge has to be worked up in the form of sociology. And because the processes and relations outside women's immediate daily lives help to create the conditions of those lives and the experiences of living in those places, only a sociology that links these two is able to make society known from the point where women stand, and to explain to them how their 'everyday/every night' lives are implicated in the actual organization of the social relations of ruling. It will then not 'explain' women's behaviour for others; it will, instead, explore, analyse and explicate a world that women know as its insiders and participants. It will also necessarily problematize the extra-local and abstracted organization of ruling as it is represented in conventional sociology.

The 'truth regime' in which childhood is implicated, and the institutionalized practices that have followed, organize for the social category of children particular locations from which they are compelled to participate in everyday social life. Through this participation, children (as any members) gain a particular range of experiences and knowledge about the social relations within which they daily live, on the locations which are theirs. This knowledge, however, is normally not articulated and therefore remains hidden, implicit, unacknowledged. Beginning from where children stand and act, as subjects, in their everyday lives, an account of society from such a point – that is, from a children's standpoint – becomes conceivable. Such an account would also not look at children and 'explain' them for others, and provide these others with information for the better ruling of the generational order. Instead, it would explore, analyse and explicate the worlds that children know as insiders, and in this continue on the groundwork laid by child-centred research. But it would not stop there, for it would also need to link children's lives with the normal everyday organization of social relations. In Dorothy Smith's words, changing 'women' into 'children', would:

> express [children's] experience and yet embed [their] experience as [children] in the generalizing relations of society. The general aim is to explicate the social processes and practices organizing people's everyday experience. It means a sociology in which we do not transform people into objects but preserve their presence as subjects. It means taking seriously the notion of a sociology concerned with how phenomena are brought into being through

the actual activities of individuals and of exploring how those activities are organized in social relations… It means an inquiry that will disclose how activities are organized and articulated to the social relations of the larger social and economic processes. (Griffith and Smith 1987, p.89)

Conclusion

At present, such a project stands in a stark contrast to the conventional adultist standpoint of both standard sociology and our everyday knowledge of children. This is a project that takes children seriously as competent actors and knowers in their everyday worlds, and even as authoritative and informative partners in defining what, in the end, are the relevances of contemporary childhoods, thereby reaching beyond the liberal and humanist attitude of respecting children's voice and vision. Realizing this project is, I think, one promising way forward in constructing a sociology of childhood.

A recent assessment from within Women's Studies states that:

> Since the mid-1960s feminism has provided some major challenges to our understanding of how the social world is constructed and the processes through which our knowledge about it might be obtained. Certainly, the significance of gender in an empirical context is now widely accepted. Women's lives have been rescued from their previous invisibility, necessitating the generation of new concepts in order to encapsulate the gendered specificities of their experiences. (Maynard 1998, p.120)

Conventionalized understandings of children and the worlds of childhood have been challenged also by Childhood Studies, and the rescuing of children's lives from invisibility has also been started. Childhood has become a respectable topic for both empirical research and theoretical studies. During this past decade, we can witness tremendous growth in the field, both nationally and internationally: research groups and centres, social-science journals, and research and study programmes have been started, and research reports, academic books and textbooks are published in increasing numbers and in different languages. Within international and national sociological associations sections have been established for developing the field, and networks between academics and practitioners are also beginning to be formed.

This last point, I think, hints also at an issue that is crucial in further developing this new field of social scientific knowledge. In the above I have made use of the links and parallels between Women's Studies and Childhood Studies. There are, of course, also differences. Childhood Studies differs remarkably from Women's Studies, or Ethnicity Studies, Black Studies, Native Studies, and any other of its forerunners, in that it did not emerge as the willed achievement of those for whom it intends to speak: children. Childhood Studies is the work of adults. Children are not, and perhaps cannot ever be, equally positioned with adults in relation to knowledge production, despite the best endeavours of researchers to redress the degree of power imbalance between children and adults. Improving the ethics and the methods in doing research with children is one route towards a better balance, and this work has been already started; much more can and needs still to be done. We need, however, to develop ways of taking children seriously on this issue, too, and this means as actors and partners with their own perspectives as to the relevances of their lives. To ensure that Childhood Studies will actually speak for children, from their standpoint, it is obvious that also the social relations between generations – between children and adults – have to change. Childhood Studies are intended to be instrumental in promoting such transformations.

Notes

1   See for example Qvortrup (1990), Speier (1976), Thorne (1987), Waksler (1991) for a discussion of this critique and an analysis of the socialization discourse also Alanen (1988, pp.56–63; 1992, pp.11–20, 80–90). Different sociological traditions and schools of thinking have their own refined notions of 'socialization'; it is not a homogeneous construct and, therefore, such critique may not apply in each case. Also, 'socialization' has its uses (as when one's concern is with what adults do when their goal is to prepare children for life in the social worlds of which adults are a part) but it is a limiting notion if the aim is to illuminate what children themselves do while being socialized, and it completely ignores the other processes and activities in which children are also engaged. Texts on children's socialization should therefore read as 'portrayals of adult perspectives while recognizing that other perspectives are possible' (Waksler 1991).

2   For example Karl Marx, one of sociology's 'founding fathers', was a vehement critic of the assumed impartiality and objectivity of the social-science theory of his own time. By criticizing it for its failures to include the essential social (class) relations of capitalism in its analytic approaches he argued the 'class question' in sociological theory (Harvey 1990). Since Marx, the 'class question' has also remained one of the central issues of sociological theory.

3   But 'gender' also is not translatable into a number of these languages; in these cases, the linguistic equivalent of 'social' has been added to 'sex' to make the distinction.

4   Stacey (1981) is one of the few.

5   The co-presence of other powerful systems of social relations (organized around class, race, ethnicity, heterosexuality, etc.) should be added here but has to be ignored in a preliminary analysis like this.

6   For Dorothy Smith (1988), this is characteristic of sociological knowledge in modern capitalist society and is explained by the fact that sociology has evolved as the contemporary of modern Western society, with its typical social structure of classes and the state and, significantly, its institutions of administration, management and polity. All of these have emerged within the same processes and have developed into a network of institutionalized social relations that mutually enforce and condition each other. The social sciences, as part of the same project, are the institutionalized forms of producing knowledge of this historical formation.

CHAPTER TWO

Theorizing Representation of and Engagement with Children

The Political Dimension of Child-Oriented Communication

Toby Fattore and Nick Turnbull

Introduction

Conventional political activity tends to exclude children from participating in politics. Common-sense understandings of childhood allow the state and adults to act for, rather than with, children. The state, and adults generally, are in a position to determine what is in the interests of children. But adult concerns and state policy often focus on ensuring that children acquire adult characteristics, that they become successful future citizens, thus deriding children's own activities and social practices. This further reinforces children and their everyday needs and practices as non-political, maintaining children's subordinate social position and minimal political power.

We propose an alternative conceptual model that addresses the exclusion of children from political processes. We investigate how we can facilitate children's participation in complex political processes and what conditions need to be met so that these processes are child-oriented. These are related problems, the first about direct participation and the second about genuine representation of children's needs by others. We utilize Jürgen Habermas' theory of communicative action to provide a framework that includes children in processes of deliberative democracy and to promote child-oriented political practice. However, we suggest certain revisions to Habermas' theory so that it is more inclusive of children and their perspectives, by drawing upon the work of Maurice Merleau-Ponty. Finally, we refer to a specific example to show how child-oriented discourse can be translated into administrative practice. In doing this we challenge orthodox practices and discourses of what constitutes politics, and the idea that children are non-political.

Childhood as a social phenomenon and weaknesses in current political thought: Identifying the problem

Children are commonly thought to be outside the sphere of politics. Politics is a field in which adults compete over controversial matters, whereas childhood has traditionally been viewed as an innocent state, uncontaminated by adult concerns. Similarly, major philosophical and sociological traditions have not paid sufficient attention to the meaning of children's actions in terms of their position within the social structure as a distinct social group.[1] James and Prout note that, in general, social and philosophical theory rarely credits children with active subjectivity (James and Prout 1990; see also Ambert 1986; Jenks 1982). Instead, conventional social theory constructs children as passive, as bearers of social reproduction (whether recipients of symbolic violence or positive socialization), or as subjects upon which genealogically constructed discourses play themselves out. In other words, these theories construct children in a particular way for the purposes of theorizing, rather than understanding children as active social participants in their own right.

Consequently, if we use these theories to inform our understanding of social institutions we rule out children's agency in advance and replicate the same biases in institutional forms. Alanen (1988) points out that the function of child-related social institutions is not to promote the everyday activities of children but to progress children through the developmental schema formalized within institutional practices. The perspectives of children are irrelevant because children act within such institutions only to acquire predetermined skills. This schema presupposes that children lack competence and require protection, which in turn serves as proof of their incapability of actively participating in society. For example, in educational philosophy, Paulo Friere (1973) points out the contrast between education that is dialogical, involving children in the process of learning about the world, and education that is passive and limits opportunities for children to actively challenge established authority.

But the new childhood studies show that children are, in fact, competent social actors. One of the consequences of this work is that we should question the idea that childhood and adulthood are two discreet ontological states (Wartofsky 1983). Once the ontological division between children and adults is questioned, stereotypes of children are also brought into question. Qvortrup points out that the differences between adults and children result more from social practice rather than some fundamental difference in nature (Qvortrup 1994). The 'adult world' does not recognize children's praxis because we define competence in relation to adult praxis. Hence we have an epistemological problem in understanding children's social practices, rather than an ontological problem that resolves itself when children become adults.

We can only deal with this problem of understanding by considering the relationships between adults and children in terms of intersubjective discourse between active subjects (see Crossley 1996). We require an ontology that acknowledges children 'as is' rather than 'as will be', and an epistemology based on intersubjective understandings between individuals across the entire age range. This means that shared understanding is possible between actors of diverse competencies, something that is important where children and adults form communicative relationships. In the next section we build upon this theory of communication to articulate a mode of political action sensitive to the diverse capabilities and needs of children. From this, we can find a path that promotes children as full citizens in a participatory democracy.

A new model for theorizing participation

Habermas' critical theory of democracy

Jürgen Habermas' work regarding political public spheres has the potential to establish a child-oriented political theory because it is based on radical proceduralism. Habermas argues that legitimate political action resides in processes of deliberative democracy (Habermas 1987; Habermas 1990). Deliberative democracy is based on the ideal of democratic association through free public argument between equal citizens. For a political decision to be legitimate it requires the right of all to participate in deliberation. So rather than legitimacy arising from an expression of an abstract (and ultimately exclusive) general will, decisions are legitimate when they arise out of a deliberative process where all who wish to participate can do so, and when they are equal in their rights to put forward opinions and debate political questions (Habermas 1992). Habermas terms this process 'political will formation'.

Accordingly, the law and institutional practices must meet the standards of a process in which everybody in the public could, with ease, self-certainty and a fear-free disposition to learn, have input into the decision-making process, either directly or via their chosen representatives. State institutions are legitimate only insofar as they establish such a framework for public deliberation (Habermas 1996). Importantly, the conditions of this framework incorporate 'the inclusion

of all parties that might be affected, their equality, free and easy interaction, no restrictions of topics and topical contributions, [and] the possibility of revising the
outcomes' (Habermas 1992, p.449).

The source of political discourses is civil society. This is important because
the starting point is the ordinary language of public life, not the élite discourses of
state or private interests (Habermas 1996). The discourses that arise out of civil
society become institutionalized as autonomous political public spheres
(Habermas 1989). Political will formation is articulated through these mediating
public spheres. For our purposes, this is an important base on which to conceive
politics because children inhabit civil society and not adult political institutions.
It also highlights how the institutions of civil society can mediate children's political concerns and enact processes that support them in expressing their political
will (for an excellent example of this in relation to working children see Miljeteig
2000).

Habermas' work is important because he suggests that we can maintain communicative relationships that are non-instrumental and non-objectifying. It is
communication that lies at the centre of his political praxis. Politics arises from
communication between individuals; hence we can include children in this just as
well as adults. Habermas' insistence on radical proceduralism, rather than the
elaboration of an 'abstract general will', means that groups in a subordinate
position, including children and children's advocates, are able to take part in deliberations that do not suppress, but include their perspectives.

What this also means is that the conditions for deliberative processes, on
which legitimate law making depends, need to be institutionalized. Habermas establishes that it is human rights that allow the public use of communicative
freedom to be legally institutionalized (Habermas 1996, pp.127–132). So, in the
Convention on the Rights of the Child, while Article 12 (the 'participation principle') is an expression of the deliberative democratic principle, it is the rights
guaranteed in the Convention as a whole – rights to cultural identity, to freedom
of expression and association, to economic security, health and education,
freedom from exploitation and abuse – that secure the private autonomy of
children, as citizens, therefore enabling them to enact their public autonomy.
Given this, social inequality undermines the preconditions for the exercise of
legal rights.

Habermas' theory broadens the meaning of participation from conventional
politics, which takes place in a narrowly defined arena, to the social and cultural
spheres as well. This expands the opportunities for children to express themselves
politically in a variety of local and organizational settings (Benhabib 1992, p.87).
Conceived intersubjectively, communication between adults and children can
proceed without one-way coercion of children by adults, taking the form of a

dialogue rather than unilateral instruction. Political public spheres therefore provide a model of political participation that can be inclusive of children's points of view and ways of acting.

Problems in Habermas' theory

While public spheres based upon 'ideal speech situations' are a positive model for democratic life because they establish a standard for communicative relationships free of compulsion and domination, there are elements of the theory that are problematic for children's participation. Given children's marginal status we must also be careful that children are not marginalized or devalued in communicative processes. This requires further consideration.

Communicative action is founded on discourse ethics. This requires that, first, the only valid norms are those that meet with the approval of all the actors involved. Second, for a norm to be valid, all the participants must freely accept the consequences of observing the norm (Habermas 1990, pp.66–71). However, taken on their own, these do not necessarily safeguard children's political involvement from being 'trumped' by dominant adult perspectives. This is because Habermas' theory relies on certain developmental and adult ideological biases and a distinction between 'justice' and 'the good life' that relegates children's concerns to a subordinate status. Only by addressing these two issues can we establish the criteria for political participation that are inclusive of children and children's perspectives.

In Habermas' theory, communicative action rests upon an individual holding particular communicative competencies. Communicative competencies are the abilities 'that make a subject capable of speaking and acting, that put him in a position to take part in processes of reaching understanding and thereby to assert his own identity' (Habermas 1987, p.138). People acquire communicative competencies, according to Habermas, through socialization. To this end Habermas adapts Lawrence Kohlberg's theory of moral development, which requires individuals to attain minimal competence to be able to partake in communicative action (Habermas 1987; see also Kohlberg 1984).

The problem with Kohlberg's, and thus Habermas' adapted typology, is that it excludes children by adopting a particular form of moral reasoning. It establishes a moral developmental norm that naturalizes the child as a subordinate (Jenks 1996, p.25).[2] From the perspective of the ethical, principled adult, children's moral reasoning is, by definition, inferior because it is the child's goal to obtain adult competence – that is, the attainment of higher stages of moral development and adult communicative ability. Hence the application of Habermas' theory maintains particular assumptions regarding the natural competence of mature and rational adults, implicitly juxtaposed against the unfinished, incomplete child. Habermas' work makes it hard to imagine children as communicative actors whose participation might contribute something to discourses about themselves and the social world.

Another problem arises from the role that socialization plays in Habermas' theory. Habermas makes a distinction between 'justice' and the 'good life'. Fraser interprets this in terms of a corresponding distinction between the public and private (Fraser 1992). Habermas has in part addressed this by arguing (specifically in relation to the feminist politics of equality) that the appropriate interpretation of needs be a matter of public debate, including determining which differences between groups are relevant for different treatment and for equal opportunity (Habermas 1996, pp.409–427). However, by constructing children as the passive recipients of socialization within the family, children's concerns are privatized and their concerns remain outside the public sphere. To redress this, private matters of the 'good life' must be transformed into public matters of 'justice', illuminating the power relations between adults and children. This would not only transform the discourses of childhood and raise public awareness of children's issues, but would also shift popular notions of the boundaries of politics. (For a fuller discussion of the parallel between feminist studies and childhood studies, see the contribution by Alanen in this volume.)

Having illuminated certain shortcomings of Habermas' theory, it is now possible to reformulate his positive insights. Our task is to explain how intersubjective communication might take place that includes children as full social actors rather than as incomplete 'human becomings'. But this task is difficult because the structure of modern political institutions means that adults will in many instances speak on behalf of children. Two considerations are pertinent here, one relating to sincerity and the other to competence. The issue of sincerity is that adults speaking on behalf of children must speak from a sincerely child-oriented perspective. The issue of competence is that communicative action must admit participants with diverse communicative competencies. The question of 'sincerity' deals with whether adults can understand children and their perspectives. We turn to this in the next section. Regarding competence, understanding communicative action as dialogical more fully allows diversely competent communicators to express themselves.

Reconstructing communicative action: Merleau-Ponty and sincerity

Maurice Merleau-Ponty's (1962; 1964) work differs considerably from other psychological theories dealing with children in that Merleau-Ponty questions the division between pre-rational child behaviour and rational, objective adult behaviour. Merleau-Ponty rejects linear and hierarchical characterizations of development; it is neither a neat continuity between childhood and adulthood, nor is it discontinuous (Lefort 1990; O'Neill 1973). This is important because it indicates how intersubjective understandings between adults and children are possible.

A child's sense of self is a product of intersubjective social interactions. That is, the subjectivity of the child is not a private 'inner-world' relation, but rather an inter-world of shared meanings created through dialogical communication with others. Hence, Merleau-Ponty challenges the prejudices of classical psychology:

> My consciousness is turned primarily toward the world, turned toward things; it is above all a relation to the world. The other's consciousness as well is chiefly a certain way of comporting himself toward the world. Thus it is in his conduct, in the manner in which the other deals with the world, that I will be able to discover his consciousness. If I am consciousness turned toward things, I can meet in things the actions of another and find in them a meaning. (1964, p.71)

This creates a shared space to understand both the other and the social world (Merleau-Ponty 1964, p.73). Children, therefore, enter the 'intersubjective order' as active participants, providing a basis upon which children and adults can understand each other.

Although the perceptual experiences of infants are strongly mediated by adults, who induct infants into a culturally specific version of the visible and social world, infants also actively construct their world in ways that adults do not expect. Research into infant imitation by Meltzoff and Moore (1991) makes both these points. Their research indicates, first, that infants play an active role in their social relationships and are not passive recipients of socialization. Second, they show that the act of imitation is evidence of an intersubjective bond between children and their significant others. Infants exhibit a complex manipulation of symbols, gestures and then later language. Imitation indicates that infants adopt adult practices and establish complex social relationships in the process.

For Merleau-Ponty (1964, p.69) the development of the self involves a series of experiences through which children recognize themselves via encounters in their environment. This 'reflection' most usually emanates from the reactions of the child's significant others towards him or her. Merleau-Ponty is less interested in stages of cognitive development than he is in the consequences of this process, which he terms the 'mirror stage'. This process through which the child differentiates himself or herself from others indicates that the child recognizes a 'public me', a 'me' that derives his or her identity in being experienced *by* others. The child thus takes the first step of experiencing himself or herself as existing for others. Under certain conditions the child can perceive this self-alienation as pleasurable and self-affirming. Alternatively, the process of becoming aware of the 'me' can be a threatening experience if the child is treated without dignity, is objectified, or loses the ability to determine the meaning of his or her own actions. In other words, socialization can be a positive process that permits infants to develop their own identity through dialogic interactions with others; or it can be an objectifying process that leaves little autonomy for self-determination on the part of the child. We can see the institutional form of this latter mode of communication in the highly administrative rationality of modern bureaucracies.

It is here that we can discern the importance of the 'emergent self' for a child-oriented politics. Precisely because the child is social and cannot isolate himself or herself from others, the development of the child may, as Elshtain points out,

> ...support the emergence of trust, autonomy, a sense of love, a conviction of inner integrity and worth and, ultimately, an identity perceived as worthy, or, it may thrust a child instead into lingering mistrust, shame, doubt, guilt, inferiority, isolation, and ultimately, stagnation and despair. (1982, p.293)

This is not merely an issue of personal development but concerns sincerity in communicative action involving children. The dialogical process of recognition and communication between adults and children provides criteria to evaluate the adequacy of our social practices regarding children – namely criteria that are indicative of the positive affirmation of the child as a person in the here and now. Here we see the connections between personal and public life within Merleau-Ponty's work.

In other words, the relationship between intersubjective communication and individual and social recognition is important for a child-inclusive politics. This is a similar point to that developed by Axel Honneth (1995 see Chapters 5 and 9 in particular; see also Honneth and Farrell 1997). Honneth argues that there is a process of social recognition between subjects that the development of human identity depends upon. He identifies three essential forms of recognition; love (emotional concern via intimate relationships), rights (as a rights bearer and morally accountable member of society) and solidarity (social esteem for individual achievements and abilities). Denying recognition leads to individual and group shame or indignation. Further, the criteria for progressive politics are not only the conditions for reaching agreement but also the conditions for forming identity; that is, whether a society provides the conditions to recognize individuals as equal, valued and unique members of society.

When we consider Merleau-Ponty's work with the political implications of recognition shown by Honneth, we see that the issue of sincerity has two aspects – that intersubjective understanding is achievable between adults and children, and that sincere communication for children reflects certain normative standards that also act as child-oriented political criteria. A child's sense of self-consciousness and self-worth depends upon the type of recognition by significant others, their broader communities, and the provision of material conditions that facilitate such processes. We should orient social arrangements that affect children, including organizational practices, towards tolerance, encouragement, appreciation, approval, trust, acceptance, and fairness. Opposed to this are personal and social structural arrangements that establish relationships with children in practice that criticize, condemn, ridicule and shame the child. We should inform our perspectives from the child's point of view with these factors in mind. This is what we might conceive as a sincerely child-oriented perspective, with implications for orienting individual action and institutional practice towards reaffirming the child's subjectivity. This provides criteria for speaking on behalf of children and for child-oriented institutional and social practices.

Reconstructing communicative action: Merleau-Ponty and competence

But we have yet to deal with the problem of children's communicative competence. We must examine the characteristics of intersubjective understanding between adults and children to account for communicative action involving persons of different competencies. In the context of adult–child communications we must be cautious of the possibility of imposing an 'adult' viewpoint upon children who are in a socially vulnerable position. Merleau-Ponty offers a solution. Rather than seeing children as incompetent, children interact with their environment in different ways than adults. Children do this in ways that are dialogically constructed between children's actions and adults structuring the social environment.

For Merleau-Ponty, children and adults reach intersubjective understanding through acknowledgement of difference and not necessarily the merging of views. Because significant differences and similarities exist between adults and children, some of which are embodied and some of which reflect different communicative competencies, interpretation is possible not on the basis of being in the other's position, but by virtue of co-acting in a shared social world. Therefore we can avoid either defining children entirely in adult terms or excluding them from social relationships. Nor need we argue that the two must be exactly the same.

Appreciating the partial nature of intersubjective understanding underscores the requirements for communicative action envisaged by Habermas, but opens it out to protect communicators of diverse competencies. This safeguards against objectifying children as a group of inferior status.

The translation of child-oriented discourse into administrative operations

So far we have provided a theory of communication that emphasizes the importance of child-oriented communication between adults and children. But now we need to outline the implications of this concept. It is important to note that this model includes both children actively participating in processes of political will formation and also adults acting with and on behalf of children by adopting child-oriented communicative practices. Adults are able to translate children's perspectives into public discourse. This is an advance on simplistic assumptions that call for children to be involved in public life in the same way as adults.

Through the model explicated here, the needs of children can be translated into organizational priorities via their involvement with institutions of the public sphere. Active citizenship is not only about individual activism in adult-defined public spheres, such as voting or taking part in public protest, but can be effected through this translation.

Let us take the difficult example of children at risk of, or who have suffered, abuse or neglect (for example, see Mason 1993; and also Mason in Chapter 6 in this volume). In New South Wales, Australia, the Department of Community Services has the main responsibility for child protection. In this department a collision occurs between the managerialist efficiency paradigm that structures departmental practice and child-oriented standards of care. This is a clash between managerial techniques that treat children as clients and practices employed by child protection workers who attempt to fulfil and facilitate the needs of children as people.

The dominance of managerialism over child-oriented standards means that strict control measures employed in the Department compromise child-protection workers' ability to deploy resources to meet the needs of the child (Rees and Rodley 1995). Before workers can allocate these resources, the needs of the child must be translated into an administrative discourse that is characterized by management's need to document and justify workers' behaviour. This is done to maintain organizational control and surveillance (for specific examples see: Cashmore, Dolby and Brennan 1994; Face 1995; Fattore, Galloway-Smith and Turnbull 2000).

However, were there an emphasis on the needs of the child, this would move away from this restrictive practice. Central to this would be supporting child-protection workers to act as advocates for children. In the context of child protection, the emphasis would be on radical and intensive casework to promote the needs of the child.

This has two aspects (Fattore *et al.* 2000). First, the *process for advocating with, and on behalf of, children*. Casework should be sensitive to the needs of children and allow for the participation of children in that casework. Other aspects include timely intervention to prevent children feeling helpless and isolated; case workers being available to provide a reference point for children; and the ability to coordinate services to meet the needs of children in a holistic and coherent way (see also Cashmore *et al.* 1994; Mason and Falloon 1999). Second, the *child-oriented content of advocacy and care of children.* This would include proactively meeting the needs of children as determined with them – for example, facilitating needs of leisure and play, material and psychological security, freedom from fear and violence, and the need to be valued, understood and respected.

This model of casework requires child-protection workers to fulfil the obligations of discourse ethics on one hand and work towards the positive affective standard suggested by Merleau-Ponty on the other. These principles establish a benchmark for practice that could become the focus of organizational activity. The organization supports its staff to allow children to express their needs and enforce moral claims with and through others. Organizational structures would therefore support radical casework as opposed to serving the more limited function of investigating child abuse.

Conclusion

A public sphere involving children and children's perspectives has considerable implications for altering the dominant tenor of policies affecting children. Such a public sphere would place pressure for the formulation of problems in a way that relates to the current life situations of children.

Intersubjective understanding enables adults to participate with children in political action. On this basis communicative action is possible between actors of diverse competencies. These measures have the potential to illuminate and safeguard against the inequalities of power between adults and children, recognizing that adults must be participants in political action that is child-oriented. Political activity can therefore legitimately include advocacy on behalf of children by adults and direct participation by children.

Child-oriented political communication opens out criteria that permit a critique of existing institutions, practices and discourses relating to children and childhood. It generates an alternative value base from which to measure political practices and structures. This has the potential to generate political practices that treat children seriously as active citizens who contribute to public life.

Notes

1   One of the major contributions of the 'new childhood studies' is to illuminate how major strands of social and philosophical thought have been predicated on particular constructions of children and childhood.

2   Habermas' theory relies on the attainment of a post-conventional ethics that, according to Kohlberg, allows norms to be judged in the light of principles.

CHAPTER THREE

Virtual Reality

Children as Constituents in Social Welfare and Social Policy Constructions

Marie Wilkinson

Introduction

This chapter considers de Swaan's depiction of a 'virtual' constituency through an examination of the construction of children as clients in child-welfare policy development and service delivery in New South Wales. In so doing, I am seeking to examine some of the paradoxes that are at the very heart of child welfare and child-protection interventions with children and families and to consider the significance of some of these paradoxes for the child constituents of such interventions.

De Swaan (1988, p.232) proposes that 'caring' professionals operate within a milieu in which their role is circumscribed by the dictates or demands of two constituencies, those of their professional bodies and of 'the state'. Both constituencies are represented as providing 'remedies' and resources for workers whilst also imposing conflicting demands. In this analysis, de Swaan further proposes that a third, virtual constituency is comprised of the actual and potential clientele of these workers. This third constituency is depicted as a 'virtual' consistency in that it has been 'constituted by the state, the labour market and the professions into well-defined categories...*whose needs and interests have been defined for them* (1988, pp.232–233, my emphasis).[1]

An examination of the history of the New South Wales state government child welfare department's own representation of its activities indicates that this department both constructed and sustained a particular representation of client

children and their families and 'managed' the discourse around those representations (Wilkinson 1999, pp.5–24). The discourse sustained certain 'beliefs' about
children and their care that can be seen to have survived transitions in nomencla-
ture, legislation, policy and practice. Some of the 'beliefs' are that:

- there are good and bad parents and good and bad children

- modes of care should, whenever possible, be family-like

- children need to be located in a relationship with 'parents'

- issues such as the significance of poverty and family are addressed, in
  both policy and practice, separately from considerations about children's
  entry to care

- the state government is, and should properly constitute the authoritative
  or 'expert' voice in decision-making about children and their care.

(pp.233–245)

Historical accounts of child welfare in New South Wales, in portraying the state's
role in supervising and controlling the parenting practices of working-class
families, or in representing the state as benevolent parent ensuring the protection
and care of needy, destitute or abused children from the inadequate practices of
the failing or pathological family, depict a range of contested claims and competing influences that have been instrumental in determining the state's role in providing for children who require care away from their families (for example,
Dickey 1980; Garton 1990; van Krieken 1992). One analysis of this history has
concluded that child-welfare legislation in Australia was never particularly
directed towards the needs and interests of children themselves but towards
maintaining order and cultural security (Brous, Green and Jaggs 1980). This interpretation suggests that the problem of defining the kinds of relationships that
should exist between the state, the family and society, and how those relationships
could be achieved, has never been resolved. In considering the state's role in the
'affairs of children', Brous, Green and Jaggs (1980) determined that the state
depended upon the interpretation of needs and the selection of objectives from a
range of possibilities about which there could 'only be uncertainty' (1980, p.37).

Dilemmas for practitioners

When child-welfare and child-protection workers have faced decisions about uncertainties, or, to revisit de Swaan's construction, when workers have been
required to manage 'competing demands', they have sought to rely upon 'informed guesses using evidence of past situations involving that child or other

children for making a prediction of the future' (King 1997, p.62). Thus, child-welfare and child-protection workers have undertaken interventions that have been infiltrated with images and expectations of 'good practice'.

However convincing the worker's identification and assessment of harm to the child, and however apparent the attribution of the causes of such harm, King suggests that a worker's decisions about a child's care can never be more than an 'interpretation' (King 1997, p.63). Workers' interpretations have been mediated through particular modes of reasoning whereby certain knowledgeable discourses have represented (thus constituting objects of knowledge) and conferred particular identities and agencies on political and social actors and made identifiable the problems to be solved (Dean and Hindess 1988). In child-welfare and child-protection interventions, such judgments have become subject to juridification, to 'technical' processes, supported by medical and/or other 'evidence' supported by seemingly scientific and objective 'truths' (King 1997, pp.63–66).

Workers have faced multiple paradoxes. They have been required to perform seemingly technical assessments, to substantiate their assessments, to support them with evidence, and to defend them. The increasing specificity and complexity of these technical machinations has disguised, or obfuscated, the paradoxes that are at the centre of child-welfare practice, and have coloured the complexity of determinations about children's needs and interests.

An authority discourse

The decision-making dilemmas faced by practitioners have been located within an 'authority discourse' of certainty, constructed by and within the state government child-welfare bureaucracy. The department identified the 'problem' of neglected and at risk children, was the architect of the naming/ identification of this issue and constructed, contained and legitimated the discourse surrounding responses to those children.

King's (1997) concept of an authority discourse is useful in analysing the operation of the state government in its role as 'parent' to neglected and at risk children. Not only is the authority discourse (such as that constructed and promoted by the state government in relation to children) the pronouncement of a privileged and authoritative account, it is also the mechanism through which the state has provided the prospect of 'certainty about the past, the present and the future' (King 1997, p.27) and embraced the impression of surety and finality.

In constructing an authoritative voice, conveying the prospect of certainty, of 'knowing', the state government's construction of 'the neglected child' or the 'child at risk', has been contained within a discourse in which the state government referred principally to itself as an authoritative and legitimating voice.

Through this process of self-legitimation or 'social autopoiesis' (Luhmann in King 1997, Chapter 1, p.27), the state government child-welfare department continually referred to itself for authority and not to any other external source. In autopoietic terms, the state government's construction and management of the discourse about neglected and 'at risk' children sustained recognition only of those elements that could be interpreted as part of that department's 'environment' and thus incorporated or recognized as part of the department's own authorized system. This authority discourse both constituted, and was constituted by, the framing of its authoritative voice within the legal/legislative and the social policy idioms.

The politics of intervention

An historical review of the politics of the discourse about 'neglected' children and 'at risk' children reveals that policy, legislative and procedural progressions have been instigated by, and occurred within, the New South Wales child-welfare department. This bureaucracy is, and has been, a site of political tension through which the needs, rights and interests of 'neglected' children or children 'at risk' are named, mediated and managed and where a political struggle over the distribution of social, political, cultural and economic resources for the care of children and families in New South Wales has been located.

The governance of this department can be read as a study of politics, where the complexities surrounding the discourse about the care of children have been reduced to a contest over meaning. In the discourse sense of politics, something is political if it is contested across a range of different discursive arenas and among a range of different discourse publics (Fraser 1989). Political activity itself becomes pre-eminently a politics of contest over meaning, comprising the disputes, debates and struggle about how the identities of the participants should be named and constituted, how their needs should be named and constituted and how their relationships should be named and constituted. The operations of the child-welfare department in New South Wales were predicated on definitions, constructs and beliefs that emanated from the 'expert' child-welfare bureaucracy, were inscribed in legislation, and underpinned the development of social policy and correlative practices.

An investigation of the construction of the discourse of the neglected or 'at risk' child suggests that child welfare is represented not as a domestic, economic or social concern but principally as a *legal* site of authority. The 'welfare of children' discourse in New South Wales has been located within a particular site of government where the complex, contradictory and contentious issue of the state's role and responsibility in caring for children, has been subject to the certainty and surety of the authoritative inscriptions of legislation. A consequence has been both the minimization and simplification of the process of contestation. The contestable precepts about what is good and bad for children, what is in 'their best interests', and what constitutes 'neglect' and 'abuse' have also been given the authority of the legal system's lawful/unlawful coding and thus rendered immutable.

These precepts have not only emerged as uncontestable constructs, but have also, through their constant invocation, lost the discursive and reflective meanings that once attached to their definition. Such assumptions have shifted in emphasis and impact during the period from 1945 to the 1990s. What has remained intransigent is the formulation of the reason for intervention as a technical, administrative and quasi-legal/legal procedure. The language that circumscribed the process of removal of the child, for example, was translated from 'neglected child' to 'child in need of care' to 'child at risk'. Through each of these progressions, decision-making was cast as a technical and rational (indeed, objective) process.

The decision to remove a child, whatever the discursive construction of that process, was inevitably a decision about those factors that have been labelled as 'amorphous' (e.g. Carney 1985b, p.203). That is, they were decisions about the adequacy of parenting, about the conduct of the child, about the child's environment and about intra-family relationships. From the 1980s, these decisions have been translated through a set of rhetorical idioms attached to the concept of 'abuse' – protection, risk factors, harm indicators – and, as such, have developed an idiomatic, technical life of their own.

Paradoxical deliberations about what is 'good' or 'bad' for children did not originate in contemporary child-protection work. They can be said to have attached to all child-welfare determinations about the adequacy of parenting, and about the suitability of the child's environment or the level of care provided to a child (Lindsey 1994).

The determinations depicted by Chisholm (1980) as nebulous, and by King (1997) as paradoxical have been the essential components of child-welfare work and the foundation upon which decisions about the removal and placement of children away from their families have been made. These interventions have been authorized by such powerful moral justifications as 'the needs of the child', 'children's welfare', 'the interests of the child' or 'the safety of the child'. In order to achieve authority, these moral deliberations have been supported by medical or scientific/technical evidence (King 1997). Over time, these 'interpretations' have been generated as paradox-free constructions within which a system of identity has been promoted for child-protection workers based on the concepts of certainty, authority and superior knowledge.

King (1997) supports Luhmann's proposition that an important aspect of this process of system-identity construction results from the very existence of paradoxes at the foundation of the system. He also notes the need to develop strategies to prevent these paradoxes from 'rising to the surface' and undermining the system's operations (Luhmann 1988 in King 1997, p.61). It is worthwhile considering King's further point that the paradox for the child-welfare worker's self-image as the promoter of child welfare stems from the impossibility of performing the task (of protecting the child) in any reliable scientific manner, given the inherent problems in harm identification and prediction. Thus, the 'problem' of child abuse is reproduced in terms that are amenable to the system's communications and operations, and where the paradoxes are concealed through the construction of a social environment in which the issues that give rise to the paradox either do not appear, or appear in an unproblematic way (King 1997).

Resolution of dilemmas

In managing the child-protection decision-making process, practice has assumed a potent interrelationship with the law, whereby the law provides the foundational truths that can be used to explain, or to interpret, protective practices (Stein 1991). The child-protection system has employed legislation to legitimate and create a reality about intervention by authoring such activities, and locating those constructions within the authoritative language of the law, which channels particular constructions of meaning and which can exclude alternative discourses and ways of reasoning (Davidson and Spegele 1991).The political construction of children and their needs has thus become circumscribed by a discourse that is both juridically potent, and technically defined.

The 'new' sociology of childhood

The analysis of discourses around childhood that has emerged through the 'new' sociology of childhood has promoted a renewed realization of the need to 'rethink childhood and its place in society' (Taipale 1993, p.7). This analysis informs our understanding of the politics of child welfare. It draws attention to the social marginalization and minority status of children in social policy, and to the lack of data available about children in research, government reports and statistics (Heilio, Lauronen and Bardy 1993; Qvortrup 1993; Zelizer 1985). The literature has also exposed the reluctance of societies to develop and conduct family policies that address the needs, rights and interests of children. So-called family-policy measures have been assessed as 'more often than not a guide for serving purposes other than children' and for devising policy measures that disguise and occlude children's interests (Qvortrup 1993). In other words, children exist as 'virtual' rather than actual constituents in the child-welfare decision-making process.

Taking children seriously

In attempting to take children seriously, we could consider the construction of the definition of the 'problem' of the 'neglected child' and the 'child at risk' and the range of strategies that have controlled the scope of the child-welfare discourse.

Yeatman (1990) proposed that states utilize a mixture of strategies to restrict and control the scope and development of the politics of discourse. The development of a child-welfare discourse in New South Wales can be read in terms of Yeatman's first proposition that core concepts such as 'needs', 'children's best interests', 'children's rights' and even the very foundational claims of 'neglect' and 'child in need of care' became authorized as ritual litanies that are not only invoked and reified through social-policy pronouncements, but undergo constant legitimation through the State's self- referral within an autopoietic process.

In considering the State's 'management' of a discourse about children who were defined as requiring 'the state's care' in an arrangement away from their families, the invocation of ritual litanies (evident in the construction of, and maintenance of core epithets such as 'children's needs', 'children's best interests', and 'children's rights') is central to the discourse by which the 'needs' of those children committed to, or admitted to, the care of the State as state wards was constructed.

This process is akin to Fraser's (1989) analysis of: the capacity and ability of members of the social collective to press for claims against one another through officially recognized idioms such as needs talk, rights talk and interest talk; vocabularies for substantiating claims in these idioms; paradigms of argumentation accepted as authoritative in adjudicating conflicting claims; narrative conventions available for constructing the individual and collective stories that are constitutive of people's social identities; and modes of subjectification. Various discourses position the people to whom they are addressed as specific sorts of subjects endowed with specific sorts of capacities, for example, as 'normal' or 'deviant'.

The state government's delimitation of the child-welfare discourse utilized such resources in the construction of the subject children of the child-welfare department's operations. The state government constructed definitions of 'neglected children', 'children in need of care' and 'children at risk' through the maintenance of definitional categorizations, through the determination of the vocabulary that depicted such 'needs' and then inscribed them in policy and legislation. Additionally, these constructions were protected from contestation.

In considering the activities of the child-welfare department, 'needs-talk' was constructed as a site of limited contestation by the department, which maintained hegemonic interpretation of certain depictions of 'needs' – that is, of the child and family subjects – thus controlling and neutralizing contestation.

Conclusion

This chapter has considered the constitution of the needs and interests of children in social-policy and social-welfare debates in New South Wales and examined the aggregation of knowledge about children that has informed decision-making on their behalf. An examination of the discourse surrounding children's needs and interests points to a conclusion that the state as parent has never addressed its 'virtual constituents', the children, but instead has constructed a system of mythologies about children's needs and interests that has remained unassailable.

The mythologies about children's needs and interests have not only survived intact in the post-war era, but have been unaffected by, or resistant to, bodies of information that have tested these mythologies. In particular, the advent of the phenomenon of child abuse (especially child sexual abuse), rather than precipitating a questioning of the mythologies about children and their care, was incorporated into a common belief system so that the foundational 'truths' about children's needs and interests remained unchanged.

In spite of research developments in sociology, psychology, social policy and social work, the actual construction of the state's care of children has changed little. Children have remained a 'virtual reality' in social-welfare and social-policy discourse. While this chapter has discussed the maintenance of this 'virtualization' of children as clients, it has also illustrated that there is no 'simple' solution to this dilemma for researchers, policy makers and practitioners.

Note

1   De Swaan's comparative historical study 'deals with the collectivizing process in health care, education and welfare', with a theoretical focus on collective action (1998, p.1). He deals with the historical contexts of this process, from early modernity to the present, covering Britain, France, Germany, the Netherlands and the United States. This paper, although concentrating on only one aspect of his conclusions, i.e. in regard to the advent of professionalism and 'expert regimes', illuminates the immense siginificance and wide applicability of his findings.

CHAPTER FOUR

Childhood and Sexuality
Adult Constructions and Silenced Children

Kerry H. Robinson

Introduction

The relationship between children and sexuality is volatile and controversial, often demanding one to exercise great caution when negotiating the discursive minefield that culturally underpins the contradictory representations and understandings prevailing in this relationship. This chapter explores the hegemonic discourses around childhood and sexuality, in which children's voices have been virtually non-existent and vigorously denied and silenced by adults. It is argued that these discourses often result in contradictory readings of the relationship between childhood and sexuality, which not only contribute to children's vulnerability to abuse and exploitation on both a familial and extra-familial level, but also deny sexuality as an integral part of children's identities (like their gender, race, ethnicity, and so on). Further, these discourses, which largely perpetuate biological and developmentalist understandings of childhood and sexuality, operate to disguise the active involvement of adults in the construction and regulation of children's sexuality and desire.

This discussion is informed primarily by recent research undertaken by the author with early-childhood educators in the metropolitan regions of Sydney and across the state of New South Wales, in Australia (Robinson and Jones-Diaz 2000). This research provides valuable understandings of how the discursive location of early childhood educators in terms of childhood and sexuality impact significantly on their everyday interactions, practices and pedagogies with young children and their families. Hegemonic discursive readings of childhood and sexuality generally prevailed amongst the early childhood educator participants, highlighting their understandings of sexuality and power as being largely considered as irrelevant to 'the world of the child'. Sexuality was generally not perceived to be part of children's identities, especially non-heterosexuality, and the perception that children were essentially 'innocent' beings and 'too young' to understand these issues was for many vehemently asserted. However, ironically, the construction of heterosexuality was a normalized integral part of the everyday practices, pedagogies and policies in which these early childhood educators engaged with children and their families.

Understanding and perceiving children as active, knowing agents in the construction of their sexual identities is rarely considered, if not totally denied, in the bulk of literature on early childhood and sexuality. Children are deemed powerless and are 'othered' from what is generally considered to be the world of adults (Ghandi 1998). Sexuality is an area of identity that is tenaciously represented as 'adults only', often carrying many cultural taboos, which in the name of 'protecting' children and childhood innocence, operate to exclude them. Ironically, the very methods aimed at protecting children often contribute to their abuse. The confusion and contradictions that surround adults' surveillance and regulation of children can result in increasing children's and youths' vulnerability to exploitation, sexual violation, and personal despair, as well as undermining their potentials of being aware, knowledgeable and competent individuals.

The social construction of childhood and sexuality

In recent times the new sociology of childhood field has highlighted how childhood is a social construction. It has also critiqued modernist, universal, biologically fixed understandings of childhood that have primarily failed to recognize the multiple experiences of childhood and the importance of viewing child development within different social, cultural, political, economic and historical contexts (Gittins 1998; James, Jenks and Prout 1998; James and Prout 1990). Similar to childhood, sexuality has also been predominantly viewed as biologically determined and linked to the development of the adult. However, sexuality as a socially constructed social relationship has gained greater prominence in the literature in recent times (Butler 1990; Connell and Dowsett 1992; De Lauretis 1987; Foucault 1977b; Weeks 1986). Sexuality as a social construction is considered to be a non-linear, multifaceted, complex, contradictory and unstable social relationship that can vary across cultures and over historical periods of time. Weeks (1986) points out that sexuality only exists through its social forms and social organization. Within this context, sexuality is primarily defined and constituted within the heterosexual/homosexual binary relationship in which heterosexuality is considered the 'norm' and a 'natural' expression of sexuality, while all non-heterosexual identities are defined as deviant and unnatural. The privilege and power associated with heterosexual relationships is perpetuated both systemically (for example, in legal, medical and education systems, as well as across religious faiths) and through the micro-relationships of everyday interactions.

Discourses of childhood and sexuality

So, if sexuality is a social relationship that is socially organized, how has childhood been positioned and represented within this relationship? There are primarily three dominant contradictory discourses that operate around children and sexuality, and it is argued that all, to varying degrees, contribute significantly to children's and youths' vulnerability to abuse and exploitation. The first discourse, represents children as being asexual, innocent and immature and is the most pervasive and influential discourse around children and sexuality, and will be the focus of discussion in this paper. This discourse is constituted within the socially constructed binary relationship between adults and children. Within this hegemonic discourse, physiological sexual maturity is constructed as the boundary between adulthood and childhood (Gittins 1998); sexuality is perceived to begin at puberty and mature in adulthood. Thus, sexuality is considered the exclusive realm of adults, in which children are constructed as the innocent and powerless 'other'. Children's sexuality within this discourse is considered to be immature or non-existent, with children being perceived as emotionally and physically underdeveloped and incapable of understanding or dealing with 'adult' concepts such as sexuality and desire.

However, ironically, it is the very innocence and purity that is constructed around children that can lead to their vulnerability (Gittins 1998; Kitzinger 1990). Childhood innocence is a commodity exploited in child pornography, where innocence becomes titillation and the perception of 'forbidden fruit' fuels the desire. This image of childhood innocence is not just perpetuated in pornography but is apparent in mainstream media representations of children (Elliott 1992; Kitzinger 1990). Childhood innocence as a more than viable billion-dollar consumer industry is certainly reflected in the success of international child-sex tourism, internet paedophile rings and the prevalence of child prostitution throughout the world (Tate 1992).

The second discourse, which intersects with the first, is constituted in the binary relationship of Madonna/whore, which has been reinforced through Freud's use of the 'seductive child' and childhood fantasy. The construction of childhood sexuality has been similar to the construction of adult women's sexuality, in which 'innocence' is gendered. As indicated by Gittins (1998 p.167), respectable Victorian women 'were idealized as asexual, domestic and pure, and such ideals were also applied to children'. Like the Madonna/whore stereotypes applied to women, young girls have been culturally represented as either 'little angels (sugar and spice and all things nice) or as little vixens, Lolitas and flirts' (Gittins 1998, p.167). Freud's seductive child has been utilized to explain away numerous sexual abuse complaints made by women. In this discourse, adult men are seduced by the allure of childhood innocence and it is maintained that in all children lurks the flirt, the Lolita, waiting to overpower the unsuspecting adult. This discursive representation of adult–child relationships takes the responsibility away from adult's behaviour. Thus, when childhood innocence is tainted, children are often held responsible. Children who have been sexually abused are removed from the innocent child pedestal and may be viewed as sullied, dirty and as useless children (Gittins 1998). The knowing child, who is no longer pure and innocent, is often stigmatized and tainted with similar, though more abhorrent, accusations and double standards as those facing the sexually active and independent woman with her own sexual desires – the whore.

The third discourse focuses on the adult 'moral panic' that exists when children are considered as sexual beings, resulting in the perception that children require constant adult surveillance at all costs. This discourse, prominent in the mid 1900s, but still relevant today, views children as sexual beings but lacking the maturity to comprehend and emotionally and physically control such behaviours. This perspective stems from historical, middle-class, puritanical, religious discourses that view sexuality as inherently immoral, sinful, and an expression of unruly and corrupt working-class public immorality. Any hint of children's sexual behaviour results in 'adult' moral panic and the belief that such urges need to be controlled at all costs. Consequently, adults have historically worked hard to police the sexual behaviour of children and youths (Gittins 1998; Jenkins 1998; Sedgwick 1998; Wolfenstein 1998). Further, Foucault (1977b) points out in *The History of Sexuality* that sexual taboos resulted in the close surveillance of individuals with the purpose of altering physical modes of behaviour.

Young children's and adolescents' sexuality and sexual agency have traditionally been perceived as a challenge to adult power and authority, where children are perceived to be assuming the 'adult role'. This discourse is very influential today. Adolescent power and autonomy is frequently expressed through active sexuality and is often viewed by others as emanating from a lack of parental control and discipline (Gittins 1998). Patton (1995) points out that adults often fear providing children or adolescents with sexual knowledge believing that it will directly result in 'causing' youth to have sex prematurely.

Children, sexuality and early-childhood educators

Research has indicated the influential role that education and educators can play in constructing children's identities, including children's sexual identities and their understandings and awareness of sexuality more generally (Corteen and Scraton 1997; Haydon 2002; Robinson 2002; Robinson and Jones-Diaz 2000; Wallis and VanEvery 2000). Normalizing discourses of heterosexuality and childhood innocence prevail in educational contexts and underpin everyday practices, policies and pedagogies. The moral panic and discourses of protection that have tended to surround children and young people are reflected and perpetuated within all levels of schooling, significantly impacting on pedagogical practices, school policies and school curricula – for example, the strict regulation of sexuality education (Corteen and Scraton 1997; Haydon 2002).

Recent research undertaken by the author with early childhood educators in metropolitan Sydney and regional areas of New South Wales, Australia, highlights the controversial and contradictory relationship that is perceived and constructed around children and sexuality, across a range of early childhood educational contexts, primarily Long Day Care and Preschool (Robinson and Jones Diaz 2000). The first project (Robinson and Jones Diaz 2000), utilizing a survey (49 participants) and interviews (16 participants), explored the perceived relevance and significance of a range of diversity and difference equity issues to early childhood education, as well as the various pedagogies and policies employed to incorporate the issues into teaching and family-support programmes. The diversity and difference areas addressed were gender, multiculturalism, bilingualism, Australian Aboriginal issues, and sexuality, including gay and lesbian equity issues. The second project, which is currently in progress, focuses solely on dealing with gay and lesbian equity issues in early childhood education. The varied responses and opinions from participants in both projects highlighted the volatile and controversial nature of addressing sexuality issues with children, especially when they transgressed from the normalizing discourse of heterosexuality. Several participants in the first project refused to complete the sexuality section, commenting that this was irrelevant to children and to their work, and/or that dealing with gay and lesbian issues in particular, was against their cultural, religious and/or moral values; overall, sexuality, generally, was an area from which children needed to be protected.

The hegemonic discourse of childhood and sexuality that constituted children as innocent and asexual beings was the most prevalent discourse operating amongst the educators in this research. For many, sexuality was considered the exclusive realm of adults and had little relevance to the lives of children, who were generally perceived and constructed as innocent, naïve and vulnerable. These perceptions were largely constituted within traditional discourses of childhood based on developmentalist understandings of child development that are central to current teaching and learning in early childhood education. Within this discourse, children tend to be viewed as being in a state of 'becoming' persons, which is considered synonymous with adulthood, rather than as active agents and persons within their own rights. Corteen and Scraton (1997, p.99) point out that 'The infantilizing of children, sustaining childhood as a prolonged denial of personhood or citizenship, is particularly marked with regards to their developing sexualities.'

Many of the participants in the research considered that children were 'too young' to understand sexuality or any other associated issues related to adult/power relationships, inequality or sexual diversity. Thus, developing children's awareness and understandings of sexuality was generally considered to be a low priority in children's education. For most of the participants, developing children's awareness of sexuality issues was considered to be the responsibility of the family and not part of their role as educators, especially as early childhood educators. Some commented that they considered this work to be more the responsibility of teachers working with youths in secondary schooling, as the issues were perceived to be more relevant to that age group. Thus, many considered that dealing with sexuality – in all its manifestations – with young children was unnecessary and that the 'exposure' of children to such knowledge would be a violation of childhood innocence. As one participant commented, 'Sexuality appears to be an issue that adults have difficulty talking about and very strong religious attitudes about rightness/wrongness…therefore [there is] a questioning of appropriateness. There is a concept of keeping children "innocent".'

Some participants were located within the discourse of moral panic around children's sexuality, which was intensified when considered in terms of children's agency or within the context of non-heterosexuality. This is reflective of the third discourse of childhood and sexuality identified previously. For some, the concept of children's sexuality was limited to being victims of sexually abusive behaviours. There was concern expressed by some participants about children who seem to know 'too much' about their bodies and sexuality and the 'appropriateness' of such knowledge, which often resulted in suspicions about the family and the 'appropriateness' of their parenting approaches. Concerns voiced about dealing with sexuality issues with young children were intensified for many when it was raised in relation to dealing with non-heterosexual relationships. It is interesting to point out that despite the prevalence of the discourse that children were 'innocent' and 'too young' to understand sexuality, the construction of heterosexuality was inherent in everyday practices, polices and pedagogies operating in early childhood settings. Mock weddings, girlfriends and boyfriends, kiss and chase, mothers and fathers, are integral to the narratives of young children's experiences of schooling. However, the normalization of compulsory heterosexuality (Rich 1980) rendered these practices invisible and they were generally considered to be a natural part of growing up (Robinson 2002). Some raised strong religious and moral objections to addressing gay and lesbian equity issues with children, in which cases homosexuality was viewed as immoral, sinful and unnatural. Adults' surveillance and regulation of children's sexual behaviour operates largely to assure that children do not fall 'prey' to homosexual behaviour, reflecting discursive myths and misconceptions about non-heterosexuals as being predators of children (see Robinson 2002 for a more in-depth discussion of these issues). This myth was expressed by several participants in this research.

What this research demonstrated was how educators' positioning within discourses of childhood and sexuality impacted significantly on their practices with young children and their families. Children's voices around sexuality were frequently silenced through the dismissal and 'dodging' of questions around sexuality that participants' considered too risky, inappropriate, and difficult to address with children. Further, educational programmes developed in the various settings in which participants worked were strictly regulated in terms of what was considered developmentally appropriate knowledge for children, particularly in relation to addressing sexual diversity issues as part of anti-bias and social-justice agendas. If they were addressed at all, which was rare, they were contextualized within family diversity. They tended to be reviewed as relevant only if settings had known 'out' gay or lesbian parents and, more specifically, if this was causing 'problems' for children in the settings. Ultimately, sexuality was not generally considered relevant to educators, as many viewed it as a private family matter.

Implications for theory, practice and research

The issues that have been discussed in this chapter have critical implications for practice, research and theory, not just in the field of education but also in other fields that involve work with children. The discursive location of educators and other practitioners working with young children and their families will impact significantly on their everyday practices and pedagogies. The role of educators in dealing with sexuality issues with young children and adolescents is a contentious issue that has raised many questions amongst schools, parents and communities (Patton 1995; Wallis and VanEvery 2000). This debate about who is responsible for sex and sexuality education – the school or the family – and what this should entail, has been ongoing in relation to all levels of schooling (Corteen and Scraton 1997; Haydon 2002; Robinson and Ferfolja 2001). It raises some serious concerns about the development of children as competent and knowledgeable persons with agency in dealing with sexuality, and capable of sorting through the many contradictions that underpin sexual identities. It is problematic when the sexuality education of young children is highly regulated by adults and dismissed as being developmentally inappropriate. This can result in young children's misinformation about sexuality. As pointed out by Corteen and Scraton (1997, p.99):

> In protecting their innocence, children's experiences and competencies are neglected – with adults directing and determining their behaviour, choices, opportunities and potential. Denied independence, or the information and experiences necessary to develop their emerging sexualities, children and young people are made vulnerable.

In order to decrease children's and youths' vulnerability to sexual exploitation and abuse it is imperative that the various discourses identified in this discussion, and the associated power relationships constituted within them (such as those operating around the adult/child binary) are critiqued, deconstructed and reconstructed. As both sexuality and childhood are sociocultural constructions as discussed earlier, it is possible to change how these concepts are currently defined and organized. The constitution of 'innocence', pivotal in the hegemonic definition of childhood, increases children's vulnerability to abuse through its contribution to the way that children are denied language, knowledge, choice and, ultimately, power within these contexts. Denying and/or restricting children's access to knowledge and to voicing their concerns in relation to sexuality issues often leaves children 'to sort out their scripts with peers, media or alone in secretive and dark corners' (Plummer 1990, p.239) or with others who prey on vulnerability. Children are rarely given the vocabulary to talk about their sexual bodies, or the permission to talk about sexual matters. In addition, Kitzinger (1990) points out that the perpetuation of childhood innocence contributes to the guilt that some survivors of child sexual assault continue to experience around the loss of their childhood and/or their perceived failure to prevent the abuse from occurring.

According to Plummer (1990, p.239) the silence around children and sexuality can have important implications in that 'the child soon comes to appreciate that sexuality is not a neutral value-free zone but one that is heavily embedded in judgments and emotion'. This point is no more obvious than in the high rates of youth suicide related to sexuality issues amongst both males and females in Australia and other parts of the world (Denborough 1996; Mac An Ghaill 1994). The silencing of children's voices in relation to sexuality generally is a problem, but the prevailing restrictions imposed through the dominant discourse of assumed and compulsory heterosexuality are particularly destructive in the lives of many young lesbian and gay people who, as a result, struggle with their sexual identities, most frequently alone.

Consequently, educators and practitioners need to be aware of their subjective locations within the various discourses that operate around the social construction of childhood and sexuality and the implications this positioning has on their daily interactions with children and their families. As demonstrated in the research conducted with early childhood educators, one's subjective location in discourses of childhood and sexuality will influence one's practices. For example, early-childhood educators' locations within these discourses resulted in a range of practices that could contribute to undermining children's power, independence, choices, opportunities and competencies around sexuality, such as:

- dismissing or ignoring children's questions around sex and sexuality

- not considering sexuality as a relevant and critical issue in children's identities

- failure to include sexuality issues within policies and practices

- excluding discussions of sexuality and sexual diversity from early childhood curricula as a result of it being considered developmentally inappropriate

- not providing a safe and supportive environment in which children can explore sexuality issues

- perpetuating myths and misconceptions about non-heterosexual identities

- perpetuating the perception that some social-justice issues are more appropriate and more worthy of support than others.

Such practices and perceptions that perpetuate childhood innocence and dependence on adults may, in turn, silence children's voices and undermine their agency, as they may inadvertently reinforce and perpetuate the inequalities that underlie children's vulnerability to adults' or older children's abusive power. Thus, early childhood educators have an opportunity, in partnerships with parents and other practitioners working with children, to increase children's access to knowledge and to develop the critical thinking skills that children require to understand the various adult/child power relations that are socially constructed and sanctioned within communities (Robinson and Jones-Diaz 1999).

The denial of children's access to knowledge and language around sexuality is often perpetuated, ironically, through programmes that aim to increase children's awareness and decrease their vulnerability to abuse. Krivacska (1992) in

his research reviewing the development and nature of child sexual-abuse prevention programmes in the Unites States since the 1970s points out that such
programmes have ignored children's sexuality and have had limited focus on increasing children's critical understandings of sex and sexuality. Rather, he argues
that these programmes often give children a negative view of these issues through
their failure to include discussions around the development of children's overall
sexuality, non-abusive sexual relations, and sexuality as an integral part of one's
identity. Krivacska comments that:

> Of great concern here is that a child's first exposure to the concept of sexuality
> takes place within the highly negative context of sexual abuse and the poten-
> tial consequence that the child may learn that sexuality is essentially secretive,
> negative and even dangerous. (1992, p.91)

Krivacska argues that child sexual-abuse prevention programmes tend to limit the
increase of children's knowledge around sexuality and sexual terminology, so as
to avoid parental and community resistance. This echoes research that has
explored the nature of sex and sexuality education programmes in schools in the
United Kingdom (see Corteen and Scraton 1997; Haydon 2002). In relation to
sex education, Haydon (2002, p.191) aptly points out that 'children's rights will
continue to be denied unless contemporary constructions of childhood, sex and
sexuality are contested'. Krivacska believes that it is crucial to increase children's
knowledge base around sex and sexuality in order for child sexual-abuse prevention programmes to be effective and to prevent the inherent negative constructions of sexuality more generally in children's eyes. His research of child sexual-abuse prevention programmes highlights that there have been cases where
children have experienced guilt relating to child sex play and have little understanding of the differences between this behaviour and sexual abuse. According
to Krivacska (1992, p.97) the message represented in many of these prevention
programmes is that 'sex is bad and you don't talk about it with anyone'. This has
important implications for practice. If children are interpreting these prevention
programmes in this manner, such programmes may be further hindering children's willingness to come forward about their experiences of exploitation and
abuse.

   Krivacska's research highlights the need to be aware of the difficulties and
contradictions faced by children as they construct their sexual identities within
an age of sexual abuse, where their knowledge, voices and agency are constantly
restricted, in an effort to protect them. These contradictions that children face
around sex and sexuality need to be given greater focus in future research in order
to understand children's experiences and concerns around these issues. Consequently, there are important implications for the development of effective practi-

cal prevention programmes aimed at dealing with child sexual abuse and critically considering the ways in which childhood and sexuality are constructed through the philosophies and approaches included. That is, it is necessary to question what discourses of childhood and sexuality are perpetuated through policy and practices that may, ironically and inadvertently, perpetuate children's vulnerability to abuse and negatively impact on children's sexual identities.

Further crucial implications of these issues for research concern the lack of legitimacy of children's voices as competent and worthy sources of knowledge. Children are predominantly the objects of research from adult perspectives, rather than subjects with critical perspectives and relevant and important contributions to make to increasing knowledge in the area of sexuality and other issues. However, the increased awareness of the exploitation and abuse of children within society in recent years has resulted in even stricter regulation of children's voices and of researching with children around these issues. The limited research that represents children's voices on issues such as sexuality often stems (rightly so) from parental and adult community concerns associated with adults' exploitation and abuse of children. Consequently, those wishing to explore children's understandings and knowledge about sexuality have to negotiate many initial social barriers, professional ethical standards and cultural fears that place the researcher under suspicion regarding their motives. Some of these fears can, on occasions, be well founded, reflecting the need for stringent ethical practices when working and researching with children. However, it is crucial to have a greater understanding of children's views and practices around sexuality, especially in terms of how children themselves, in conjunction with adults, construct their sexualities in the early years of their lives, as well as regulate the sexual identities of their peers. This process does not just begin at puberty, but is a part of the everyday lives of very young children and is intimately connected with the constructions of other aspects of their identity such as gender, race and ethnicity.

Conclusion

The double-edged sword of 'protection' has often silenced children's voices, possibly hindering the development of more appropriate and effective approaches to the prevention of children's exploitation and abuse. As Plummer (1990, p.240) aptly comments: 'What is important is the mode of approach: looking at sexuality through the child's eyes to grasp how it actively has to construct a sexual world. What matters is how the child interprets sexuality. Of this we know very little.'

PART 2

Policy

CHAPTER FIVE

The Social Condition of UK Childhoods

Children's Understandings and Their Implications

Berry Mayall

Introduction

This chapter provides some reflections on childhood in the UK. First, I introduce two inter-linked topics; these provide a context for the second part of the chapter. These topics are: the status of children and childhood in the UK and the division of responsibility between state and parents for children's welfare.

The status of children and childhood in the UK

A major stumbling-block in the path of those wishing to work for children in the UK is the status of children and of childhood itself. Children have for a hundred years been constituted through a body of psychological knowledge as incomplete persons. They are projects for adult attention. An important feature of the adult project is the surveillance of children: measurement, assessment and categorization; and an important goal is to establish whether a child is normal (Rose 1985). If a child is abnormal, then intervention to return her or him to normality is appropriate. As developmental projects, children are not regarded as persons with socially recognized roles so they are not regarded as contributors to the social order (La Fontaine 1999). UK social policies, rather, seek to protect children and to exclude them from the dangerous physical and social worlds that adults have developed. A corollary of these understandings is that children who are seen to transgress social and psychological norms are regarded either as victims of adult behaviour or as threats to the social order (Hendrick 1994; 2003).

Second, again through psychological spectacles, children have been understood to lack the tools of reasoning and the experience and moral sense necessary for status as moral agents in the social order (Burman 1994). And, again, the implications of these ideas are that children's knowledge and experience is commonly disregarded. A further implication arising from this line of thinking is that children are not ready to participate in decision-making and so their rights may be generally discounted. A particularly worrying point here is that many adults regard children as morally suspect and unreliable (Mayall 2002).

The third point concerns the individualization of children. Since children are understood principally through the lenses of psychology, they are generally regarded as individuals; any identified problems are regarded as individual cases to be solved at individual levels. The social condition of childhood in the UK, its character and quality, is not seriously addressed by those governmental agencies providing services. To do so adequately would require lifting children (conceptually) out of the family and looking across childhoods. It would require understanding children as a minority social group, as citizens deserving of resources in their own right; and it would then require a concerted effort to devise and implement measures to improve their social condition.

Fourth, under this general heading, adult interests take precedence over children's interests. Children have very low priority in the minds of policy makers and planners in the UK. The interests of adult social worlds predominate, for instance, in transport and traffic policy, advertising, housing. Even services ostensibly planned for children are provided mainly in the interests of adults. For instance, education policy subjugates the health and welfare of children now, to the production of useful citizens in the future. Increasingly, instrumental educational policies over the past twenty years focus on children as products to be taught, rather than as learners and as people with rights to good experience now.

In making the above statements, I am purposefully offering a very broadbrush account. The aim is to point to dominant understandings and to dominant social arrangements. It is, of course, also arguable that there has been considerable progress on children's rights in the past dozen years or so, since the ratifying by the UK government of the Convention on the Rights of the Child (Franklin 2002). In the UK, as in other European countries, there is now a large body of research that argues in favour of children's rights, notably to the 3Ps: protection, provision and, especially, participation (Alderson 2000; Cloke and Davies 1997). At lip-service level, too, there is some recognition of children's participation rights in decision-making (Freeman 2000) There is an increasing body of work, broadly within the sociology of childhood, that documents children's agency, their contributions and their abilities to reflect on their experiences and to offer reasoned arguments on moral issues (Alanen and Mayall 2001; Mizen *et al.* 2001). How far this research work has currency outside the readership of like-minded people is debatable. So, opinions may differ on how far the above points have been challenged in policy and practice.

Public and private responsibility for children

The second broad theme here is the division of responsibility between the state and parents for children's welfare.

THE DIVISION OF RESPONSIBILITY FOR CHILDREN AND CHILDHOOD

Within the UK welfare state, health and education services have traditionally been universalist, and social (or welfare) services have been residualist, so the division of responsibility between the public and the private for children's health, education and welfare differs accordingly. But even the health and education services are less universalist now than they were and they are not adequately backed by financial and care packages to enable parents to rear healthy children. As to the residualist welfare services, increasingly the balance of financial and social responsibility has been shifted away from services and towards parents. State responsibility for health and welfare stops at provision of surveillance and monitoring, prevention and cure. However, care (for instance, of a disabled child) is mainly a private parental responsibility. Provision of adequate financial and material resources to ensure reasonably good-quality childhoods was off the political agenda after 1979 and is only slowly coming back. A highly significant marker of this neglect is that proportions of children living in poverty increased from about 10 per cent to 30 per cent between 1979 and 1997, far and away the worst in Europe. The Labour government in power since 1997 has made a range of policy initiatives to tackle child poverty; again, opinions differ as to how many children, or what proportion of children have been lifted out of poverty (Bradshaw 2002; Hendrick 2003).

State responsibility for the education and care of children at school is increasingly at bare-bones level. Parents are asked to contribute, not only by fundraising for extras but also by taking on the central functions of the school – providing books, picking up ill children from school, working free as helpers round the classroom, paying for and accompanying school trips and working with children in the evening. Mothers rather than fathers do most of this. In the UK the high costs of rearing healthy children are unequally borne by parents as compared with the state. These are the costs of keeping children safe, feeding and clothing them, providing home, comfort and stability, enabling children to acquire cultural capital, paying for tuition and experience in areas of knowledge that have been pushed out of the schools (such as music and art and sports and drama). Of course, all this means that equality of opportunity has decreased with increases in income inequality.

The education measures put in place by the Conservative government in the early 1990s, have been reinforced by the Labour government, and have increased inequalities. Thus, frequent testing of children at school, publication of the results, parental right to choose schools at any distance from the home, the establishment of selective schools, and the continuance of charity status for private schools, all lead to children's educational experience becoming dependent on parental income, knowledge, ability and willingness to shop around.

THE FAMILIALIZATION OF CHILDREN AND CHILDHOOD

It can be argued that in the UK childhood has become privatized or 'familialized'. The rhetoric of social policy insists that children are to be understood mainly within parent–child relationships and that children's success depends on parental child-rearing. Emphasis is on 'parenting' (including 'parenting' classes), emotional values, and individual child development. Of course, 'parenting' means mothers. Yet under current Labour government policies, mothers are being encouraged to go out to work, even though daycare services remain insufficient and expensive. So mothers are caught in a double bind, as ever: asked to take on double responsibilities, both for earning and for producing successful children and, of course, doing housework on the side. Children in this scenario are invisible, subsumed within the family and children's visibility to professionals is largely achieved when they deviate as victims or as threats.

Comparisons between UK and European child-related policies

The ideology and politics of the UK welfare state provide a distinctive division of labour between the state and parents as compared with that in some other European countries. States such as France and the Nordic countries intervene much more fully and take a bigger share of responsibility for child welfare in the private domain, in the public domain and across the private and the public (Pringle 1998). Indeed, distinctions between the private and the public are far more blurred than they are in the UK. Social policies in Nordic countries, for example, take account of child and parent welfare and of the need for coherent financial and social packages to support home life. Planning for school services includes input from health and social-welfare services as well as education services. Policies consider child welfare in conjunction with parental work hours so after-school care is designed to serve both children and parents (Mayall 2002).

In the name of rational organization of the lives of children and parents, and to some extent in the name of children's rights, some European countries regard children as a social group, as the target of policies (Therborn 1996). They take more financial responsibility for children than the UK does. It can be argued that some European policies not only collectivize and institutionalize children, they also standardize their childhoods. There may be downsides as well as considerable upsides, whether by design or not, in wholesale state intervention.

In summary, this very brief and extremely sweeping discussion of some aspects of social policy in the UK serves as an introduction to the second part of this chapter, for children effectively provide a commentary on those policies.

What children say

In the late 1990s, I carried out a study with nine-year-olds and twelve- year-olds. This was part of a large programme of research in the UK that asked researchers to focus on the child as social actor.[1] The information presented here comes from discussions with 57 children aged nine attending schools in inner London. The children are a multi-ethnic, mixed-social-class sample of girls and boys. In UK cities, we have children from all over the world; some are themselves first-generation immigrants and may be refugees; some are people whose parents or grandparents came to the UK. Through 'mixed' marriages and partnerships, increasingly British citizens have their roots in more than one society, in more than one culture. In many classrooms, especially in inner-city areas, white 'English' children are in the minority and are part of a hugely diverse school population. My reason here for pointing to this diversity is that it is a basis for an important finding – that children from a range of backgrounds share experience, knowledge and judgements. There is more commonality than there is difference.

The aim of my study was to explore how children understand and experience childhood. This is not a common research topic and I confronted it both directly and indirectly. First of all, in friendship pairs, I asked them to reflect directly on childhood: the status of childhood, what childhood is like, how it differs from adulthood, and how they understand and experience child–adult relations. And then, second, some of them talked with me individually or again in pairs and I asked them to describe their everyday life and reflect on it, on what the issues were that their everyday life raised for them. Here is an extremely brief summary of some of the main points they made (see Mayall 2002).

Mothers and fathers

The children expressed very traditional views about the social positions and functions of mothers and fathers. This is in spite of the fact that in one classroom, for instance, of 28 children only half actually lived with both their mother and their father. All described motherhood as involving absolute, total, final responsibility for children and for the home. Fathers were understood as responsible for the financial status of the family. It is fathers who go out to work. Children saw that parents work hard; and almost all argued that adulthood is hard by comparison with childhood: an interesting point. Motherhood was particularly hard because of its many conflicting responsibilities and, of course, also because many mothers have to finance the family. While fathers can, and do, walk away from their responsibilities, mothers, they say, cannot.

The social position of childhood

The salient and central point in children's discourse is that they understand child–adult relations, not just in individual terms but as relations between the social positions of childhood and adulthood. Adults have authority over children and children must obey adults, notably, of course, parents and teachers. It is a parental job to teach children morality and to punish and reward accordingly, as Montandon (2001) also found in Geneva. And children say they have the right to care, protection and provision from parents and that on the whole, though not in all cases and at all times, they get it. In their emphasis on social status, and on points they think hold true across cases, you could argue that children are more sociological than many adults.

Responsibility

As stressed above, children propose that mothers in particular but also fathers have total, absolute responsibility for keeping the family afloat, both financially and socially. When I asked children whether they too had responsibilities, many said they had none. For them, part of the condition of childhood is not having ultimate responsibilities. They then went on to talk about their daily activities – housework, food preparation, child-care, fetching and carrying, organizing and carrying out their school work. When asked whether these were responsibilities, they generally suggested that these were assigned or delegated responsibilities and not absolute ones. The children are presenting themselves as subordinate, as dependent, not as autonomous (see also Thomson and Holland 2002).

Free time

A striking feature of children's accounts is the high value they put on what they term 'free time'. This, as they describe it, is time when they are freed from the tasks of childhood. Childhood, as they present it, is heavily controlled by adults most of the time, so they highly value 'free time', and describe it as a right. During free time, one may do many things: reading, watching TV, listening to music, being with friends and playing. Notably children understand play as something children do, in free time.[2] So I asked children to explore this topic. 'Do adults have a right to free time too?' The common reply was that, yes they did but, of course, adults were not much good at 'free time'. They don't know how to enjoy themselves.

Negotiation

Negotiation, after all, was the proposed theme of my project: Negotiating Childhood. When I planned it, I hypothesized that children participated, through interaction, in constructing their childhoods. Children's accounts indicate that negotiation comprises working with adults and with other children on three main tasks. The first one relates to the point outlined earlier – that childhood is a dependent social status. Children clearly explained that an important part of the job of childhood was to work towards becoming a 'good enough person' within the cultural norms of the home and the social network. Autonomy is not something that is being sought at this age. That was true of the twelve-year-olds too.

The second negotiation is the character of personal, social relations: participation in constructing and reconstructing relations within the family and with friends. The family is critical and central to the lives of these children. Friendships are important not only because they provide happy social relations, but as a defence against the adult-ordered regime of the school. Friendships also provide a forum for discussing personal and family problems.

And, third, they work on the project of their own life. This may include plans for the future, making the most of one's abilities, thinking of school work as a pathway to future ways of life. So they present three strands in their interactive lives, of which the third is slightly more individualistic than the others – that there is, after all, their own life to be considered and what they are going to make of it.

Apprenticeship

During this research project, I early on learned that an important strand in children's thinking was a traditional one: that childhood is a period of time when you learn what you need to know to face the adult world; you do that at home and school. As regards school, children welcome the opportunity for education at school and by and large they are conformist. Some of us adults regret very much the prescriptive, competitive agendas imposed on children's experience in our schools, but the children themselves consider they are getting a good education that will be useful for their futures; they accept the domination of teachers and the curriculum (though not instances of adults' unjust behaviour). They regard themselves as having absolutely no choice at all about what they do at school, except at playtime.

Moral status

The next two points are about moral status. This is a central issue in considering the social condition of childhood. There are two competing components in their moral status: the assignment of moral status and their own moral agency. Children find that they are commonly regarded as morally subordinate to adults and that they are morally suspect. They accept moral subordination to adults, who control their lives while also caring for them.

Yet children are also expected to take moral responsibility and their accounts indicate they do act as responsible moral agents. This emerges not so much from their own identification of their moral agency but more from their accounts of their daily life. Children work within, towards and as restructurers of, their own social identity. They carry out work in maintaining the social order of the household through participating in housework and child-care. In particular, they are participants in family relations, sympathizing, caring, worrying, keeping in touch with relatives who live elsewhere and, in particular, of course, fathers. Additionally, children show moral agency in maintaining their friendships with other children and acting as confidants and helpers when friends are going through difficult times. Many children told me how they share their problems in relation to school and to home life. And finally, children's agency is expressed in taking responsibility for activities related to school, getting the work done, organizing their belongings and doing their homework.

Summary – What children say

It can be concluded from this research that these children are indeed social actors. Indeed, they can be described as social agents, in the sense of making a difference. For they regard childhood as a period of life when one charts a course. Within the social constraints of child–adult relations, children participate in constructing their childhoods. Childhood can be understood as a deliberate course of actions, balancing adult control with freedom, and at school, enjoyment of friendships and orientation to the future, building one's identity as part of the family and as one's self. Children therefore see themselves as participators in the structuring of their own lives and the lives of their family and friends. Thus childhood, in their accounts, includes orientation to both present experience and future life.

An important point in their accounts is that (though they do not use the language of rights) children think that they are entitled, they have a right, to be protected and provided for; carrying out that responsibility towards them is one of the functions, the central function, of parents. Most, but not quite all, of them did feel secure in parental protection and provision, but their participation rights are more problematic. Children find that their participation rights are not routinely, in all circumstances, respected. I heard many stories from children about how they were pushed aside and refused a voice. This was especially so at school. School is given; you have no choice about determining what happens at school. At home children have more mixed experiences because some parents do listen to them sometimes; but parental agendas, busyness and authority diminishes children's ability to make themselves heard and responded to. And, as I have stressed, a particularly worrying explanation for this is that children find themselves regarded as morally suspect.

Thus children confirm that childhood has a particular character in the UK – it is understood as preparatory, as inferior to adulthood. It is also a 'familialized' childhood. These children stress the centrality of family, of home. We do not know how far children in other societies talk on this topic – but there are competing views. For instance, in Finland, a society where the state has a much larger part in providing for childhood in its own right than the UK has, Leena Alanen found that some children put very great stress on friendship or on their particular interests, rather than on family relations (Alanen 2001; Mayall 2002, Chapter 8).

Some general points

I reflect here on some general points emerging out of several studies I've carried out over the past twelve years or so (Kelley, Mayall and Hood 1997; Mayall 1996; 2002). All in all I've listened to children from the age of five up to sixteen in various settings and with particular focuses, talking about their daily lives at home and at school. These are all just ordinary children living in London, and going to state schools, not children selected because they were special in some way.

My general purpose in this enterprise has been to fill in gaps in our understanding of how the social order works, because you cannot achieve an adequate idea about this unless you take account of the views and experiences of every member group; and it is children who, of course, have been neglected here (Stacey 1981). I've also been concerned with policy-oriented issues – the rights and wrongs of children and how to right them. Four general points emerge out of this work.

First, I think children think sociologically. They are concerned with the social status of children and of childhood now; with the present tense of childhood in its social relations, not with childhood as a pre-social becoming.

As sociologists, children divide the social order into two groups of people, adults and those whom adults define as non-adults, that is children. They are very clear about this. Many of them reflected in sophisticated ways about what being called a child means. They arrived at these definitions through contrasting childhood with adulthood; by definition as a person sited within the definition 'child' you do not have the characteristics of adults.

They also, therefore, regard childhood as relational, the point made initially. That is, they see the character and quality of childhoods as structured through relationships with adults, most importantly parents and teachers. This, I think, is an extremely important point, which is, to some extent, neglected in psychological approaches, because they focus so much on 'the individual child', and on the development of the child towards adulthood, through processes thought to be determined by biological maturation (see Greene 1999 for discussion). From the children's point of view, what they are, in the here and now, derives from relational processes.

The second point I have already outlined. Children subscribe to a paradox. They agree with adults that childhood is a period of life, an apprenticeship, when people are rightly subordinated to those with more experience and knowledge. Being protected by adults from absolute responsibilities is one kind of right that children identify and childhood should include free time and fun. But apprenticeship is only part of the story of childhood. Children's accounts forcibly indicate that they are moral agents who carry out important activities, both in the structuring and progressing of their own lives and in making and remaking relations within the context of family and friends.

Third, I emphasize this central point, which requires adults to rethink child-adult relations. Children emphasize that their moral status and, in particular, their participation rights, are constantly in question. Adult conceptualizations of children as incomplete people and adults' assumptions that their own agendas matter more than children's do, lead them to downgrade children as moral agents and, in turn, children's own subordination sometimes leads them (as they tell me) to adopt whatever tactics they can to assert their rights, such as wheedling, lying, demanding and refusing. The fact is that in the UK children are regarded as adult responsibilities in public places; children are decreasingly allowed out on their own (Holloway and Valentine 2000). This social exclusion further serves to solidify adult views that children are incompetents.

Fourth, and most grandly, children have important lessons for moral philosophers on issues of autonomy and interdependence. Western liberal thinkers, all of them men, have regarded the autonomous, independent moral agent as the highest form of life and many of them have found it very hard to include women as possible candidates, let alone children. It has taken feminist philosophy in the past twenty years to point to interdependence as the value by which most of us live and to note that the man in the ivory tower is not autonomous, but relies on others, mainly women, to wash and clean, to provide food and to engage him in personal relations (Grimshaw 1986).

Children, too, like women, regard relations as the cornerstone of their lives. It is of crucial importance to them to work with and through family relations and to care about those who live elsewhere (non-resident fathers, grandparents) as well as those they live with. Children's accounts centre on such matters, on the health and well-being and problems of the people they love. And, of course, as they said, the best thing about school is friends because while the formal school agenda is dictated by adults, relationships with friends provide the forum that allows you to make sense of school, to put up with it and even enjoy it.

In summary, children provide us with a unique and specific set of takes on the social, which both help us to understand how the social order works and provide pointers towards ways of improving childhoods.

Making children visible: Addressing the issues

If in the UK children have been routinely excluded and invisible in planning and policy-making, then what can we do to make children visible? I think more is being done in Australia, in New Zealand and in many European countries than is being done in our country. How can we work towards putting children's welfare higher on our national agenda? Other chapters in this book discuss policy measures. I end by noting proposals from a recent outstanding report.

Save the Children UK (1995) contextualize their proposals in the UN Convention and, since they work all over the world, they take an international perspective, which draws especially on Articles 12 and 13: the right of the child to express an opinion in matters concerning him or her and to have it taken into account; and the right that actions concerning the child should take full account of the child's best interests. The report made six main points:

1. The need for child-specific data.

2. The need for recognition of children's productive contribution.

3. The need to include children as participants in policy-making.

4. The need for more appropriate conceptualization of children and childhood.

5. The need to give serious attention to child interests.

6. The importance of gender and generational issues.

Conclusion

In Sweden, at the very beginning of the twentieth century, Ellen Key (1909) wrote an influential book: *The Century of the Child.* She argued (within the eugenics movement) for women's responsibility to ensure a healthy generation of children. At the end of the twentieth century an acerbic commentator noted that what we got was not the century of the child but a century of the child professional (Stafseng 1993) – that is, the child as adult project. I think it is our duty and our task to help make the twenty-first century more like the century of the child. None of us knows what this would look like – nor did Ellen Key. A start is the rights of the child. My view is that these can derive a solid theoretical foundation in the sociology of childhood (Mayall 2002).

Notes

1   The study in question was funded by the UK Economic and Social Research Council as one of 22 projects on the Children 5–16 Programme. It was called 'Negotiating Childhoods' and ran, formally, from September 1997 to August 1999 (ESRC ref. no. L129 25 1032) (see Prout 2002.) A series of books under the title 'The Future of Childhood' is being published by RoutledgeFalmer. Apart from those in the reference list (Alanen and Mayall 2001; Christensen and O'Brien 2003; Mizen, Pole and Bolton 2001), others so far are: R. Edwards (ed.) (2002) *Children, Home and School*; I. Hutchby and J. Moran-Ellis (eds) (2001) *Children, Technology and Culture*; A.-M. Jensen and L. McKie (eds) (2002) *Children and the Changing Family.*

2   I briefly note here that children's understanding of play as activity out of ordinary adult-controlled life not only accords with Huizinga (1949), but also acts as a commentary on adult formulations: that children's play is educational – they learn physical and social skills through it. (For discussion, see Mayall 2002, pp.132–5.)

CHAPTER SIX

Child Protection Policy and the Construction of Childhood

Jan Mason

Introduction

The way we construct or understand childhood is closely related to state policies around interventions in some families for the protection of children. Child-welfare and child-protection policies have been key discursive spaces for the way in which childhood and adult–child relations are structured. In implementing state policies child-welfare practitioners function as mediators between the state, children and their families. In this capacity professionals have been key agents for reinforcing, through their interventions with individual children, ways of defining childhood and appropriate adult–child relations within the broader society.

Historically, in English-speaking societies child-welfare policy has been influenced by the developmental, adult-centric paradigm and has reinforced that paradigm through its interventions. This paradigm has constructed childhood in terms of a contrast with adulthood, as a time of 'becoming' and incompetence. Children have been conceptualized as 'lesser than' adults and fused within families as passive dependents. Childhood has been constructed as universal, across cultures.

In recent years the emphasis on child participation, highlighted in the codification of child-participatory principles in international and national legislation, has challenged thinking about child-welfare policy and practice. This challenge is given impetus by a construction of childhood identified with an alternative paradigm. According to this alternative paradigm (James and Prout 1990) children are 'beings' who are actors in their own lives and have individual ways of experiencing the world.

In this chapter this alternative paradigm is the lens through which the influence of the dominant paradigm on child-protection policy is analysed. By applying this paradigm retrospectively we can sharpen the focus of the lens on contemporary practices and thereby assist in rethinking current practice.

Children as 'becomings' – A future orientation

Applying the lens of the alternative paradigm to child-welfare policies and practices highlights the way that the emphasis of the developmental approach on children as 'becomings' has justified child-welfare policies based on the value of children as *future adults* and thereby ignoring them as 'beings' with experiences in the present.

Historically, the future orientation on childhood has been exemplified in Australian policy supporting particular child-protection practices. For example, a 1911 statement of the Aborigines Welfare Board claimed that removing children from Reserves was justified in order to prevent them becoming, as adults, 'a positive menace to the State' (Reed undated, p.7). In the United States, Charles Loring Brace a key child-welfare reformer of the mid-nineteenth century, believed it was important to 'rescue' children of the 'dangerous' classes and place them in middle-class families so that they would grow up and become reputable citizens, alleviating the threat of civil disorder, occurring in other countries at the time (Bremner 1970, p.401).

In more contemporary terms, similar future-oriented concepts were articulated as a rationale for child-protection policy in Kempe's (1975) keynote address to the first Australian national conference on child abuse. Kempe argued in this address that it was important for Australia to develop policies against child abuse for 'its young children who are, after all, the nation's future and therefore its most valuable resource' (Kempe 1975, p.4). More recently, Carter, (2002) in a report on foster care, cites human-capital issues as a pragmatic reason for child-welfare reform and describes the current human-capital approach to child development as viewing investment in early childhood as 'ultimately an investment in the future human capital of a society and its future productive capacity' (p.53).

Child-welfare rhetoric that constructs children as assets and highlights the symbolic value of children as society's future, thereby ignoring their experiences in the present, can be seen to be associated with policies that contribute to children being treated as 'object(s) of concern', in the way critiqued in the English

Cleveland report (Horne 1990, p.102). Such policies have legitimated practices where children's present realities as experienced by them have been trivialized and discounted. Some blatant examples of the impact of the implementation of this phenomenon have been exposed in investigations into the 'stolen generations' of both Aboriginal children and children who were the subject of forced migration from England to the then colonies (Goddard and Carew 1993).

More generally, children who have been the focus of child-welfare interventions have expressed, sometimes graphically, how they have felt objectified by child-protection and welfare policy. For example in a video scripted by children in New South Wales who were state wards and entitled 'Wardies Supermarket', the children depicted themselves as being like products on a supermarket shelf (ACCA 1980). That children continue to experience objectification as a result of child-protection policies is indicated by comments in discussions of more recent research, such as 'they didn't treat you like people' (Cashmore and Paxman 1996, p.40) and 'another kid is just another case' (Butler and Williamson 1994, p.75).

The fusion of children with the family

The normative, developmental approach to childhood conceptualizes children as fused within the family. This has meant that children have been invisible, existing only as minors or dependents (Makrinotti 1994). Parents share responsibility with the state for 'growing up' of children, based on their mutual interests in re-production of both family and society and so children have not generally been recognized as recipients of policies except in child-protection situations. In the case of child-protection policies, families departing from the norm have been labelled 'dysfunctional' or 'deviant'. Because of children's fusion within the family, many young people removed from families carry with them the stigma attached to these families, feeling condemned because they do not have 'normal' families (McNeish and Newman 2002; Mason and Gibson 2004).

The conjunction within the developmental model of the fusion of children with families and the emphasis on normative 'ideal' families has influenced the dominance within child-welfare of policies promoting placement of children removed from their own homes in 'substitute' families. These substitute, or foster, families have typically been 'approved' on the basis of their proximity to the norm of 'ideal' nuclear families. These policies were exemplified in late-nineteenth-century Australian foster-care practices. For example, when foster care was introduced in the state of South Australia, it was described as being about 'select(ing) homes for our destitute children among the better class of our labouring population...to restore them as far as possible to that family life which is the institution of our Great Creator Himself' (Ramsland 1986, p.165).

An emphasis on the idealized family as the place for children has continued during the twentieth century to influence child-welfare provisions in Australia and other English-speaking countries, through the promotion of foster care over institutional care as the preferred placement option for children removed from their parents. This option has been implemented through a process that has high-lighted the negatives of residential care, while typically ignoring, or glossing over, the deficiencies of foster care (Frost and Stein 1989). Foster care has been accepted as the appropriate response to abusive and neglectful family situations, making it unnecessary for policy makers to confront the association between parental abuse and institutionalized inequality in adult–child relations inside (as well as outside) the family (Mason and Falloon 2001). This is in spite of contem-porary reports of ongoing vulnerability to re-abuse of children in substitute families, as demonstrated, for example, in allegations of current widespread physical and sexual abuse of children in the Queensland foster-care system (e.g. Qld's foster care condemned. *Sydney Morning Herald* 2003).

The notion of a 'universal' child

The focus of the dominant paradigm on normative stages of child development contributes to the discounting of children as individuals, through assumptions about the *universal* child – a child existing independently of historical and cultural contexts and of social relationships (Hogan 1997). Although as Burman has observed '(t)he normal child, the ideal type…is a fiction or myth' (Burman 1994, p.16), this ideal has influenced child-welfare and child-protection practices aimed at monitoring any deviancy in children from 'normal' paths to adulthood. In this process, child-protection work has been about observing, categorizing and standardizing child-rearing practices through child-protection interventions (Thorpe 1994).

The assumptions inherent in the conceptualization of a normative childhood have been based on a white, middle-class set of ideas of childhood, in which chil-dren's social contexts and their individuality, have been ignored. Historically this practice was characteristic of early-nineteenth-century child-welfare policy, which attempted to inculcate white European values in Australian Aboriginal children through their removal to institutions specifically designed for this purpose (Mason and Noble-Spruell 1993; Ramsland 1986). This practice has also been exemplified in the way racist assumptions and stereotypes about appro-priate parental practices have influenced and continue to influence child-welfare decision-making about children in Black and ethnic-minority groups (Frost and Stein 1989; Roberts 1999).

The association of a normative childhood with particular white ideals of parenting has meant that child-welfare policy has generally ignored the socio-economic dimension of child-protection interventions that has historically been evident in the strong association between poverty and the entry of children to care (Frost and Stein 1989; Mason and Noble-Spruell 1993; Roberts 1999; Schneiderman *et al.* 1998). Instead, policy has been about 'blaming' parents in poverty and placing them under surveillance. In examining state intervention in the United Kingdom, Thomas (2000, p.55) notes that 'surveillance and intervention fall more extensively and heavily on the working class or the poor' and that children in out-of-home care 'originate overwhelmingly from certain social groups: poor working class families in inadequate housing, often with disrupted parenting and disproportionately of mixed ethnic origin' (Thomas 2000, p.73). Of the contemporary American child-welfare system, Roberts concludes that it appears as a 'system designed to regulate, monitor, and punish poor families, especially poor Black families' (1999, p.64), while poverty and lack of support for parents is a major factor in the entry to care of a disproportionate number of Black children in the United States for reasons to do with poverty.

Child protection policy and inequality in child–adult relations

The conceptualization of children as *lesser* than adults has legitimized adult–child relations where adults are considered to have a 'natural' right to impose authority on children as part of the social order. Analysis by sociologists of childhood, such as Alanen (1994), has identified the asymmetry in power relations between adults and children. Child-protection policy can be seen as a mechanism for the institutionalization of this asymmetry. This institutionalization occurs in various ways through child-welfare practices.

First, the reliance on the 'best interests' rhetoric reinforces paternalistic decision-making and legitimates adult power or authority over children. This power of adults has been justified in terms of children's biological immaturity and dependency, which has typically ignored the fact that children become less physically dependent throughout their non-adult years and has masked the ways in which children's diminishing biological immaturity is replaced by socially determined dependency, based on economic and other factors (Kitzinger 1988; Morrow 1994). 'Best interests' policy has inbuilt assumptions that adult–child relations are based on adult concerns to protect children's best interests. Such assumptions have been challenged by Franklin (1986), who highlights the extent to which adult–child interactions are characterized, even defined, by unequal or asymmetrical power relations. Further, these assumptions work to camouflage the extent to which 'best interests' decision-making is based on individual adults' discretion and therefore subjectivities.

Second, child-welfare interventions built around monitoring of parental behaviour frequently use the power and authority inherent in professionals' statutory roles, in a manner that research has shown reinforces the 'authoritarian' or patriarchal 'premises on which an abusive parent's behaviour is based' (MacKinnon 1998, p.234). Third, in those instances when child-welfare workers, as agents of public patriarchy (Hearn 1990), remove children from their parents they rarely increase the power of these children. Rather, they redistribute power over children from one set of adults to another set of adults (Chisholm 1979). The reinforcing of asymmetrical relations by child-protection interventions that relocate children with substitute families is evidenced in the frequency with which further abuse occurs within these homes (e.g. Owen 1996; *Sydney Morning Herald* 2003).

Finally, when child-protection policies ignore the interconnections between dependency and power, in accepting as their premise that children are weak and victims of adults, they may promote (as Kitzinger (1988) has noted in the case of sexual abuse) surveillance of children and the curtailing of their freedom and autonomy by parents and professionals. The paradox is that this restriction of freedom may actually increase children's vulnerability. For example, children's activities may be limited to places where abuse is known to be prevalent: the home and school. Placing controls on children's lives by responding to them as victims avoids threatening the power of adults. As a consequence, children who experience child-welfare interventions may see themselves as to blame, and experience interventions as punitive (Mason and Gibson in process).

The concept of incompetence and the trivialization of children's knowledge

The construction of children as passive dependents – as not adults and therefore lesser beings than adults – enables adults to discount and marginalize children's knowledge. Placed at the bottom of a hierarchy of cognitive authority, children have been excluded from contributing as 'knowers' to child-welfare practice relevant to their lives. Instead, they have been 'protected' from discussions around interventions into their lives and their perspectives have been conveyed and interpreted by intermediaries: mothers, fathers and various professional experts such as social workers, teachers and psychologists. These intermediaries, as Oakley notes, 'all have a stake in the business of knowing about children' (Oakley 1994, p.30). Expert adults have defined child abuse, the abusers and the abused while silencing children as victims. This has been evidenced in the recording of child-protection interventions on official files. For example, Parton, Thorpe and Wattam (1997) report that in the files they examined children's voices were missing – except where they were brought in to support practitioner decision-making. Numerous examples attest to the fact that when children subject to child-welfare policy have tried to speak out about abuse both in the past and present, they have been disbelieved (ACCA 1980; Owen 1996).

Taking into account children's knowledge will challenge child-protection policy and practice, as findings on their feelings of objectification and vulnerability to further abuse are placed alongside what we know of their construction of child abuse. For example, children defining child abuse have placed it firmly within the context of inequalities in adult–child relations. In research on children's definition of child abuse they conveyed their belief that 'we're all oppressed by our parents' by virtue of being children, because 'adults can treat them (children) however they want' (Mason and Falloon 2001). These children believed it was the inequalities in power between adults and children that enabled adults to behave towards children in ways which they, as children, could not reciprocate. As one child said 'you're not allowed to smack anyone else but children...' and 'I can't smack (back)' (pp.106–108). Actions of adults towards children that they could not reciprocate they defined as child abuse. Similarly, Butler and Williamson (1994) report that in their research where children spoke about trauma and social work they defined 'safety' differently from the way adults define 'protection'.

Conclusion

The mechanism for changes to the way child-protection policy is implemented is that codified in children's right to participation in child-welfare policy and practice. This codification has given impetus to discourses on children's participation in child-protection decision-making. It makes possible the re-conceptualization of children according to the 'alternative' paradigm as active, individual and competent, acknowledging children as beings with 'rights' to participate in decision-making. Taking children and their knowledge seriously will mean confronting structural inequalities in child–adult relations through child-welfare policy – and, more broadly, social policy – as a fundamental strategy for reducing adult abuse of children.

CHAPTER SEVEN

'To Know Them Is To Love Them', But Instead Fear and Loathing

Community Perceptions of Young People

Natalie Bolzan

Introduction

Various social indicators such as employment (Dusseldorp Skills Forum 2003) and suicide rates (Mission Australia 2003) suggest that young people in Australia are a marginalized group. Concern has been expressed that the community of adults may be prejudiced against young people, thereby preventing their full inclusion in society. In order to explore community attitudes to young people and the sources of these attitudes, the National Youth Affairs Research Scheme (NYARS) – formed of representatives from the government youth bureaus in each Australian state and territory – commissioned research into the area. NYARS hypothesized that negative stereotyping was associated with prejudice that contributed to community behaviour disadvantaging and marginalizing of young people. The research they commissioned is reported here.

Stereotypes can be seen as social constructions that are in common use in a community. The social construction of young people refers to the manner in which they (like most groups, issues or topics) are 'constructed' or contingent, rather than 'pre-existing givens' (Hastings 1998, p.194). Such constructions are underpinned by the use of certain language, knowledge and power, which are interconnected at the level of discourses (Foucault 1977a). Negative stereotypes can then lead to prejudice – defined as an antipathy based on faulty and inflexible generalization that may lead to discriminatory treatment (Allport 1954). By exploring the discourses around young people we come closer to knowing how young people are constructed (Fairclough 1998), that is, the stereotypes that lead to prejudice affecting the way young people are treated in and by society. Discourse here is used in terms of its wider definition of implied social relationships (Macnaughten 1993).

It is not easy to identify those discourses that construct young people in a society. At a most fundamental level, language constructs issues or situations (Fairclough 1998; Hastings 1998); the words available to describe an item or situation are responsible for how we understand it and therefore respond to it. Thus to understand how a community is constructing young people we need to explore the words the community are using to describe young people.

The process by which a thing is named and the manner in which a community takes up this naming is not clearly understood. Certain sites of naming, or discourse production, have been identified as influencing the community and creating public opinion. These include: the media (Webber 1998); public inquiries (Macnaughten 1993); conversational context (Moir 1993); and policy makers – those who hold sway in powerful institutions, the enforcers of legislation, professional groupings, academic writers and researchers (Tucker 1997). Consequently there may be many sites producing the discourses that construct young people. The research discussed in this chapter explores the construction of young people evident in one common site of discourse construction, the media, and compares these with the discourses around young people in the general community.

Methodology

In May 2003, Media Monitors (a national media-survey company) were commissioned to identify and collect any items in the national electronic and print media that mentioned 'young people', 'adolescents', 'kids', 'youth' or 'teenagers'. Three hundred and ninety-three items were identified in this one-week media snapshot.

One week later AC Neilsen, a well-known market-research firm, was commissioned to conduct a national omnibus survey to elicit community perceptions of young people. One thousand one hundred and ninety adults over the age of 24 from rural and urban locations throughout Australia were surveyed. The age of 24 was chosen as the cut-off age, because of its use by the Australian government in formal social-policy definitions of young people. Table 7.1 describes the sample.

Table 7.1 Sample for survey of community opinion

Sex	No.	%
Male	593	50
Female	597	50
Total	1190	100
Age groups		
25–39	497	42
40–54	385	32
55+	308	26
Total	1190	100

As this was exploratory research aiming to capture community attitudes to something that had not been explored elsewhere, an open-ended question was developed to identify people's attitudes (Haddock and Zanna 1998). The advantage of this was it minimized the influence of researcher biases and assumptions about how the community perceived young people.

The community survey was introduced with 'We'd now like to ask you some questions about young people in Australia, that is people between the ages of 12 and 24. What three words, images or phrases best describe your personal view of young people?' This was then followed by a question concerning the source of this view 'People's views about young people are probably influenced by a range of factors. What sources/factors do you think have influenced your views about young people?'

The collection of media accounts of young people preceded the survey of adults as in previous research by the author (Bolzan 2003) in which community members identified the media as an important influence in the formation of opinions or the creation of discourses of young people. Sercombe (1995) argues that newspaper texts about young people provide insights into the discursive information about youth and young people that are articulated for a mass audience. Tucker (1997, pp.92–93) observes that media scrutiny focuses on specific aspects of youth activity that highlight illegal activities such as drug-taking and sexual experimentation or the rejection of 'meaningful' forms of activity by participation in activities such as 'joy-riding'. The events that are defined in this way are then used as the norm to describe the behaviour of young people. The application of certain characteristics observed in some instances ensures that a few isolated incidents are taken as 'typical' of young people's behaviour. Davis and Bourhill (1997) argue that the media portrayal of children and young people's involvement in crime is central in creating and reinforcing public perceptions of young people. The media is seen to be influential in creating the everyday talk (Van Dijk 1987) by which young people are constructed.

Findings – Community attitudes to young people

Young people needing help

The media reviewed in the current project constructed young people, in the main, as in need of assistance. Just over half (54%) of all items reviewed presented young people as in some way disadvantaged, ill-equipped or ill-prepared for the responsibilities of adulthood. In 213 out of 393 items young people were constructed as needing: care or protection; education or instruction; or improved services and facilities. In exploring the 'vulnerability' of young people a set of items created a discrete and strong discourse around young people as needing help or being 'incomplete'. There were three facets to this discourse. The first was concerned with describing the help provided to young people. It contained items describing programmes and services necessary to help young people become competent healthy adults, such as: computer programs to teach children to save; school-retention programmes; programmes to reduce anti-social behaviours; the destruction of records of young offenders who reform; and programmes to encourage more active participation in the community. Other items in this category described immaturity as a factor in drug use; unemployment; bullying; reckless driving; daredevil behaviour; the need for programmes for homeless kids; and industrial problems. A second facet of this discourse described problems created for the vulnerable young by a society's lack of care for them, for example: in not protecting young people from paedophiles; through too much sugar in breakfast cereals leading to obesity; through legalizing cannabis; and locking children up in detention centres. A final facet of this discourse dealt with information for parents on how to help children to become healthier and safer. It dealt with issues concerned with parents teaching children about; dieting; sex; surfing; fishing; playing outdoors; following their dreams; and learning about consequences of their actions.

Young people as victims

The very strong discourse emerging of young people needing the help of the community was reinforced by 14 per cent of items that very clearly constructed young people as victims. Young people were victims: of other young people; of hit and run drivers; of fashion; of businesses; of carers; of paedophiles; of rural unemployment; and of increases in fees for higher education.

Young people as problematic

The other strong discourse evident in the media identified young people as problematic. In 20 per cent of the items (77 stories) young people were presented as behaving badly with no ameliorating social context. For example young people were discussed in terms of: gang activity; attacks with a knife at school; car crashes; rapes; running away from home; selfishness; sloppy speech; disobeying laws; criminal acts; bomb hoax; alien hoax; and increasing debt. This discourse constructed young people as bad and causing trouble.

Young people as successful

A final construction of young people was evident in the media whereby 10 per cent of items described young achievers and those who have succeeded in some way. There were several stories of individual achievers and successes that celebrated achievement and congratulated these young people. Such stories were concerned with young people making a film; running a festival; making video clips; involved in traditional trapping activity; playing music; winning sports awards; getting work; advisory group meetings and participating in civic activities. Of the 393 items appearing in the one-week media snapshot, 38 (10%) portrayed young people in this way.

Summary

In summary, 68 per cent of all media items dealing with young people constructed them as 'vulnerable' or victims and as needing assistance. This strong discourse was often linked to the message that young people needed constant surveillance and intervention in order to enable them to grow into competent, self-reliant adults. Whilst, on the surface, a discourse about the community working to help young people appears supportive, there is a different message that one might take away from this discourse. The notion of young people needing help serves to construct young people as ill-formed and needing guidance, training, direction and a 'firm hand' to ensure they grow in the right way. A construction of young people as needing to be influenced or even controlled emerges. Such an interpretation is aided by stories that quite clearly describe young people as acting badly, breaking the law or transgressing social norms. The dichotomous view of young people as either victim or threat is not new and has been discussed in the literature (see, for example, Goldson 2001). In the current media sample it is not tempered by a corresponding emphasis on the achievements or contributions of young people. The 'take-home' message is 'if we do not contain, train, teach or control young people, there will be trouble'.

The power of the media to rely on simplistic generalizations serves to focus attention on a few stereotypical understandings of young people that then lead to a limited set of discourses around young people. What is missing from the creation of this discourse is the understanding of young people themselves, as well as the voices of adults who know these young people. The complexity of the lives of young people around their motivations and their interpretations is remarkable in its absence from media representations. The question then remains as to how much the limited discourse presented in the media is reflected in the broader discourses in the general community of adults who may have a variety of experiences of young people.

Findings – Survey of public opinion

The first point that must be made is that responses to the open-ended question about personal attitudes produced a diversity of responses. AC Neilsen, the company who collected the survey data, reported that they are usually able to code open-ended question responses into 15 categories, the current sample required 90 response categories.

In reviewing the responses it became apparent that the responses could be grouped into five clusters: three main clusters; and two smaller clusters. These were:

- a cluster containing words such as: positive, ambitious, hard working; well educated; innovative; and caring. This 'personally positive' cluster could be seen as similar to the media discourse around young people as 'successful', but contains many more descriptions of young people that are positive and not necessarily limited to achievement

- a cluster in which young people are described with words such as: frightening; lazy; selfish; immature; rude; angry; no work ethic; no respect; no values; impatient; weird; plastic; and silly. In this paper this cluster is referred to as 'personally problematic': 40 per cent of responses were of this type, which has parallels with the young people constructed as problematic in the media sample

- comments about young people as full of potential but placed in a problematic social context. These fell into a cluster of 12 per cent of responses and are referred to as 'socially negative', which mirrored some of the media reports describing young people as victims. These included: devalued, victimized or neglected, a labour market unwilling to employ them; having to grow up too fast; lacking security; having no loyalty from business world; and the community placing no trust in young people

- a neutral cluster, not apparent in the media sample, of responses (2%) in which young people were not judged or assessed by a comment, including responses such as: 'wide variety of characters'; 'short'; 'being different'; 'human nature is what it is'; 'jeans'; 'multicultural' and 'fashion'

- a smaller cluster that described a social context of young people offering great opportunities. This cluster is referred to as 'socially positive' and contained approximately 1 per cent of the responses and is closest to the media cluster that described the many programmes and services offered to young people.

The responses that fell into each of these three clusters are presented in Table 7.2.

It would seem that the community has a mixed perception of young people, with a slight bias towards positive images. This bias is even more apparent if we look at the ordering of responses. Respondents were asked for three words images or phrases that described young people. The first response given by 627 people was of the personally positive type, while 507 of the first responses were personally negative. Table 7.3 shows the responses in the order in which they were made. If we assume that the first response made coincides with the strongest opinion then we may more confidently state that the community has a slightly more positive perception of young people. This assumption has not, however, been tested in this project.

Table 7.2 Community perceptions of young people

Community perceptions	Count	% Responses	% Cases*
Personally positive	1449	46	126
Personally problematic	1252	39	108
Socially positive	38	1	3
Socially negative	371	12	32
Neutral	66	2	6
Total responses	3176	100	–

*   Percentages exceed 100 due to multiple responses by which any 'case' could potentially have three responses recorded in any one cluster.

Table 7.3 Images of young people in order of mention

Mention	Personally positive	Personally negative	Socially positive	Socially negative
1st mention	546	421	14	128
2nd mention	469	444	12	113
3rd mention	434	387	12	130

In summary, the general community described two very distinct discourses around young people. These were as: enthusiastic, positive and energetic on the one hand; and as problematic, on the other. A lesser discourse emerged around young people, that of being disadvantaged by social arrangements, mirroring the discourse apparent in the media survey. There was very little evidence in the general community of adults, of the dominant media discourse around the services or programmes provided to assist young people on their path to adulthood. The various constructions apparent in the two samples are presented in Table 7.4.

Table 7.4 Constructions in the media and community samples

Construction	How present in media	How presented in community
Vulnerable/needy	Very strongly present describing (54% of items) <ul><li>Services to help</li><li>Society's lack of care</li><li>How to help young people</li></ul>	Few comments describing young people as immature, but not otherwise apparent.
Victims	Young people as disadvantaged by social arrangements (14% of items)	Young people as being disadvantaged by social arrangements (around 12%)
Problematic	Young people as dangerous and clearly problematic (20%)	Describing bad, dangerous and anti-social behaviour (40%)
Successful	Successful young people (10%)	Positive attributes of young people (46%)
Opportunities	Not apparent	Opportunities for young people (1%)

Where opinions come from

The second question asked of the community sample was concerned with identifying the source of opinions. Just on half of all respondents noted their opinions
were formed, in part, by young people known to them. Table 7.5 presents the
findings of this second question. It would seem that the sources of opinion can be
clustered into five categories:

- personal contact; made up of 'being a parent' and 'Young people known'

- media; comprising 'TV', 'Newspapers', 'News', 'Talkback Radio',
  'Current Affairs Programmes'

- information; made up of 'politicians', 'things my neighbours and friends
  tell me'

- observation of young people; and

- memories of being young.

Table 7.5 Source of influence

Source of influence	Count	% Responses	% Cases
Young people known	540	21	50
Young people they see	536	21	50
TV	349	14	33
Memories of being young	199	8	19
Being a parent	252	10	24
Newspapers	199	8	19
News	162	6	15
Neighbours/friends	128	5	12
Talkback radio	94	4	9
Current affairs programmes	71	3	7
Politicians	20	1	2
Totals	2550*	101	240*

*   Respondents could nominate up to three sources of influence. Hence total exceeds number of
     respondents surveyed and percentages exceed 100.

When the data is collapsed into these categories of influence and cross-tabulated with images of young people, an interesting pattern emerges.

It would seem that where community members have personal contact with young people they are inclined to be more positive and considerably less negative in their opinions of young people (51% of responses by people who had contact with young people were positive and 34% were negative). If one adds to this percentage the comments that suggest young people are disadvantaged by their social environment, 63 per cent of all responses are accounted for.

When 'observation' is noted as a source of opinion a different pattern is noted. As shown in Table 7.6 community perceptions when informed by observation are fairly evenly poised between negative and positive impressions of young people. Furthermore, of all the sources of information 'observation' is the least strongly associated with placing young people in a negative social context. It would appear that when young people are observed without the benefit of personal knowledge of young people there is a stronger negative impression of young people.

The results generally suggest that opinions associated with personal contact with young people tended to be more positive than negative, whilst those people with the least intimate contact with young people – whose opinions were associated with observation alone – tended to be more equivocal in their opinions of young people.

Discussion

The dominant discourse constructing young people in the media, in the terminology of the 'new sociology of childhood', predominantly constructs young people as 'becomings'. Fifty-four per cent of items in the media sample were concerned with young people as needing guidance, help and instruction across a variety of areas in order to be ready for adulthood. The existence of this discourse is particularly interesting given the prominence in the media of a discourse of young people as villains. Cohen talks about the process by which the demonization of children as villains is followed by a reaction in the form of 'rescue' and 'remedy' (Cohen quoted in Goldson 2001, p.39). The construction of children as 'becomings' needing rescue and remedy is clearly an example of this process and is not value-neutral. Young people were described as needing assistance that suggests that they are 'inadequate' in a range of important areas such as finances, drugs, driving, sex, employment and citizenship. Such young members of the community are, by virtue of their 'incompleteness', bound to cause problems.

The discourses presented in the media of young people as victims or becomings was to some extent challenged by the discourses present in the general

Table 7.6 Source of influence by perceptions of young people

Source of influence	Personally positive	Row %	Personally negative	Row %	Positive environment	Row %	Negative environment	Row %	Neutral	Row %	Total
Contact	913	51	608	34	26	1	222	12	27	2	1796
Media	539	46	441	37	18	2	147	12	32	3	1177
Information	170	46	134	36	7	2	57	15	4	1	372
Observat'n	633	43	642	43	27	2	156	10	32	2	1490
Memories	249	47	186	35	17	3	69	3	7	1	528

* Totals do not equal numbers of responses because of incomplete responses to source of perception.

community sample, which was predominantly sympathetic to young people (describing them as: happy, creative or coping with a hostile social environment), but also twice as likely as the media to report views of young people in clearly negative ways (with nearly 40 per cent of responses describing young people as problematic). The dominant media construction of young people as needing or receiving help was to a large extent absent in the general community sample. Very few comments from the community described young people as vulnerable or needy.

One way of reconciling the conflicting media and community constructions of young people is to view the dominant community perceptions of problematic young people as a reinterpretation of the media construction of young people as ill-equipped. Where the media discussed the issue of young people requiring drug education, the general community described young people as having a drug problem. Media items that dealt with young people being offered driver-training programmes, appear in the community discourse as young people being bad drivers. Various areas of need as presented by the media emerge in the community sample as problems. The process by which a dominant media discourse influences but does not define a dominant discourse in the community is interesting.

The existence of parallel themes but varied constructions of young people in the two fora of the general public and the media suggests that discourses do not simply transfer from one site to another. Two factors appear to play a role in the manner of the transmission of discourses. First, the discourse that gains dominance needs to be understood in terms of the variety of knowledges used to inform the site in which it occurs and, second, the accommodation of a new discourse into an already existing set of discourses requires a degree of interpretation that may well alter it.

Knowledge that informs discourses

In terms of the knowledges used to inform discourses, the media rely on established and often routine sources of information, selecting items on the basis of news-worthiness. Often the demands of tight media deadlines mean that certain sources of information such as courts, police, and written press releases are privileged, '(C)hildren's meaning and motivations are persistently ignored, as is the position of adults, both familial and professional, as powerful definers of deviant behaviour' (Davis and Bourhill 1997, p.31). The bias set up in such reporting lends itself to the production of the dominant media discourses around young people as victim, villain and becomings. The community, on the other hand, reports their sources of influence as: personal experience; memories; and 'information from others', in addition to the media.

In exploring the range of sources from which community opinions were formed the place of personal experience was prominent in determining positive opinions. In the absence of personal experience the images of young people were more negative.

Discourse re-interpreted

It is significant that of all community responses 40 per cent described young people as personally problematic. Parallels between the media discourse and the community discourse of young people as bad are clear, with 20 per cent of all media items describing young people problematically. This discourse, however, is much stronger in the community sample than in the media. It is possible that the media discourse of young people as becomings has been reinterpreted by members of the community who do not have personal experience of young people as young people being inadequate and therefore problematic.

Van Dijk (1987) explains this process in the case of racial prejudice when he argues that for most people there is no access provided to alternative forms of talk or text other than that which exists in the dominant discourse, consequently information that does not conform to the general discussion as formulated by the media has no model for talk that differs from the dominant construction. Journalists describing young people produce news stories in which news-worthiness, informed by sensationalism and popular appeal and relying on official sources of information, create the discourse by which young people can be known. This is a process named by Scraton, Jemphrey and Coleman as the 'vocabulary of precedence' (quoted in Davis and Bourhill 1997, p.29). People who have access to alternative forms of talk through meaningful personal experience develop different understandings and constructions of young people. Those with no personal experience are more likely to construct young people in terms consistent with media representation and to interpret their observations in terms consistent with these dominant constructions. As Van Dijk says 'information tends to be selectively attended to and memorized under the influence of stereotypes people already know or share' (1987, p.128). It is in this way that everyday observations of young people are constructed in terms of problematic behaviour until personal experience offers a challenge to those stereotypes.

This sits comfortably with the finding that those who cite 'observation' as their source of information are the most inclined to perceive young people negatively, or to interpret what they see in the language provided by the dominant media discourse in terms of young people needing to be managed or directed.

Conclusion

The current work has identified an extension to the media categorization of young people in the form of a discourse concerned with young people as 'becomings'. Young people were discussed in the Australian media in terms of the services, programmes, guidance and attention they needed to fully and appropriately grow into responsible adults. Such a focus has not previously been identified in the media but was very strongly present in the current sample, with the majority of items of this type.

The current research has determined that in contrast to the media sample the general Australian adult community describes young people in more positive than negative terms but that there is, none the less, a strong discourse in the general community constructing young people in very negative ways. The presence of this strong negative discourse appears to have its roots in the media discourse that describes young people as victims, villains or 'becomings', and which provides the talk by which young people are constructed as being inadequate or problematic.

The very strong positive perception of young people in the community sample is explained by the contribution of personal experiences of young people in attitude formation. Personal experience was identified as the single most common source of influence in the formation of opinions of young people and tended to be associated with images sympathetic to young people. Where respondents identified 'young people I know', and/or 'being a parent' as influencing their opinions, young people were described positively or as being disadvantaged through social arrangements that had let them down or acted against the interests of young people.

The combined influence of all media is, none the less, seen as the greatest source of opinion formation. This is an important finding given the dominance in the media of discourses constructing young people as either needing help or in negative terms (74% of all items surveyed). The influence of the media can be seen directly in general community discourses that problematize young people and those that describe young people as victims, or it can be seen indirectly in the everyday talk that community members have available in which to describe young people. This is consistent with research that discusses the role of the media in developing the everyday talk by which events are constructed. In this way, observations are interpreted to be consistent with shared information and beliefs as proposed by the media.

Opposition is offered to the everyday talk by the personal experiences the community of adults has of young people. Through such experiences the general community has developed a further discourse constructing young people as happy, vibrant and creative. The challenge to those working in the youth field lies in discovering how to enhance the opportunities young people have in contributing to the discourses that define them. It is apparent that when young people engage with the sites of discourse production a different discourse is created from that developed in their absence.

CHAPTER EIGHT

The Objectification of the Child through 'Physical Discipline' and Language
The Debate on Children's Rights Continues

Bernadette J. Saunders and Chris Goddard

Introduction

In recent years the physical punishment of children has received considerable media coverage in Australia and Britain. In spite of this attention many people continue to condone the physical assault of children in the name of discipline. Indeed, analysis of media coverage suggests that challenges to this unnecessary and misguided parental right deserve little more than a humorous response (Saunders and Goddard 1998). Further, the choice of language used to describe the physical assault of children, such as 'smacking', 'spanking' or 'reasonable physical chastisement', and the choice of language used to refer to children, such as 'kids', 'effectively reframes and minimizes the seriousness of offences committed against children...and may degrade children, thus impeding full recognition of their rights' (Saunders and Goddard 2001, p.446).

Drawing on the 'New Childhood Studies' literature, we suggest that 'physical discipline' of children is permitted because of society's construction of childhood, rather than because of the oft-quoted justifications based on pedagogy or the best interests of children and society. The child's inferior status permits and condones violent and hurtful responses to a child that are neither legally nor socially tolerated as a response to adults. Indeed, it may be argued that:

> the social and legal endorsement of hitting children is one of the most
> symbolic indications of their low status in our society [and] until we cease to
> endorse it as legitimate punishment, we will…perpetuate children's vulnera-
> bility to the abuse of adults. (Lansdown 1994, p.43)

In policy and practice, children's lives may be adversely affected by a perception
of them as 'incomplete vulnerable beings' who need to be turned, often by violent
coercion, 'into mature adults' (Mayall 1994, p.3).

This chapter, drawing on recent media debates, suggests that community education and holistic family services are required to bring about the attitudinal and
legal changes necessary to protect vulnerable children, to recognize each child's
right to dignity and self-esteem, and to encourage adults to become more
child-focused.

The prevalence of 'physical discipline' and the social construction of childhood

Historically, children have been considered the 'property' of their parents
(Lansdown 1994). Violence directed at a child who is owned may be considered a
right rather than a questionable act. Further, discipline by physical force may be
considered an obligation, a response to children that is expected of 'responsible'
parents (Gough and Reavey 1997; Hodgkin 1997).

Childhoods do, however, 'differ from one another' (Dencik 1995, p.105). In
some countries, 'children are legally entitled to certain rights, for example, the
right not to be physically disciplined or humiliated by parents or other adults'
(Dencik 1995, p.107). In contrast, in Australia, England, and the United States,
physically painful discipline is perceived to be 'normal' and is an experience
common to many childhoods (Department of Health 2000; Duke and Aitkinson
1992; Newell 1994; Nobes and Smith 1997; Straus 1994). Many babies have
been hit before their first birthday and some parents continue to assault their 15
to 17-year-old children (Smith 1995; Straus 1994). Studies in Britain revealed
that two-thirds of a large sample of mothers had 'smacked' their babies (Newell
1994). Fifty-two per cent of one-year-olds were hit at least once a week by their
parents and 29 per cent of parents had used implements to hit children. More
than 20 per cent of parents admitted to severely physically punishing their
children (Nobes and Smith 1997). In 1994, 66 per cent of parents believed they
were entitled to punish children however they chose, without interference
(Creighton and Russell 1995).

Daily 'spanking', Straus (1994) suggests, is common in the US. In Australia,
one study revealed that 94 per cent of children aged between 4 and 14 had been

'smacked' and 36 per cent had been hit with an implement. Ninety-seven per cent of parents reported being smacked as a child (Duke and Aitkinson 1992). In 1995, 20 per cent of Australians surveyed believed that hitting a child with 'an implement [is] not harmful' (Editorial Opinion, *Sydney Morning Herald* 1995, referring to research by Cashmore and de Haas). These figures only represent a partial view of this issue. The exact nature and extent of physical punishment, particularly of very young children, is difficult if not impossible for researchers to accurately ascertain.

Adults often appear to be indifferent to children's experiences as children. Painful experiences, such as the bruise or cut from a cane, belt or wooden spoon, or the sting from the hand of the 'loving' parent or caregiver, may be justified as being in the best interests of the child – a part of every child's socialization into adulthood, or perhaps personhood. In this context, 'physical discipline' is for many parents an indispensable means of shaping and controlling children's unacceptable or disturbing behaviour. A child's 'need' to be disciplined, even by harsh physical punishment, is arguably a social and cultural construction (Hendrick 1997) designed by adults to enforce conformity. Of particular concern, however, is the 'abuse of [this] power over children' given the 'existence and maintenance of that power itself' (Kitzinger 1997, p.185). Adults may justify violence directed at children as 'teaching the child a lesson', in the child's and society's best interests. In this context, adult attitudes of superiority may motivate behaviours that not only degrade children, denying them physical integrity and respect, but may become severely abusive. Childhood as an institution makes children 'vulnerable': 'assault and exploitation are risks inherent to "childhood" as it is currently lived' (Kitzinger 1997, pp.184–185).

This chapter will draw on research in both the UK and Australia in which children were consulted and included as active participants (Saunders and Goddard 2003a; Willow and Hyder 1998). Children's voices are essential to any debate about the acceptability of parental physical punishment.

'Physical discipline' as a form of assault: Children's voices

'Physical discipline' is an infringement of children's human rights to physical integrity and to protection from physical and emotional harm. These rights are clearly set out in Articles 19(1) and 37 of the UN Convention on the Rights of the Child 1989 (see Van Beuren 1993). 'Children *are* hurt when they are smacked, both physically and mentally' (Willow and Hyder 1998, p.89; emphasis in original). Twelve-year-old girls commented that 'you can see a bruise but you can't see how it mentally affects someone and they'll carry that right through their childhood, right through their adulthood', and 'I wouldn't want [my children] to feel that way against me' (Saunders and Goddard 2003a, p.8). Children perceive 'physical actions such as smacking to be abusive because they are experienced as related to their subjugated positioning as children' (Mason and Falloon 2001, p.106). A 13-year-old girl described feeling 'slightly subordinate to adults', and remarked that:

> I think you should respect all people…I personally don't think it's appropriate…to physically punish me anymore…that should be my say really, 'cause I think I am becoming a bit of a person, not a child anymore. (Saunders and Goddard 2003a, p.8)

A nine-year-old boy gave his perception of being owned and therefore powerless and vulnerable:

> If [an adult] physical contact with [another adult], like punching 'em, it's against the law…And that's exact same for smacking. But if it's in your house, if you're a kid…it's OK because they're your kids…if you are a kid, it doesn't really matter, because you don't…you barely have any say. (Saunders and Goddard 2003a, p.4)

'Physical discipline' and 'smacking' are two of several euphemisms for assault by a larger, more powerful person on a smaller, more vulnerable person. Six- and seven-year-old children described a 'smack' as 'a hit…and it hurts you' (Willow and Hyder 1998, p.26); 'you might get a bruise or a lump. And it's horrible' (Willow and Hyder 1998, p.80); and 'it makes you feel ashamed inside' (Willow and Hyder 1998, p.47). A nine-year-old girl revealed that parents get 'really mad so they start hitting you…and it really hurts…[children] may understand or they may not…sometimes it leaves red marks, it's that hard' (Saunders and Goddard 2003a, p.5). A 12-year-old girl said physical punishment makes children feel 'embarrassed, hurt… Smacking is really cruel and child abuse' (Saunders in preparation). Children are the only people against whom violence is sanctioned and justified as discipline. Adults similarly assaulted are victims of crime.

Many parents have been both 'victims' and 'perpetrators' of parental violence toward children. An adult who works with children recalled in Saunders' research: 'when I smacked that child…it was like I felt I had lost control and was like my father'. This person acknowledged that being hit as a child had harmed her. She commented, however, that other people who have been hit as a child may think:

> 'well if that child does that, then I will smack that child, that happened to me, that did me no harm', but they don't actually realize it's like they're, you know, talking about reacting violently…so the harm is in the fact that they actually will do that to their own child.

Another adult in Saunders' research physically punishes children

> because that's all I know and that's what everyone around me does, that's what happened to me. Not so much in a violent way…that's how I was disciplined and I turned out okay, so that's an effective way.

It is significant that the word 'violence' is rarely used by parents to describe 'disciplinary' actions that inflict pain on a child. Words such as 'violence' and 'assault' appropriately describe unlawful, irresponsible acts that are unacceptable in humane, civilized societies but these words are rarely chosen to describe parental 'physical discipline'. One mother maintained that 'a little touch of violence is a part of every child's security' (Saunders in preparation). Children may be made painfully aware of their inferior position in relation to adults.

The role of the media

Language is powerful in maintaining society's acceptance of the physical punishment of children. Language also has the potential to be powerful in changing attitudes, beliefs and behaviour:

> Language…may be a vehicle of disregard, denying the child personhood, dignity and respect. When critically examined, however, language may also 'expose' injustice and provide the impetus for 'change'. (Saunders and Goddard 2001, p.445)

The media have played a major role in many child-protection issues in Australia and the UK. Goddard and Saunders contend that the media appear 'to have more influence on child-protection policy and practice than professionals working in the field' (2001a, p.1). While much media coverage may have a positive effect (Goddard and Liddell 1995; Saunders and Goddard 2003b), the media are also a powerful force in creating and reinforcing limited social constructions of childhood (see, for example, Goddard 2003). The language used by the media in the UK and Australia may deny the child 'personhood, dignity and respect' (Saunders and Goddard 2001, p.445). In turn, the child may become an object and thus 'less than a subject' (Goddard and Saunders 2001b, p.30), resulting in the minimization of children's painful experiences (Goddard and Saunders 2000).

It is notable that, when a child seriously assaults another child, media questions about childhood itself inevitably arise. Yet a child's experience of physical pain or even injury at the hands of his or her parent may be reported as both reasonable and defensible. Parental assault of children appears to be within the bounds of what may be considered 'normal' in childhood. It seems that within the context of 'normal' socially constructed parent–child relationships a child's right to physical integrity challenges established family power structures.

In this context, the media's response to the physical punishment of children at times trivializes the issue. Rather than using the power of words to promote the rights of children, the physical punishment of children appears to be regarded as a source of humour in addition to a parental right. This small selection of headlines from Britain and Australia is instructive: 'Give the NSPCC a clip around the ear, somebody' (Hume 2003); 'Top judge's swipe on child smacking' (de Kretser 2002); 'Judges must stick to judging: Family Court Chief Justice Alastair Nicholson deserves a smack himself' (Gray 2002); 'Rod not spared in discipline rethink' (McIlveen 2001); 'Gentle spanking can hit the spot' (Giles 26/8/01); 'Smacks take a beating in UK' (Hickley 2001); 'British get to bottom of child discipline' (Hall and Ward 2000). Treating violence directed at children so frivolously denies children the dignity to which they are entitled.

In the media debate in Australia stimulated by the release of our discussion paper entitled *Why do we condone the physical assault of children by parents and caregivers?* (Saunders and Goddard 1999a) journalists' reports and letters to the newspapers were notable for an abundance of euphemisms and appeals to common sense. Note the following headlines from one tabloid newspaper, the *Herald Sun*: 'Child experts plead for curbs on parents who spank: Ban the smack' (Coffey and Dent 1999); 'No more smacking' (Morrell 1999); 'Smacking controls kids' (Letter 1999, 11 June); 'Parents must control kids' (Letter 1999, 15 June); 'Be sensible on smacking' (Letter 1999, 16 June); 'A lesson in discipline' (Letter 1999, 19 June, the letter begins: 'A SPANKING story; Undermining parent's rights'); and, finally, 'Smacks not necessary' (Letter 1999, 21 June).

The *Herald Sun* may have hoped to present a balanced perspective but letters to the editor overwhelmingly reflected the views of adults who cling to their right to hit their 'kids'. Adult motivations and justifications for hitting children such as duty and pedagogy, ownership and control, and 'it never did me any harm' were all powerfully expressed (Gough and Reavey 1997; Saunders and Goddard 1999b). A *Herald Sun* poll on 9 June 1999 prompted 2,499 responses to the question 'Should parents be allowed to smack their children?'. In response, 2,385 callers (95.4%) answered in the affirmative. Clearly influenced by the inevitable burst of outrage from threatened pro-smackers, the *Herald Sun*'s editor bowed to the numbers. The editorial headline, 'A good move on road rage…but a bad one on smacking' (Editorial 1999, 10 June) highlighted the irony of the readers' support for proposals to denounce road rage while they opposed proposals to denounce adults hitting small children. Aldridge, the letters editor, concluded that 'so far consensus has supported stiffer penalties for road rage, but…child discipline in the form of a smack must be the parent's prerogative' (Postscript 1999).

Similar media reporting was evident when New South Wales debated and passed legislation maintaining parents' rights to hit children, even with an implement. Note the following headlines: 'Rules spell out how to smack a child' (Lipari 2000); 'Law to spank parents who smack' (Ellicott 2000). More recently, a woman in New South Wales was convicted of assault after hitting her child across the head; the headlines revealed considerable sympathy for the offender. 'Three slaps made this mother a criminal – "I did smack him but not hard"' (Goldner 2004); 'NSW: Damned if you smack, and damned if you don't' (Conway 2004); 'Mother convicted but community split on smacking kids' (AAP 2004); 'Helpless mum hit toddler' (Goldner and Taylor 2004). The stories themselves gave clear indications of how language can be used to minimize the seriousness of the crime: 'give the little brat a hurry-up' is how hitting a child was described in one piece (Conway 2004).

Such reporting stands in stark contrast to coverage of events where a child is seriously or fatally injured as a result of excessive physical punishment, or 'reasonable' physical punishment 'gone wrong' (Saunders and Goddard 1999c, p.124). The tone of media reporting in such cases aptly reflects the seriousness of this issue: 'Space games in morning and death in the afternoon for three-year-old' (Binning 2003); 'Severe blow probably killed boy, court told' (Adams 2003); 'Toddler basher guilty' (Howell 2003); 'Child-killing bully jailed for six years' (Ross 2002); 'Dad fined for beating' (Calvert 2001); 'Appeal lodged on child belting' (Greber 2000); 'JAIL for letting dogs die; FREE for bashing a child' (Titelius and Dolan 1999); and 'Accused "hit baby 10 times"' (Cant 1999).

The following headlines, appearing in *The New Zealand Herald* within one week, present stark evidence of the ambivalence in the media's reporting of violence directed at children: 'Cruel "disciplinarian" goes to jail' (Gower 2001); and 'Ban on smacking is hitting too hard' (Editorial 2001). Until all media reporting of physical punishment reflects the true nature of parental assault, as children themselves have described it, the protection of children from harm will continue to be undermined in deference to parent's rights.

The social positioning of children

Children continue to be the only people against whom violence is considered to be acceptable. The idea that 'physical discipline' of children is a parent's right needs to be continually challenged both publicly and privately. We contend that the physical punishment of children is always abusive and an infringement of children's rights. In some cases, there appears to be:

> a point along a continuum of physical punishment when a smack or tap esca-
> lates into spanking into beating and so along the line to the point where abuse
> laws, or the criminal law, can be invoked. (Boss 1995, p.28)

Indeed, many deaths and severe injuries, particularly of young children, may be
linked to 'confusion about, or reluctance to condemn, corporal punishment of a
child' (Goddard 1996, p.182). Victoria Climbié's death in the UK is a recent
example. Lord Laming, Chairman of the Victoria Climbié Inquiry, when
examined by the Health Committee of the House of Commons on 27 March,
2003, made the following comments:

> The issue of how we value children does not relate to how we treat children
> within law and what we can do to children that I could not do to my col-
> leagues round the table (physical assaults)… It seems to me from reading the
> Report and what happened to Victoria that discipline and punishment was a
> major context for the abuse that took place… Victoria's abuse began with little
> smacks. The great aunt told the inquiry that there was nothing wrong with
> smacking. My personal experience has been going to court on a number of
> occasions with child-abuse cases and losing cases on a defence of reasonable
> chastisement. I have made a number of recommendations to protect children.
> I have not used the phrase 'reasonable chastisement' which I take to be a
> phrase which is subject to a great deal of interpretation by a number of
> people… I would have thought that people would come to the conclusion
> that violence towards children should be taken as seriously – or more seri-
> ously – than violence towards adults. (House of Commons 2003, Question
> 71 in the Minutes)

In this context, it may be argued that:

> [i]f there is an immediate point to childhood studies, it is the improvement of
> childhood conditions. Child abuse, however understood, has provided the
> impetus, and children's rights the context, for evaluating the government of
> childhood. (McGillivray 1997, p.16)

This chapter has drawn attention to the importance of physical punishment as an
issue that affects the lives of many children, from infants to young people in their
late teenage years. Children's low status and subservience to adults may be perpetuated through a social construction of childhood that views children as less
than adults (Jenks 1996). Within this social construction of childhood, adults'
common use of euphemisms for 'physical discipline' serves to rationalize and
justify degrading and disrespectful treatment of children and young people, and
to disguise actions that would be described as assault if directed at an adult.
Examples were drawn from the print media to illustrate how the physical punish-

ment of children may be trivialized, reinforcing children's subordination to adults, and their exemption from universal human rights (Mason and Falloon 2001).

Miller has observed that children 'have a capacity for recognizing injustice even when they can do nothing about it' (1997, p.xiv). Children's views, however, are rarely sought on anything (Goddard 2003), and physical discipline is no exception. Fortunately, in the UK and in Australia, children have been given an opportunity to document their thoughts about 'smacking'. Children commented that 'no one should smack anyone' (Willow and Hyder 1998, p.63), 'It hurts [children's] feelings and physically' and 'It's giving the message that it's OK to smack... It's just a big cycle' (Saunders and Goddard 2003a, p.8).

Conclusion

In Sweden physical discipline of children was banned in 1979. Since then many other European countries have followed Sweden's example. In 1965, 53 per cent of people in Sweden thought that smacking children was acceptable; in 1999 only 10 per cent of people thought it was acceptable (Durrant 1999). As noted by Palmérus (1999), attitudinal change occurred in Sweden through various means in addition to legislative change. Recognition was given to the difficulties of parenting by the provision of social-welfare supports for families that decrease the likelihood of parental stress, frustration and anger that may result in violent responses to children. These supports included home-visitation by nurses to provide parenting advice and to give parents devices that would ensure safety in the home, such as locks and electric outlet plugs. Parenting education also occurred through the provision of a brochure, written in various languages, that provided information about alternative means of discipline, and detailing sources of further information and assistance. Education of parents via information on the sides of milk cartons and through responsible media reporting was particularly effective. In Sweden, 'there is a more respectful, holistic approach [to child welfare], with children seen as "social capital", of which the prohibition of hitting is a small part' (Clark 2001, p.27, quoting Judy Cashmore).

In recent years, several events have occurred in Australia that had the potential to improve the status of children and provide protection from physical assault in the guise of punishment. These included: the 1990 ratification of the UN Convention on the Rights of the Child (1989); the release of discussion papers on physical punishment (Cashmore and de Haas 1995; Saunders and Goddard 1999a); and a strong rebuke about corporal punishment from the UN Committee on the Rights of the Child (Summary of the 404th meeting: Australia. 24 December 1997). In addition, law-reform processes in New South Wales and

Tasmania generated considerable debate about hitting children (Gawlik, Henning and Warner 2002; Standing Committee on Law and Justice 2000). The results, however, have been uninspiring. It is significant that in New South Wales the result of the law reform is that parents may still legally hit their children with implements (such as a wooden spoon or belt) to cause harm to the child for 'a short [undefined] period' of time (Crimes Act 1900 (NSW) S.61AA (2) (b)).

Research about the physical punishment of children and the inter-generational transmission of child abuse, funded by the Australian Research Council and the Australian Childhood Foundation, is near completion at Monash University, Australia (Saunders in preparation). This research enabled Australian children, parents, grandparents, and professionals who work with children to describe their experiences of physical punishment of children. Further debate that incorporates children's views about 'physical discipline' is required (and education and holistic family services are needed) to bring about the attitudinal and legal change that will advance the protection of vulnerable children from abuse, and recognize each child's right to dignity and self-esteem.

The media have a crucial role to play in this change. Much violence is learnt at home and a great deal of that violence is meted out in the name of discipline; the home, therefore, is where we must begin to arrest this process (Goddard 1994, p.12). Rather than taking a flippant attitude towards violence against children, perhaps the media and others should listen to what children themselves have to say: 'You shouldn't hit people, because there's a better way…than hurting someone' (12-year-old boy, Saunders and Goddard 2003a, p.10).

CHAPTER NINE

Children's Democratic Rights
What We Can Learn From Young Workers Organizing Themselves

Per Miljeteig

Introduction

The world-wide implementation of the Convention on the Rights of the Child (CRC) (UN 1989), as well as the process to establish a new ILO Convention against 'the worst forms of child labour' (ILO 1999), have created a climate that is conducive to viewing child labour and work-related exploitation of children in new ways. First, the CRC has an article especially devoted to the right of the child to be protected from economic exploitation and work that is hazardous or interferes with the child's development or education. Second, the whole text of the Convention and the spirit behind it establishes an exhaustive framework for protecting children from *any kind of exploitation*. The CRC offers several principles that promote the child's well-being and integration into society.

The CRC also reiterates that *all* persons below the age of 18 enjoy central civil and political rights: the right to freedom of expression, the right to freedom of thought, conscience and religion, the right to freedom of association, the right to protection of privacy and the right to access to information. An important innovation brought by CRC is the *right to be informed about the rights* established by the Convention. If we want to address issues concerning the situation of working children and youth in a child-rights perspective, it is crucial to keep in mind that 'participation rights' include all of these rights. That means to accept that children are capable of having opinions, that these should be listened to and taken seriously into consideration. It also implies that children can act on their own, take action to protect their own interests, and act as stakeholders in efforts to address their situation. In several countries around the world working children and youth have actively made use of their rights to form organizations and demand to be heard in the child-labour discourse. Are we ready to take them seriously as partners in the further efforts to address the problems associated with child labour?

The 'participation rights' have been the subject of much interest as well as controversy since the adoption of CRC in 1989 (Miljeteig 1992; 1994; see also Flekkøy and Kaufman 1997; Franklin 1998; Kjørholt 1998; West 1997). It is only when participation rights are understood as civil and political rights, or as democratic rights, that participation rights gain full meaning and become possible to implement. I will raise issues related to the changed roles of children and adults *vis-à-vis* each other in the perspective of the Convention on the Rights of the Child and discuss some pressing challenges both for adult society in general, and for those who work professionally with and for children: How to alter our attitudes and behaviour if the principles of the Convention are to be fully observed with respect to children's participation rights or – as I would prefer to describe them – their democratic rights? My discussion is to a large extent based on a review I recently have been doing for the World Bank, examining the involvement of working children and youth in efforts to improve their own situation and to address issues of economic exploitation (Miljeteig 2000).

Influenced by the CRC, the child-labour discussion has become more focused on *exploitation*: how to prevent exploitation through, for instance, education, social mobilization and poverty-reduction initiatives. Furthermore, it has become accepted that it is necessary to include the perspective of working children and youth as well as that of their families, if we are to fully understand child-labour situations (Miljeteig 1999; Woodhead 1999). Working children have made statements such as: 'We are against exploitation at work but we are for work with dignity with hours adapted so that we have time for education and leisure' (Kundapur Declaration 1996). Taken together, these developments have brought us a significant step further in understanding the complexities and realities of child labour. But we will not see a genuine child-rights approach emerge until working children and youth are allowed to influence policies and programmes through active participation and partnership, and until we have fully realized the important resource they represent.

Working children and youth organizing themselves

The very vocal and visible entry onto the scene of working children and youth speaking out on their rights created several reactions. It took most of the other participants in the 'child-labour discourse' by surprise, and created some uneasiness because they were not used to dealing with young people and their direct language. In some cases, young workers caused particularly strong reactions, because they made claims for their 'right to work' and the right to be respected as workers. Statements from international gatherings of working children and youth use very straightforward language and are not easy to respond to with clear answers (Dakar Declaration 1998; Kundapur Declaration 1996).

In general, however, the public appearance of working children and youth has helped give child labour 'a face' and contributed to a more nuanced and diversified understanding of what 'child labour' is. They have demonstrated that, despite being in extremely vulnerable situations, they have resources to make informed decisions about their lives, and that they are not just passive *victims* of exploitation.

Organizations of working children and youth around the world share many things in common.[1] First, they share a strong foundation in an activist approach that supports empowerment of poor or otherwise marginalized and disadvantaged people. They are focused on workers' rights and poverty reduction. They have a strong grassroots nature, with little trust in government and formal structures. They have grown gradually and spontaneously from small initiatives. Even if they have large numbers of members, their main organizational units are small, local groups. It would probably be more appropriate to label them as *movements* rather than organizations in the strict sense. This is also how they perceive themselves, and is consistent with the way they grow to include several communities, states and regions in a country. They are democratically organized and place importance on election of office bearers and those who represent them. Some have introduced membership identification to identify and protect their members, and to gain acceptance as workers. Another remarkable thing is the effective international networking among the organizations globally, including several international gatherings of representatives from the various movements.

Achievements of working children and youth in the child-labour discourse

Local level

In order to describe the achievements of organized working children and youth, it makes sense to distinguish between the local and international levels. It is at the local level that the main focus of activity lies. The organizations seem to grow through attracting new members and supporters, and tend to spread gradually from country to country within a geographical region. They appeal to those working children who have the energy and the resources to participate in causes of collective concern. The members who join become activated and energized. Many of them decide to stay on, even after they, technically, are too old for the organizations, and become supporters in some capacity or another.

A common goal for the organizations is to support the members in their daily lives. This is typically done through small, focused discussion groups, inspired by the Participatory Rural Appraisal (PRA) approach used by many non-govermental organizations (NGOs) in development work. Here, they share their thoughts about the situation they are in, the kinds of problems they meet in their work situations, and how to deal with the daily hassles. Joining others who are in the same situation creates a sense of belonging, self-esteem, and group solidarity. Many of the members work in the informal sector – for example, as domestics – and work in isolation from others of their own age. These young people are particularly prone to exploitation, and need to learn about their rights and possibilities. Manthoc, in the Latin American context, has supported young workers to have a sense of dignity associated with work, and in being able to make a living from decent work. It is assumed that those who achieve better understanding about their situation as children or adolescents, and as workers and citizens, will be better able to protect themselves from exploitation and seek less harmful types of work. For that reason Manthoc has made it a specific part of its philosophy to promote what they call *formación*, an educational approach that is focused on giving information about society and skills that are useful in their particular situation. For the same reason, most of them have paid great importance to disseminating information widely among their members and externally. The West African Movement and Bhima Sangha both have newsletters with wide circulation. ENDA-Jeunesse Action and Bhima Sangha have also started using electronic communication.

In some cases, informal training in literacy and vocational skills is organized within the smaller units of the organizations. Sometimes it is as basic as those who have reading and writing skills sharing it with those who do not. Working children's groups in West Africa have successfully negotiated access to classrooms for literary classes after hours (Mali), or organized literary courses outside working hours for their members (Côte d'Ivoire). To address health concerns, they have collaborated with local health services to set up a scheme whereby working children can seek consultation at the hospital at the same price as school children (Côte d'Ivoire), won access to the same services as public servants (Côte d'Ivoire) and set up a mutual savings scheme for health care (Senegal). In Senegal, young workers have also organized joint purchases of material they need for their work, for instance as shoe-shiners.

Both at community and national level, the organizations have worked to influence legislation relating to children and youth in general, or more specifically to child labour. The most striking and well-publicized example is probably how the National Movement of Street Boys and Girls in Brazil significantly influenced the inclusion of a reference to children's rights in the new constitution and the drafting of national legislation on children and youth in the late 1980s (Gomes da Costa and Schmidt-Rahmer 1991). Working children's organizations have participated in local child-rights campaigns, and established partnerships with local NGOs and trade unions. In Senegal, the Movement of working children and youth has become an official partner in the local IPEC[2] programme and is represented in its governing body.

International level

The young workers who gathered, for instance, at Kundapur,[3] or in Dakar,[4] or sent their representatives to large international conferences in Amsterdam,[5] Trondheim,[6] Oslo[7] or Geneva,[8] have presented themselves as quite different from what was expected of 'child labourers'. They have very effectively contrasted the picture of working children as sad and suffering victims, unable to protect themselves. They gave coherent presentations of their own situations, what has led them into the work they are doing, the problems and hassles they face, and how they are trying to relate to all of this. They presented ideas about what needs to be done, and gave warnings about well-intended, but not carefully thought-out, efforts from the international community to 'solve' the 'child labour problem'. The essence of their messages is reflected in the declarations from their meetings in Kundapur and Dakar (Dakar Declaration 1998; Kundapur Declaration 1996). Their clear message is that child workers can no longer be seen exclusively as passive recipients of protection and special services. They are able to take action to improve their situation, and should consequently be consulted and involved in the development of measures to assist them.

At international meetings and conferences, the awkwardness of including the young representatives in the regular proceedings has been very obvious. The young people are not familiar with the, often, formal setting and protocol. The other participants are not used to dealing directly with young people in this setting and seem to be uncomfortable with the language and impatience of the young people. There has sometimes been uncertainty about what 'status' the working children and youth have at such events. In Amsterdam, they were treated as 'working children' and given a special place at the conference in the form of a 'working children's panel'. In Oslo, they were 'regular NGO participants' in the conference. It is significant to note that in both cases there were separate children's meetings that, among other things, were meant to serve as support for the young people who were to participate in the conferences.

One of the critical views against such participation is that these children and young people are not representative of working children. Typical comments include 'How can they represent all working children?', 'Some of them are not even children any longer!'. Regarding representation, technically they cannot speak on behalf of *all* working children. However, their organizations have been through very careful processes to identify who should represent them. On the question of age, it is correct that some of the spokespersons are above 18. Again, they have been elected by the organizations to speak on behalf of them. That should be acceptable, particularly when they do not pretend to be 'child workers'. Some of them have a history as child workers, and have continued to work for the issue. The age issue has also been used the other way around. At the Oslo conference, one of the government delegates publicly accused the representative of lying about her age. He was making the point that a 13-year-old would not be able to speak at an international conference the way she did.

Another point that has not been raised as often – but is a more relevant criticism of representation – is that the young workers who speak at international conferences or to the media are probably the most resourceful among the young workers. In that respect, they might not be representing all their fellow workers. This should be borne in mind, so that one does not expect the same involvement from all working children and youth.

It should be noted that the promotion of 'children's participation' is continuing – world-wide – in a snowballing fashion. Working children's organizations are taking an active part in this, and serve as examples. This was seen at the UN General Assembly Special Session on Children that was held at the UN headquarters in New York, 2002. Several of the working children's organizations actively participated in the preparation and in the Special Session itself, including as members of Government delegations. Their efforts to influence the text of the outcome document concerning child labour or other issues of special interest did not succeed, despite active lobbying from the African Movement of Working Children and Youth. It is too early to assess the impact of children's participation in the World Summit for Children process. It could be seen as an acknowledgement of the principle that children have a rightful place in such exercises. How much will trickle down to the local level and influence day-to-day development, and also at government level, remains to be seen.

Spontaneous vs. planned participation

Working children and young people have not waited for an invitation to 'participate'. They have acted on their own, and implemented their own rights in their own way, in some cases as a response to information about these rights. Also, they have exercised their right to freedom of association, a right that one normally does not attribute to children. The organizations have typically developed slowly and organically, according to the needs of the people involved as defined by themselves. That makes these organizations difficult to describe in organizational terms, and sometimes difficult for the surrounding world to relate to. They do not always have formalized structures as many adult organizations have. It is also interesting that labour organizations, both locally and internationally, have been quite negative to the notion of recognizing these organizations as labour unions. This is a discussion that cannot be taken further here, but it is interesting to note that the International Confederation of Free Trade Unions is now launching a 'youth campaign', where they are encouraging labour unions around the world to recruit young workers as members.

The way these young people act fits very well with the definition Hart (1992) introduced, when he made one of the first and influential efforts to specify what children's participation means in light of CRC, and what qualifies as *genuine child participation*. He defines 'participation' as

> ...the process of sharing decisions which affect one's life and the life of the community in which one lives. It is the means by which a democracy is built and it is a standard against which democracies should be measured. Participation is the fundamental right of citizenship. (Hart 1992, p.5)

Manthoc introduced the term 'protagonism', from the Spanish *protagonísmo*, to stress the interactive and responsibility-taking aspects of participation. The word is now being increasingly used in English, with the meaning it carries in Spanish underscoring some of the associations normally not linked with participation – such as a capacity actively to take part in the definition of the choices of a given community (see, for instance, Cussianovich 1997; Sanz 1997; Swift 1999; Tolfree 1998; Torres 1994). To take this a bit further, one could say that a protagonist is a partner.

Tolfree (1998) studied the role of children in various programmes and organizations for working children, and concluded that the direct involvement of children in the running of the organizations creates a sense of responsibility:

> ...it is through the collaborative work with others – children and adults – that young people learn to exercise responsibilities. It is in this context that concepts such as protagonism...are important, for they emphasize that the exercise of active participation goes hand-in-hand with the exercise of responsibility...it is this more active exercise of responsibility which tends to promote positive changes in working children rather than mere participation. (Tolfree 1998, p.47)

In addition to taking responsibility for themselves and others, members of the working children's organizations also exercise their right to access to information. Seeking and promoting information about issues relevant to their situation play an important role in the activities of organizations of working children. Manthoc has from its inception used *formación* (creating knowledge and awareness beyond regular education) as a key conceptual tool in its work, next to protagonism. The philosophy is that without sufficient and relevant knowledge about their situation and the society in which they live, the working children and their families will not be able to improve their situation. If they are to have impact on polices and programmes developed by local and national governments, or international organizations, they also need access to information about how such agencies work. Without in-depth knowledge of these rules and the procedures for decision-making, it is difficult to gain any direct influence.

Furthermore, organized working children and youth creatively interpret Articles 12 and 13, when they insist that information they present *as a group* must be taken into consideration. Taken literally, the text of CRC undercommunicates the right of children to *provide* information. In the case of exploitation of working children and youth, it should be obvious that the information they could give us would be a very important input to planning interventions aimed to improve their situation.

Conclusion

The road forward

Organizations of working children and youth are like living laboratories for participation rights and democracy. In theorizing about how to facilitate and arrange for children's participation, it might be worth taking a closer look at how these organizations work, what strategies they develop and their achievements. It would be misleading not to mention the important role of adults in these organizations. They have often been key inspirers. Often they share the same background as the working children, and have a genuine insight into their situation. They have been very conscious about their role as facilitators, and made great efforts to establish the principle that the organizations are to be lead by the children and youth, and that they should have only an advisery or supportive role. Most of the organizations have organized, or been involved in organizing, training courses for adults working with children. They all have on-going internal debates on the relationship between adults and the children, and what the roles of adults should be. These experiences can be analysed to learn about how children and adults can collaborate towards common goals, and what kind of adult support is conducive for child-led activities.

The reason behind success at the local level is that the organizations use the actual needs of their members as the entry point for their activities. Thus, they focus on very concrete and real issues or problems that need urgent attention and where the results might be of immediate importance in their daily lives. There is no need to 'construct' themes for collaboration between the young people, or between the youth and the adults.

This success has not been matched internationally. The main reason is probably a clash between languages and methods of work. However, there is also quite a bit of scepticism and lack of empathy from the adults. For instance, when some of the working children claim that they have 'the right to work' many adults and their organizations react negatively and refuse to have discussions with them. They have already taken the non-negotiable position that children and work are incompatible. If they listen, they would also hear that the majority of working children say they want education, time for play, recreation and cultural activities. But they may have a different opinion about what kind of education serves them best or the optimal combination between work and school.

Working children who have participated in international conferences report they feel they have been listened to, but also that there is a big distance between themselves and the adult participants. Two typical comments from the young people were:

> They said they want to abolish child labour, put children in schools because children have to go to school, have to play, and that if a child works then he or she is no more a child, while we have organized ourselves to fight against poverty and improvement of our working conditions. (Faye 1998)

or 'Several researchers presented the results of their studies. They talked a lot and we understood very little of what they were saying.' (Dakar Working Children's Association 1998). We should listen carefully to what such statements are telling us.

At the local level, there are already initiatives to include working children and youth in programmes and operations aimed at improving their situation or assisting them in various ways (see, for example, Johnson et al. 1998; Tolfree 1998). Local organizations such as Manthoc, Enda, Fundaciòn Olof Palme (The Olof Palme Foundation) in El Salvador and Concerned for Working Children, Bangalore, India, have pioneered by giving working children influence in their work, and some have also substantially supported groups or organizations of working children. International NGOs such as members of the Save the Children Alliance have followed suit, particularly in making measures to include children when relevant and appropriate by taking a 'child-centred approach'. Organizations that work both at local and international levels, such as Save the Children

and UNICEF, could play an important role in two ways: first, by using their resources to develop models for genuine and culturally sensitive participation of
working children in the planning and programming that relate to their situation,
and, second, by serving as advocates for working children and youth and helping
to convey their views and opinions from the local level into relevant international
fora.

   Since the organizations mentioned above operate, for the main part, at the
local level, they should develop strategies for partnerships with organizations of
working children and youth. Other organizations that operate internationally,
such as the World Bank, have included participation of their beneficiaries as an
important principle in their operations. They should be challenged to apply the
principles they have developed for working with other disadvantaged groups
such as poor people, or women, to working with young, exploited workers as
well.

Challenges

Looking at the experience gained by the organizations of working children and
youth and their encounters with the 'adult world', the following challenges need
to be addressed urgently, if we mean to take children's civil and political rights seriously.

1.   In order to show respect to children and young people and prove that
       we take their rights seriously, we need to *establish a culture of listening
       to children*. As Roger Hart has put it: 'Children's participation is often
       promoted as a 'children's voices' movement, but it should equally be
       an "adult ears" movement' (Hart 1998, p.147). This means that we
       are obliged to respect young people's right to have different opinions
       from our own, and that we are willing to examine them without
       prejudice.

2.   The next challenge follows almost automatically if we take the first
       one seriously: the need to *establish a dialogue* with young workers
       based on respect. At the local level, where children and adults work
       very closely together in the movements, this seems to function.
       Further, we need to examine the *language* we use. Well-intended
       adults and their organizations talk about abolishing child labour,
       making work below certain ages forbidden by the law, rehabilitating
       child workers. Many working children and youth find this language
       offensive because such phrases do not reflect respect for them as
       individual human beings. In a joint statement addressed to the 1999
       International Labour Conference,[9] some of the movements

commented on the language in the convention on the worst forms of child labour: 'Instead of talking about "return into society" we prefer "active participation" in the community and in society.' No wonder that young people who contribute actively to the economy of their societies and families feel provoked by indications that they are outside of society! Trying to establish a common language that avoids the unnecessary confrontations and misunderstandings should be the ultimate goal. Where a common language is not possible, or desirable, one should at least establish an understanding of what is meant by the words and phrases used, and the reasoning behind them.

3. If there is willingness to establish a dialogue there might also be a willingness to *find ways to include representatives for working children and youth in international proceedings,* and include them in implementing such proceedings and the resolutions from such proceedings. The regional movements of working children and youth have had several international gatherings and have managed to reach agreements. Why should they not be able to take part in negotiations with adults? It probably has more to do with willingness than with ability.

4. *Working children and youth can provide valuable information and insights about their work;* they can also tell us something about which interventions works and don't work. Some programmes for working children have started to include the 'beneficiaries' as partners in the design, implementation and evaluation of the interventions. Some researchers have tried to develop ways to seek information directly from working children (for example, Johnson *et al.* 1998; Tolfree 1998; Woodhead 1998). I see a big challenge in finding ways to collect such information in a systematic way, and to make use of it as an important tool to improve the situation of working children.

5. What are the *roles of adults vis-à-vis* working children? There will be many different roles: those of parents, employers, facilitators in working children's programmes, local authorities, representatives of local and international organizations. One central question relates to all: 'How far are they/we willing to regard children and young people as partners worth listening to, and including in our reasoning and planning?' There is a need to marry the experience from fields such as environmental care and planning with the experience of working children and youth. Young people are reaching out to meet us. Are we ready to meet them on equal terms?

6.   This leads us to the ultimate, and unavoidable, question of whether
      we are willing to revise (or even change) our *understandings of*
      democracy. Are we willing to change our perceptions about who
      defines the 'reality' in such issues as child labour, and who makes the
      decisions? Are we willing to give up power and admit that sometimes
      young people come up with better explanations and better solutions
      than we do? Cockburn has suggested a new model for democracy,
      based on children and adults being interdependent. Such a model
      might provide theoretical grounds for arguing that all children carry
      some responsibilities and duties. This is the case that working
      children and youth are making. If we can accept that even the
      youngest members of society have the responsibility and duty to
      reproduce themselves, it is only fitting that the awarding of rights
      and citizenship should be returned. The youngest children might be
      more 'dependent' upon some adults. This should not necessarily
      exclude them from citizenship as we are all in some sense or another
      dependent upon others, including the youngest of children
      (Cockburn 1998, p.113). Maybe this is a way to go?

Notes

1   For more detailed accounts of the individual organizations and their histories see for instance:
     Swift (1999) and Tolfree (1998). The organizations that I have drawn my examples from are
     Manthoc and the Latin-American movement of working children and youth; Enda-Jeunesse
     Action and the West-African movement of working children and youth; MNMMR – The
     National Movement of Street Boys and Girls (Brazil); Bhima Sangha (India). To a large extent I
     have also made use of their newsletters and other information material, as well as personal com-
     munications as sources for my work.

2   The International Programme for the Elimination of Child Labour (IPEC) is a special programme
     under the International Labour Organization (ILO). It is implemented through a series of country
     programmes based on an agreement between ILO and the national government and with
     multiple local partners.

3   First International Meeting of Working Children, Kundapur, India, 27 November – 9 December
     1996.

4   International Movement of Working Children, meeting in Dakar, Senegal, March 1998.

5   Conference on the elimination of the most intolerable forms of child labour, Amsterdam, 26–27
     February 1997.

6   Urban Childhood Conference, Trondheim, Norway, 9–12 June 1997.

7   Working Children's Forum, Oslo, Norway, 21 October – 2 November 1997 and International
     Conference on Child Labour, Oslo, Norway, 27–30 October 1997.

8   Forum of working children and youth held in connection with the International Labour Conference, Geneva, June 1997.

9   Declaration addressed to the 87th Assembly of the ILO, held in June (1999) from the NAT's movements of Asia, Africa, Latin America and the Caribbean on the new ILO Convention and Recommendation on child labour.

PART 3

Practice

CHAPTER TEN

Taking Young People Seriously Means Giving Them Serious Things to Do

Roger Holdsworth

Introduction

Young people are held in schools for longer and longer periods of time. The nature of the activities provided for them within schools generally lack productive outcomes: serious purposes that go beyond the classroom or the school. Instead, they are asked to defer important outcomes: to 'learn for later'. Yet, at the same time, we know that young people lead complex lives outside schools in which they exercise high levels of responsibility. How can schools recognize the present value of young people? How can schools develop approaches that provide serious, valuable, purposeful and productive outcomes for all young people?

In thinking about the implications of taking young people seriously, I wish to raise some basic issues about the ways in which educational structures respond to young people. I want, first, to ask some questions about school structures that either support or deny the serious 'voice' of young people; second, I want to question whether 'voice' is enough and look at what serious things we give young people to do. These are issues that are concerned not with questions of whether young people have anything important to say, nor with the capacity of young people to speak up, but with asking whether anyone is listening seriously.

Why is this an issue?

Over the past decade at least, there have been several intersecting concerns in education: about young people's cynicism about political processes and participation (Mellor 1998a; 1998b); about student alienation; and about the connectedness of young people to their schools, communities and their society. These have appeared in debates on Civics and Citizenship (Holdsworth 1997; Owen 1996); on the 'new citizenship' (Rimmerman 2001); on Middle Schooling (Australian Curriculum Studies Association 1996); on 'Full Service Schools' (Semmens and Stokes 1997; Stokes and Tyler 1997); on Health Promoting Schools (Mukherjee, Stokes and Holdsworth 1997); on the Youth Allowance (Dwyer *et al.* 1998); on social capital (Cullen and Whiteford 2001; Putnam 2000; 2001), and so on.

Rather than looking at such ideas from the perspective of whether young people themselves are cynical or alienated or have a sense of connectness, I am interested in the ways in which institutions, such as schools, act to either alienate or connect students. In particular, what do students learn from the way school is organized, and from their prescribed or implied place within that school? At one stage, this was often referred to as 'the hidden curriculum', though it has now become more common to talk of the impact of the 'school ethos' – policies, programmes, organization – on student learning.

Such an ethos is developed at a number of levels, from the form of decision-making in the school as a whole, to the degree and nature of curriculum negotiation within classrooms, to the nature and purpose of learning tasks. When we consider how we organize our schools and how we organize learning and knowledge, what are we saying to students about how seriously we take them, their opinions, abilities and learning?

Deferred outcomes...or real roles?

There are fundamental and continuing changes occurring in the perceived role of young people in our society. For example, Wyn points to the invention of 'youth' as a category that is positioned in relation to a future based on a static notion of adulthood:

> Conceptually, the positioning of youth in this way obscures the experiences of young people by relegating them to a less significant realm than those who have reached 'adult' life… They are citizens of the future, rather than citizens in the present. (1995, p.52)

Most school-based learning activities provide purposes for students that are deferred. Students are told: 'Learn these abstract ideas because they will be valuable to you later'; 'Study because it will help you get a job in the future', 'Learn about citizenship because one day you will be a citizen'. Some students will be content to defer the outcomes of their learning – because they recognize they have a secured future. Others faced with greater uncertainties will become passive collaborators, or active resisters. But all of these students are learning that education and its organization through schools devalues their experiences, knowledge and present situation.

By deferring the outcomes of learning, and by devaluing students' present situation – by not taking them seriously, or providing serious things for them to do, we are conveying strong messages to students about how Australian institutions regard their participation. We are, in fact, teaching about 'active citizenship' in the most negative way.

Passivity...or agency

Coleman, writing in 1972, also pointed to change in the roles of young people, and to its consequences. Coleman suggests that the student role has been expanded in place of education within the family and productive activity through work. However, the student role is a passive one:

> The consequences of the expansion of the student role, and the action poverty it implies for the young, has been an increased restiveness among the young. They are shielded from responsibility, and they become irresponsible; they are held in a dependent status, and they come to act as dependents; they are kept away from productive work, and they become unproductive. (pp.5–8)

In response, there has been some recent attention to classroom curriculum processes including getting students more involved in curriculum implementation and curriculum and classroom decision-making – for example, approaches that emphasize the role of students in negotiating curriculum. Beane (1993) points out that these approaches help young people broaden and deepen their understanding of themselves and their world, and begin with questions and concerns they have about these two areas. The curriculum themes are organized around the questions and concerns about self and the world that intersect.

Yet these approaches can devolve into trivial exercises in temporary engagement. Negotiated curriculum processes have concentrated largely on the what and how of the curriculum: about what we will learn, how we will make such decisions, and (in the presence of increasingly specified external frameworks) on how we will learn. Little attention has been paid to the more difficult issue of encouraging and supporting student participation in why learning something is valuable or useful.

It is no surprise then that students continue to bemoan the lack of relevance of the curriculum, even as we seek ways to make the activities we design more relevant to their perceived interests, and seek to centre the curriculum in student interests and needs. We need to recognize that students are asking for their work within schools to be concerned with serious issues, and with more direct engagement in the immediate purposes for their learning. The curriculum must include the capacity and willingness of students to act upon their learning: to produce something of value, to be valued and to value one's self as someone who can 'make a difference' – a difference that goes beyond the teacher and the classroom.

Value

These views argue for approaches in which student roles of community value are created about real and serious issues.

In deferring learning outcomes and in 'negotiating' trivial curriculum pursuits, we are teaching students their lack of value to our present society. We are allowing creativity, commitment and enthusiasm little or no place. We are saying that 'being cool' is about being irrelevant and disengaged. In developing a 'theory of the value of youth', Pearl has suggested that 'If youth are to be valued, they must be of the society – participants, not recipients. That is the crux of any theory of valuing youth.' (Pearl, Grant and Wenk 1978, p.24).

In Australia, school-based approaches that respond to issues of agency and value occur within the arenas of classroom curriculum and school governance under the general heading of 'student participation'. These approaches see young people as partners in the learning process, as bringing skills, views, and experiences to their education. They recognize and reinforce effective learning that is active, relevant to the needs of the learner, recognizes the background and present situation of the learner, and takes the learner seriously.

Student-centred approaches in education are not new. Almost a century ago, Dewey (1916) articulated principles and approaches that are now being rediscovered. While building upon these principles, ideas of student participation go further to assert that schools must develop ways in which their students' education can contribute to outcomes of recognized community value.

Student voice

More recently, similar ideas have been advanced under the heading of 'student voice'. Proposals for consulting with young people – for establishing and supporting forums in which young people can 'speak out' – have been debated and advocated. By enabling greater 'voice', it is argued, improved practices within schools (and broader areas of society) will be enacted.

Yet, the talk of 'providing a voice' for young people may serve, if taken literally, to limit the possibilities for real participation by young people. A simple focus on 'speaking out' can merely serve to make it appear that young people are active participants; it may serve as a 'safety valve' to ease pressures for real changes in decision-making processes and structures. It may simply be a way of making decision makers feel as if they are 'doing the right thing'.

Some challenges to the notion of 'voice'

Voice... or action?

Some recent student forums have realized the limitations on 'youth voice' and are explicitly making bridges from the concept of 'voice' to ideas of 'agency' or 'action'. One such student-run network changed its name from 'Teenroar' to 'Teenaction' – 'The idea is to build on what we know and – rather than just "roar" – "act" on implementation of programmes which will positively address relevant issues in the youth culture' (Osmotherly quoted in Holdsworth 1998, p.15).

For many years, the concept of a community or youth 'participation ladder' (e.g. Hart 1992, p.9) has been used to explain that ideas of 'consultation' and 'involvement' are more limited than ideas of 'participation' and 'action'. In a similar way, we can distinguish between views of 'youth/student voice' and characterize stages to the real inclusion of young people in their communities:

- youth/student voice: 'speaking out'

- being heard

- being listened to

- being listened to seriously and with respect (including a willingness to argue with students with logic and evidence)

- incorporating youth/student views into action taken by others

- sharing decision-making, implementing action and reflecting on action, with young people.

This development has been seen as a move in focus from 'youth voice' to 'youth agency' – that is, towards development of the capacity and willingness of young people to act upon issues that affect them.

It has also been recognized that student groups tend to work in modes of 'do', 'ask' and 'share' (Holdsworth 1998, p.16). While there are some things that student groups can do (by themselves), these tend to be relatively trivial in most cases; while there are some things that student groups will need to ask others to do these tend to lead to rejection and to reinforcement of students' powerlessness.

While it is recognized that the capacity and willingness to both 'do' and 'ask' is important for the development of a student's agency, the more important challenge has been to encourage a movement towards the 'share' role in which students (as other parties do) work with others through accountable, decision-making partnerships.

At the moment, however, with very few exceptions, students (and young people generally) remain locked out of such partnerships – relegated to asking, encouraged to have a 'voice', but no more.

Inclusive or exclusive: Which young people are taken seriously?

There has been a disturbing trend to take only some young people seriously: those who 'present themselves well' or with whom we agree. There has been a language movement from 'participation' to 'representation' and then to 'leadership' – and a shift to developing the skills of the few students elected or appointed to élite positions. Similarly, while curriculum programmes such as cross-age tutoring have traditionally been inclusive (and even provided alternative positions of responsibility and value to students otherwise excluded and marginalized) there has been a similar degradation of such programmes in favour of the already advantaged students 'who will best represent the school'. For some schools, caught in situations where every action is thought of as 'selling' the image of the school, educational outcomes have become secondary to those of public relations. In a process of choosing only the 'best students' the forms and activities of participation hide a commitment to the selection of the few for continued success. The loss of equity criteria is alarming.

This observation is reinforced by recent research at the Australian Youth Research Centre (University of Melbourne), in which many young people alienated from schooling were highly disparaging of student organizations, seeing them as neither effective nor as representing them (ACEE and AYRC 2000; Dwyer et al. 1998). Similarly, some schools are now recognizing that the forms of student organizations that ostensibly support and encourage 'student voices' have, in fact, served to exclude the majority from access (Little 1999). In forums that enable students to 'enact their voices' we need to ensure that all voices are heard and that all students are enabled to walk the bridge from voice to action. Further, it will be necessary to ensure that opportunities for collective action be established to promote inclusion. That will mean taking specific measures to overcome the legacies of silence, distrust and inactivity that have traditionally locked some students out.

Serious about what?

The nature and extent of topics on which it is thought appropriate for young people to be taken seriously can become limited and limiting. It is, unfortunately, still common to find that both students and teachers think that student voice through some form of student organization is 'what student participation is all about' – and that the prime concerns of such organizations are school support (fundraising, social) activities.

Even relatively forward-looking approaches to Civics and Citizenship Education have talked as if 'representative democracy' defines the total scope of what being an 'active citizen' is, rather than acknowledging that having and exercising a valuable role within communities is at the core of our citizenship. School-based approaches have consequently focused on the need to build on existing examples of 'student democracy' and 'leadership', but to the exclusion of curriculum initiatives. Learning about active citizenship in schools will include support for active student voice and participation through student councils and within various areas of school governance, but it must also include fundamental changes to the ways in which we structure teaching and learning in classrooms – particularly, as has been argued above, towards rethinking how we share purpose and demonstrate authentic outcomes.

Rethinking schools

Being taken seriously: A curriculum issue

Being taken seriously is about being involved in the governance of a community and about having a valued and recognized role within that community. These issues are inherent to discussions of citizenship: about distinguishing between 'civics' or the study of institutions, and 'citizenship' or the practice of social participation. Hannam (1999, p.5) draws a similar distinction between mainstream political activity including voting in elections – what the French describe as the *citoyenne* aspect of citizenship, concerned with constitutional rights and legal status – and participation in voluntary or communitarian activities, clubs or societies – the French *civisme* aspects of citizenship (Hannam 1999, p.5).

If it is 'the array of roles that individuals can play in forming, maintaining and changing their communities' (Owen 1996, p.21) that shapes citizenship, then the role of citizenship education is to ensure that young people have opportunities to participate in those roles. Arguments about recognizing and supporting the active citizenship of students therefore have bearing across the curriculum, not just within the subject areas mandated to teach Civics and Citizenship content. Thus the critical challenge in thinking about how and what students learn about their roles within our society is how can we develop curriculum and governance approaches that take young people seriously, and enable students to build upon their civic competences. How can we ensure that we build both 'learning about' and 'learning to' into education?

In taking students seriously, all subject areas will be judged by the respect and consideration they give to students within their teaching approaches, but also by their capacity to support and create real roles of community value for young people as part of the learning within those subjects – that is, by how far they give young people serious and important things to do.

Student participation

In education, the word 'participation' has been used in various ways. For example, it can mean 'being there' (as in participation or retention rates); it can mean 'taking part' (as in doing activities over which students may have no say); or it can mean 'having a say' or 'student voice' (students speaking out about issues). 'Student participation' here means:

> an active role for students in decisions about and implementation of education policies and practices and of the key issues that determine the nature of the world in which they live. (Holdsworth 1986, p.6)

Student participation must involve activities that are valuable and make sense in three ways:

- *to the participants:* students are working on issues they choose, that make sense to them, and in which they are valued

- *to the wider community:* the community sees the issues as valuable ones to be worked on, and in which students can add something of value to and as part of that community

- *academically:* the participation meets the academic or curriculum goals that schools are required to achieve, and involves learning and development.

This implies that participation must: value the contribution that students make, meet genuine needs (that is, be about real things), have an impact or consequence that extends beyond the participants (that is, outside the classroom), be challenging to participants, and provide the opportunity for planning, acting and reflecting.

Arenas of student participation

There are two major arenas in which student participation is developing: in school governance and in curriculum. Participation in both these arenas is important and complementary.

IN SCHOOL GOVERNANCE

Here, students are taken seriously in their direct or representative participation in school decision-making about educational issues. This occurs through students being on committees such as school councils, curriculum committees or regional boards, and also through student-run organizations such as student representative councils (SRCs), junior school councils or student networks, where students can discuss, debate and decide their position on issues.

In both areas, students' views are taken seriously, and students are supported in developing democratic structures that ensure the views of all students are represented. Earlier in this chapter, attention was drawn to the development of governance approaches that attempt to be inclusive and participatory rather than exclusive and 'representative'.

There is now emerging further evidence of the importance of such aspects of the school curriculum to the development of active citizenship. Owen reports on a recent US-based study of 'civic voluntarism' that suggests (on the basis of some 15,000 preliminary interviews and a further 2500 in-depth interviews) that it was opportunities for participation – and therefore learning – in the processes of school governance, together with opportunities to discuss contemporary political issues of interest to the students, that were more important than actual civics courses. The US study suggests, very forcibly indeed, that it is how we run our schools rather than what we teach in them that will determine levels of active citizenship (Owen 1996).

Many schools have some form of student organization, and these have recently developed most rapidly in primary schools. While such student groups have traditionally been seen as having limited functions, schools that are serious about supporting student participation continue to grapple with issues involved in extending the role of a student organization as a vital part of the school's overall decision-making structure. Some of the concerns being explored include when the student groups meet; who is elected; how processes of selection and organizational structures influence opportunities to participate; how schools recognize and credit students' participation as part of the school's curriculum; and what other organizational options there are to engage all students, rather than a select few.

Student representation also occurs within the broader decision-making structure of the school and raises further issues for representatives about reporting back and seeking direction from other students, in the SRC and then through discussion at home group or sub-school levels.

IN CURRICULUM

Students are also taken seriously in decision-making and action through classroom learning partnerships, and through specific 'student participation' projects or approaches that deal with real issues for purposeful ends. The process of curriculum negotiation is basic to all such approaches and can occur at all levels, either informally or formally (though it has been described most clearly – and formally – in senior school curriculum e.g. Holdsworth 1986, p.30; 2002). Curriculum partnerships between teachers and students have taken joint responsibility for setting goals, canvassing needs and background, identifying appropriate content, devising learning methods and putting appropriate assessment and evaluation measures in place.

The most extensive examples of student participation are seen in the wide range of curriculum projects that have been developed within schools. These can be community-development projects in which students create resources and services of value to their communities. Examples have included cross-age or peer tutoring in which students teach other students; media productions in which students have produced community newspapers and directories, resource guides, oral histories, or radio and television programmes; and job-creation initiatives within school-based 'incubators' through enterprise education. There have also been significant community-research and action projects in which students investigate and act on issues facing their community. These have included student action teams that have undertaken research and action projects (as part of their curriculum) around issues of community safety, environment, and so on (see Holdsworth et al. 2001; Holdsworth, Cahill and Smith 2003). There are many practical examples available in all these areas (see Holdsworth 1988; 1999; 2000; Pearl and Knight 1999).

Implementing participatory approaches

When we look at the suggested structural and curriculum ways of 'taking students seriously' we see that these go beyond ideas of 'student-centred education', 'active learning' or 'creative teaching'. Student participation involves more than student activity. Active learning may be only the first step of the dance; when we talk about student participation we actually mean doing a two-step.

Step 1: Moving from passive instruction to active engagement

Inquiry-based learning approaches are characterized by an active role for young people in investigation and presentation. These are characterized by teachers asking: 'How can I organize for the students to do it instead of me doing it?' For example, in a lesson about the nature and range of local mental-health services (within MindMatters, a Mental Health Education programme), a teacher-centred approach would involve providing students with a list of the appropriate organizations; classroom activities might then be focused on answering worksheet questions about this information.

The first step towards participation would be to change this approach by organizing for students to carry out the local investigation. They might, as a group or in small teams, compile the list of services (asking and answering questions about where to find information) and perhaps interview services to write descriptive paragraphs about what they do. This information would then be disseminated within the class and discussed. The teacher role has moved from presenter of information to one of organizer of learning. The student role has moved from recipient of facts to active searcher for information and meaning. But this is just the first step.

Step 2: Moving from activity to value-creation

When we talk meaningfully and seriously of developing student participation, we really need to be thinking of approaches that go beyond this. Approaches should also involve creating real and recognized roles of community value for the students and for their learning. Active learning can be 'pushed' a step further to create engagement with meaningful outcomes.

To pursue the curriculum example above, we could start by asking questions about the collection of information about the services: 'Why do we want to find this out?' and 'What are we going to do with the information?'. What might then emerge from class discussion are several possible outcomes: the students could publish the information they have discovered in a school newspaper, in a community forum or newspaper, or through a small booklet or pamphlet that is distributed in the area. Students are now learning for a direct purpose. They are adding something of community value to their learning, and are being seen as valuable community members, doing valuable things. These are all indicators of being taken seriously, by being given serious things to do.

Conclusion

The challenges for teachers in doing the student participation two-step, and in taking students seriously, are to be:

- inventive: teachers must always be seeking ways for real and valuable outcomes (authentic assessment) of learning – and that might mean recognizing and seizing local opportunities as they arise

- bold: be willing to leave 'safe' or meticulously pre-planned territory and embark on exciting uncertainty – a dance of learning with the students

- serious about the approach: be committed to and understand that young people can and must tackle important issues as they learn.

CHAPTER ELEVEN

Negotiating Competing Versions of 'The Child'

A Preschool Child's Competence in Parent–Teacher Talk at the Preschool

Michele J. Leiminer and Carolyn D. Baker

Introduction

Parent–teacher conversations in early childhood settings are activities where parental and (preschool) teacher versions of children, and social life at home and preschool, meet. These conversations are events where parents, teachers and children are engaged in the work of constructing the home–preschool relationship. Children could be in a very unique position to contribute to the construction of this relationship because they are members of both the preschool and the home. To varying extents, parents' and teachers' versions of social life at the preschool (or at home) may coincide or differ. Similarly, and accordingly, their definitions of what it means to be a competent child may coincide or differ. As potential participants in these events, children could contribute to, navigate their way through and manage these versions of life at home or school. Whether and how their competence is recognized in the event is open to analysis.

This chapter examines how a child, Mitchell, successfully negotiates his way through the different versions of social life in the preschool, as prescribed by the preschool teacher and his mother, by studying an instance of parent–teacher–child talk. For Mitchell to be perceived as competent by both his mother and the teacher requires that he also juggle their competing versions of 'Mitchell the child'. He manages to do so by negotiating between the parent and teacher versions of social life at the preschool. This negotiation involves a considerable amount of careful monitoring of and participation in the conversation by the child, as well as strategic action. He manages not only to negotiate between these versions of 'himself as child', but also to assert his own version. Mitchell's work in this parent–teacher conversation is exceptional in that children rarely do get the opportunity to present their own version of affairs in the discussion about a problem at preschool. We can consider his actual participation as an instance of the possible ways that children's competence in mediating between the home and school might be found.

Children and competence

In the 'new social studies of childhood' and the 'new sociology of childhood', children are taken seriously as active and competent members of childhood and adult cultures (Alanen 2000; Alanen and Mayall 2001; Corsaro 1997; Hutchby and Moran-Ellis 1998b; James 1998; James and Prout 1997; Mayall 1994; Prout and James 1990; Thorne 1987; Waksler 1991). Whilst recognizing children as active and competent agents, this new area of theory and research also acknowledges that various social contexts and participants within these contexts may constrain or enable the competencies that children are able to display or have recognized (Hutchby and Moran-Ellis 1998b).

Mackay (1974) suggests that within education adults and teachers 'simultaneously assume and interactionally deny' the competence of the child (p.27). Danby and Baker (1998) clearly demonstrate this phenomenon in their analysis of instances of conflict in play that attracted teacher intervention in a preschool classroom. In their analysis, the teacher is shown to rely upon the children's competence 'to enact her discourse of care and consolation' (p.159) whilst at the same time her intervention in the conflict suggests her presupposition of the children's incompetence in maintaining their social order.

Leiminer and Baker (2000) demonstrate how all participants actively construct the child as competent, including the preschool child himself, in their analysis of parent–teacher–child talk in a preschool setting. A number of competing versions of competence are identified and presented in this prior analysis. In this chapter we will examine more closely this adult–child interaction for competing versions of Mitchell as child, focusing on describing parent, teacher and child versions, and the position/s the preschool child is offered, and adopts throughout the talk.

A child's perspective on home–(pre)school relations

Edwards and David (1997) highlighted the absence of a child's perspective on home–school relations, calling for a child-centred approach that focused on the 'child' as the unit of study. Edwards and Alldred (2000) then explored the issue of parent involvement from the perspectives of children and young people, focusing on how they talked about prompting, cooperating, obstructing and resisting parental involvement in their education. Most recently an increase of emphasis has been placed on children as social actors and understanding how they negotiate between their home and school worlds (Alldred, David and Edwards 2002; Edwards 2002; Ericsson and Larsen 2002).

Edwards and David (1997) noted also a range of issues that required investigation from a child-centred viewpoint, including the issue of children's participation in communications between school and home. At present there is a minimal amount of research that examines the specific topic of children's work in home–school communications, especially in terms of analysing the actualities of how children participate in home–school communication. An example is a study by Baker and Keogh (1995). In their analysis of parent–teacher interviews they describe the secondary-school students who were present at interviews as an 'overhearing audience'. Silverman, Baker and Keogh (1998) study the 'silence' of the child in such interviews more specifically. In the area of early childhood, Leiminer and Baker (2000) analyse how one child actively participates in a home–preschool communication by examining a particular occasion of adult–child interaction conducted in a preschool setting. (See also a further analysis of this data in Baker and Campbell 1999.) This study extends that work to examining more specifically this child's competence in mediating between the home and preschool in a parent–teacher–child conversation.

Methodology and procedures

The study

Data reported in this chapter are part of a larger study exploring how children participate in home–preschool communications, predominantly parent–teacher conversations in three preschool settings that conduct programmes for children in the year before formal schooling commences. This study utilizes the methodological approaches of ethnomethodology (Garfinkel 1984), conversation analysis (Sacks 1974; 1984; 1992) and membership categorization (Hester and Eglin 1997; Sacks 1992; Silverman 1998). These approaches are primarily concerned with the study of common-sense knowledge and the ways in which members of society 'make sense of, find their way about in, and act on the circumstances in which they find themselves' (Heritage 1984, p.4). The focus of the analysis is on *how* something is said, rather than what is said, and what is socially realized in the process (Gubrium and Holstein 1997). This focus on the 'how' of the talk and action reveal 'the practices by which social order is accomplished' (Silverman 1994, p.180). According to this position, members, through their talk and actions, are seen to be competently and artfully constructing the social order.

As outlined by Hutchby and Moran-Ellis (1998b) conversation analysis has much to offer the sociology of childhood. It can demonstrate in close empirical detail the ways in which children competently use language to create social organization. It also allows us to appreciate the details of children's social worlds as they are negotiated and constructed.

The data

The study commenced with a six-month period of participant observation during which each preschool service was visited for one day per week, followed by a ten-week period of data collection. The conversations among parents, their children and preschool staff were audio-taped in the mornings and afternoons and at parent/staff committee meetings. Written texts were also collected in the form of newsletters, parent handbooks, and notices to parents. The data analysed in this chapter is taken from a parent–teacher–child conversation that occurred in the afternoon at a government-run preschool. The conversation has been transcribed to produce a representation of the talk, and it is to this text that our analysis refers. All names have been changed to ensure anonymity. A key explaining the conventions used in transcript notation can be found in the Appendix.

The parent–teacher–child conversation

The parent–teacher–child conversation took place at the front door of the preschool at the end of the day, when Mitchell's mother arrived to collect Mitchell. The analysis will demonstrate how participants in this conversation construct different versions of the social life of the preschool, and relatedly of Mitchell as child through their talk and actions. First, the versions of Mitchell the child constructed by Mitchell's mother and the preschool teacher will be outlined. Mitchell's demonstration and construction of Mitchell the child will then be explored. His version of himself as child will then be compared and contrasted with both his mother's and the teacher's. This section of the analysis will focus on how Mitchell competently negotiates his way between these competing versions. This, we propose, is the extremely challenging and delicate task of mediator of the home and the preschool.

The mother's construction of 'Mitchell the child'

Mitchell's mother's construction of Mitchell the child is demonstrated in the design of her talk commencing in Line 75 below, which, in effect, skilfully initiates and orchestrates her child's entry into the parent–teacher conversation. She constructs 'Mitchell the child' as one who is 'capable of presenting his own evidence'.

69. PT: and (0.5) you know (0.75) and we had a little sess today about caring for its blah blah and sharing but it's (0.25) a bit

70.   0.5

71. P: yeah

71. PT: um (0.5) it's been (talking) about their feelings (0.5) on the way (0.25) but he certainly (0.5) you know (0.75) (won't find it difficult) to find someone

73. P: yeah

74. PT: [[to play with] =

75. C: [[ohohuh ((noise))]

76. P: =to play with him if he's being left out? or something from what he (says)

77.   (4.0)

78. PT: you've? always got someone to play with here?

First, the mother powerfully sets up her son to gain the floor by reporting Mitchell's assessments as evidence to the preschool teacher. This work commences in Line 76 where the parent reports '=to play with him if he's being left out? or something from what he (says)'. We know this is Mitchell's evidence and not the parent's because it is marked by the 'from what he (says)'. This is said with Mitchell overhearing. Whilst the packaging of the parent's report states Mitchell's evidence, it also very importantly appears to prompt cross-examination by the preschool teacher. The 'or something' may be hearable as 'something I missed or may have misrepresented in Mitchell's evidence'. The preschool teacher, to ensure the reliability of the evidence, might want to cross-examine. The possibility of discovering the 'or something' may also be achieved by questioning Mitchell.

A very important turn for the course of the conversation is Line 76. Mitchell's mother appears to have packaged her report in a way conducive to the teacher inviting Mitchell into the conversation, to be questioned, but it depends on how the preschool teacher takes this up. The mother's management of her turn appears to further implicate the preschool teacher to question Mitchell, and give him the floor, as indicated above.

A very significant silence of 4.0 seconds is presented in Line 77, and demonstrates very clearly 'the power of the pause', for the parent's apparent decision not to self-select to continue speaking presents a compelling space for the preschool teacher to enter as the next selected speaker. This silence, in combination with the parent's turn design in Line 76, powerfully sets the stage for the preschool teacher to commence cross-examination, thereby inviting Mitchell to 'gain the floor'.

The preschool teacher's construction of Mitchell the child

The preschool teacher, by her actions, also constructs a particular version of Mitchell the child as an accomplishment of her talk. In this case, however, her version is different from that of the parent's. Her version of Mitchell the child, in part, is one who is capable of being agreeable and compliant with her version of how the preschool should function. This is demonstrated by analysing turns where the teacher compliments Mitchell. From this point it is possible to identify her version of Mitchell the child. The first of these occasions occurs in Lines 81–84, where the teacher offers the following assessments to Mitchell, that he has 'a good way of asking people' and that he is 'a fine boy to them'.

79.   (1.0)

80. C: yeah

81. PT: yeah (1.0) it mightn't be the one you've chosen in your mind ((noise)) but there's always somebody there (0.25) because you've got a good way of asking people and you are a fine? boy to them

82.   (0.25)

83. C: yes

84. PT: you are

In effect, in Lines 81–84 the teacher proposes some counter-evidence to the mother's assertion and seeks Mitchell's agreement with it. What does seem to be sought by the teacher is Mitchell's compliance with her counter-evidence that he 'always has someone to play with here'. He agrees, demonstrating in his actions his agreement and compliance.

The second occasion of complimenting occurs in Line 121 where the preschool teacher says Mitchell is 'a kind boy' after he helps tidy up the preschool classroom. On these occasions, the preschool teacher describes Mitchell as one who is kind, communicates well and is nice to his classmates. This suggests that he is capable of being agreeable and compliant with her construction of how the preschool should work.

It appears that the preschool teacher may not share to the same extent the parent's version of Mitchell the child – as one who is 'capable of presenting his own evidence'. This is demonstrated by the reluctance on the part of the teacher to allow Mitchell to enter the conversation, as evidenced by the amount of work the mother needed to do to achieve this action (as outlined above).

Mitchell's construction of 'himself as child'

Mitchell's construction of himself as child is demonstrated in his actions as a language-user. This demonstration of Mitchell as a language-user occurs in lines 85–95 of the parent–teacher–child conversation, when he becomes an active speaker in the talk. Just after Mitchell's mother and the preschool teacher discuss Mitchell's reported difficulty in finding a friend at preschool, Mitchell manages to 'do disagreement' with the preschool teacher. He eventually 'wins' the point at issue. He achieves this 'victory' with his competence in language, specifically in debating. In the sequence below, a number of actions performed by Mitchell demonstrate his competence in language, and simultaneously his own construction of himself as child.

84. PT: you are

85. C: but but Ta I wanted Tarrant to be my friend and he keeps keeps saying no no no

86. PT: mm do you know what I say to those sort of things?

87.   (0.25)

88. C: what=

89. PT: =you need to find a friend who'll say yes? and that means you've found a kind friend (1.5) doesn't? it (1.5) there's plenty of other kids (.) remember there's Jason (1.0) [Wayne (--)]

90. C: [yeah I I I'VE BEEN] ASKING EVERY KID

91. PT: Lachlan

92.   (0.5)

93. C: but they all say no

94.   (6.0)

95. PT: next time you come we'll see who can play with you where do you want them to play in the sandpit or somewhere different to that (0.5)

Mitchell begins actively contributing to the parent–teacher talk in Line 80. First, by agreeing to participate in the conversation, Mitchell has presented himself as 'a competent child' and one who is 'confident with his language ability'.

He then demonstrates that he is also 'capable of representing himself verbally'. This demonstration of verbal capability is clearly occasioned in the talk between Mitchell and the preschool teacher in Lines 79–85 where he skilfully initiates a disagreement with the preschool teacher's assessment. First, in Line 79 there is a significant silence of 1.0 second producing the delay device of no immediately forthcoming talk. This response of silence by Mitchell may constitute a turn shape for disagreement when an agreement is invited (Pomerantz 1984). He then responds with a weak agreement form, 'yeah' in Line 80. Mitchell's weak agreement may display that the preschool teacher's initial version of her assessment is not adequate for acceptance (Davidson 1984). The preschool teacher then presents a subsequent version in Line 81. She repackages her assessment (previously presented in Line 78), by presenting a compliment of Mitchell's social competence at the end of the turn as an interrogative. Her turn is shaped to invite agreement. Once again (as in Line 78) the preschool teacher may perhaps restrict Mitchell's second assessment possibilities. A restriction of second assessment possibilities may be achieved because Mitchell (as addressee) should supply the second pair part to the compliment, in this case an acceptance. Mitchell complies and agrees with 'yes' in Line 83, fulfilling his second pair-part obligation, but the agreement is slightly delayed. The preschool teacher then confirms her compliment in Line 84, 'you are' (a fine boy).

This time, in Line 85 however, Mitchell commences doing disagreement by not supplying a second pair part to the preschool teacher's compliment confirmation. Instead, he presents an evaluation that is in direct contrast to the preschool teacher's, using 'but' as a preface to a disagreement: 'but but Ta I wanted Tarrant to be my friend and he keeps saying no no no'. He reframes the issue from the teacher's assessment that he always has 'somebody to play with' to being turned down by Tarrant in Line 85.

Prior to this turn Mitchell and the preschool teacher have presented their competing versions of 'social life at the preschool', juggling for the power to define it in their own terms. The preschool teacher's version is that children at preschool always want and have 'someone to play with', whilst Mitchell's version is that he does not. Specifically, it seems, Mitchell wants Tarrant or some particular friend. Mitchell's version of social life at the preschool is partly taken up by the preschool teacher in Line 89 when she suggests Mitchell could 'find [another] a friend', supplying the names of specific children. For the first time she uses his version, finding 'a' friend. By partially taking up Mitchell's version of social life at the preschool, the preschool teacher provides Mitchell with the opportunity to then reply with his conflicting evidence in Lines 90 and 93, 'yeah I I I've been asking every kid but they all say no'. This produces a huge standoff in the form of a six-second silence.

The teacher's attempt at retrieval

93. C: but they all say no

94.   (6.0)

95. PT: next time you come we'll see who can play with you where do you want them to play in the sandpit or somewhere different to that (0.5)

The teacher's recourse in Line 95 is to deny Mitchell's evidence by proposing that next time Mitchell comes, things will be different, and more in line with her version. We see this proposal continued in Lines 98–108.

96. C: arr (0.5) I WANT TO PLAY (0.5) down at the home corner?

97.   (1.5)

98. PT: okay (0.75) well there's usually plenty people in there (who want to play) but you you ask me when you come next time (0.5) Tarrant doesn't play a lot in the home corner (2.5) he plays a lot with the blocks

99.   (3.5)

100. C: oh yeah

101. PT: mm (0.25) so that's probably why he's (yet to) to know him because he doesn't want to go ((laughy)) with you to the home area (and play) ((laugh)) (HEY) (0.75) do you think that might be why he says no?

102.   (0.25)

103. C: no

104. PT: no

105. C: I think that=

106. P: =(if you're gonna fool around)

107.   (2.0)

108. PT: well there's a lot of other kids there's Aaron, and there's Ned and there's Adriana no[w]

In Line 101 the preschool teacher proposes that Tarrant may not be agreeing to play with Mitchell because he does not want to go to the home area and play. Her turn is shaped to invite a 'yes'. However, in Line 102 there is a delay of 0.25 seconds. In addition, in Line 103 Mitchell produces 'no' as a strong disagreement with the teacher's proposal. He then starts to say something further in Line 105. At this point his mother interrupts, producing a reprimand directed at Mitchell. A significant silence of 2.0 seconds follows in Line 107. By Line 108 the preschool teacher has retreated again, supplying the names of specific children.

109. C: [I']VE BEEN TALKING TO EVERY ONE OF THEM

110. P: oh (0.5) oh well (0.25) you try again next time hey

111. PT: yep you come back if you're having a problem you see me next time okay

112. C: next time

113.   (1.0)

This allows Mitchell (as it did in Lines 90, 93) to present his personal experience as conflicting evidence in Line 109, 'I've been talking to every one of them. At this point the teacher's argument and evidence have been defeated. Mitchell has been able to claim that he has tried the teacher's solutions and they have not worked. He has actively demonstrated his competence as a language-user and that he is very capable of presenting his own evidence. His version of himself as child is one who has tested the teacher's theory and 'presents his own version of affairs'. In addition, his version of himself as child extends beyond mere presentation to acknowledgment by the teacher of his version of affairs.

Mitchell's negotiation of competing versions of 'himself as child'

Mitchell negotiates his way between his mother's version of Mitchell the child and the preschool teacher's. Constant monitoring and shiftings of his position in the talk enable him to walk the tightrope that is the child's challenge in participating in the adult world, on this occasion parent–teacher talk. His task is difficult enough when parents and teachers agree on their version of Mitchell the child, but when they do not an added dimension of challenge is present. Given these obstacles, Mitchell still manages to juggle these positions competently. In addition, he is also able to present his own version of himself as child. In so doing he is contributing to a redefinition of the 'preschool child'.

Mitchell initially accomplishes the management of these conflicting positions by entering the conversation (Lines 75–84) and demonstrating how to be a 'compliant pupil', by presenting his talk within the conventions of the preschool teacher's requirements. According to her own definition, Mitchell could be assessed by the preschool teacher as being competent. At this point he is also adhering to his mother's version of Mitchell the child as being 'capable of presenting his own evidence'.

Mitchell disagrees with the teacher's assessment in Line 85, and presents his own conflicting evidence until Line 105. During this segment in the conversation (Lines 85–105) he is actively constructing Mitchell the child as being capable of presenting his own evidence, the version of Mitchell the child his mother presents. He also commences work on constructing his own version of himself as child, which includes his mother's version along with the addition of requiring that his version of social life at the preschool be acknowledged.

Mitchell continues to present his version of himself as child between Lines 105–113. Mitchell has 'won' his disagreement with the teacher by Line 111. Simultaneously, his definition of the social life of the preschool has been acknowledged by the teacher, and his version of himself as child defined. His mother, however, in Line 110, appears to distance herself from his version of himself as child by downplaying his win, and agreeing with the teacher's suggestion that he 'try again next time'. Mitchell's version is outside both his mother's and the teacher's acceptable versions in this particular situation. The preschool teacher, in Line 111, agrees with the parent's reiteration of her proposal. At this point Mitchell's mother and the preschool teacher (the adults) join forces to maintain their version of the adult world. Mitchell has crossed the boundary between competent preschool child and adult language use and participation rights. That Mitchell has oriented to this illicit boundary crossing is evident in Line 112 when he repeats the adults' direction 'next time'. It could be seen as a capitulation to the combined forces of the mother's and the teacher's 'next time' solution.

114. C: WHA ((loud yell))

115.   (1.5)

116. PT: oh? (0.25) oh that's come <u>out</u> of (0.75) <u>a</u> (0.75) <u>bed</u> I think (2.5) we had it wrapped up

117.   (2.5)

118. P: come on mate (.) say goodbye then

119. C: <u>there</u> you go (0.25) I fixed it

120.   (1.5)

121. PT: he <u>is</u> a kind boy (0.5) he <u>is</u> he's kind (for a lot)

122. P: yeah

From this point in the conversation Mitchell proceeds to identify a classroom toy in Line 114 that needs to be fixed and put away. He claims then, in Line 119, to have fixed the toy. By taking this course of action Mitchell repairs his previous breach of encroaching into the adult world beyond the invitation extended to him. These actions may also be seen as a way of aligning himself with the preschool teacher's version of Mitchell the child as one who helps in the classroom, and therefore is compliant with her version of how the preschool functions. By taking this action he manages not only to avoid sanctions, but also to be rewarded by the teacher in the form of a compliment (Line 121).

A child's competence as mediator between home and preschool

Mitchell manages to negotiate his way through the differently constructed versions of social life of his home and the preschool. Correspondingly, this negotiation requires that he operate both within and outside his mother's and the preschool teacher's versions of Mitchell the child at different times. This negotiation is by no means a simple process – even identifying these different versions of competence is difficult. Mitchell, however, competently mediates between these competing versions of social life, constantly monitoring and shifting his position in the talk. He also manages to assert his own version of himself as child. Even when his mother and the preschool teacher join forces to maintain their version of the 'adult' world, Mitchell is able once again to competently renegotiate his position, taking into account that the adults have now together limited his participation rights in the adult world.

Deciding what to say and do at a particular point in time in this conversation is the very difficult skill involved in this conversational participation for Mitchell. Throughout the conversation Mitchell continually monitors the talk for these appropriate times. He manages to walk the line between home and school, even managing to be complimented by the preschool teacher at the end of the conversation. Receiving a compliment from the teacher is possible even after he has 'won' a disagreement with her and succeeded in presenting his own version of himself as child as one who 'presents his own version of affairs and requires that they be acknowledged'.

Conclusion

Research on home–preschool communication has largely ignored the part that children play in these communications. However, it is possible to examine closely how children competently participate in these conversations by analysing a parent–teacher–child conversation in a preschool.

In this particular conversation, the analysis demonstrates how all participants actively construct different versions of Mitchell the child in this context. Mitchell the child to the preschool teacher involves his compliance with her version of social life at the preschool. To Mitchell's mother, Mitchell the child is one who is 'capable of presenting his own evidence'. Finally, Mitchell defines himself as child in terms of his ability to 'present his own version of affairs and have them acknowledged'.

Parent–teacher conversations are a site where home and school versions of children, and social life at the preschool meet. This analysis demonstrates how a home–preschool relationship is constructed in, and through, this type of talk. In this case, the lack of continuity between the home and the preschool also, is evidenced in the talk. Mitchell, however, is competent and actively contributes to, and influences, the home and preschool communication by his participation in this event. As the person who is physically present in both the home and preschool contexts, Mitchell has a stake in the negotiation of home and preschool constructed versions of himself and social life. Given the discrepancy between his mother's and the teacher's initial stances on his problem, Mitchell demonstrates an additional competence – that of mediating between the home and school. Through his talk and actions he is actively contributing to defining and redefining 'the competent preschool child'. As such, he is contributing to his own evolving membership in the social world of the preschool and also affecting the participation of adults and the formation and re-formation of their adult social world.

Acknowledgements

We wish to thank the participants in this home-preschool talk for their agreement to participate in the study and have their talk audio-recorded.

Carolyn Baker died after a short illness on 12 July 2003. I remember her as my supervisor, friend and colleague. In particular, I appreciated her attention towards always locating the 'good sense' of interactants. This was one of many practices that Carolyn shared that I work from.

Michele Leiminer

CHAPTER TWELVE

Using Computers at Home and at School

Children's Views and Perspectives

Toni Downes

Introduction

Of all the technologies currently available to children[1], and others in society, computers have particular social and educational significance. Together with a range of other communication and information technologies (such as the mobile phone, television, CD, DVD and video recorder/player and radio) they are becoming a part of the fabric of children's daily experiences. This is occurring through their progressive presence in homes, educational settings, arcades, local libraries and other public and private spaces. For example, the Australian Bureau of Statistics estimated that in 2000, over 70 per cent of Australian Households with children had working computers in their homes, and over 40 per cent had Internet access. Many Australians now use the Internet and mobile phones daily to conduct both their business and personal transactions, and in 2000 the Australian Bureau of Statistics estimated that nearly 50 per cent of children (5–14 year olds) used the Internet either at home, school or in other locations (ABS 2003).

This increasing access to, and use of, computers by children attracts much discussion about the benefits and problems associated with such use. Invariably, such discussions – and even much of the research and policy development surrounding such use – draws on adults' conceptions of technology, education and childhood. For example, much of the rhetoric around issues of concern from politicians and parents about children's playing of violent computer games (Dietz

1998; Fling *et al.* 1992) stems from conceptions of children as, on the one hand, innocent and in need of protection and, on the other, as vulnerable to corruption and even potentially dangerous. Furthermore, much of the theoretical framework that is embedded in the research and discussion around children's use of computers has strong elements of techno-determinism (for example, Subrahmanyam *et al.* 2000) or social-determinism (for example, Dietz 1998). Only a few accord 'agency' to the child and/or recognize how the differing social constructions of childhood, as well as technology and education, interact with access to and use of computers to shape the social environment of children's computing.

In order to better understand the complex relationships between the social, the personal, and the cultural artefacts that are generated when children use computers in their homes and schools, Downes (1998b) developed a blended theoretical framework by drawing on key concepts from various traditions. The key concepts were:

- childhood and technology as social constructions

- children as active in constructing and determining their socio-cultural life within the home and school while simultaneously being constrained and enabled by the context they are helping to shape

- the computer as offering a range of affordances shaped by its symbolic meanings and instrumental features; and

- the home and school as micro-systems of the child, with their own socio-cultural practices, beliefs, gendered relations and resources.

Importantly, the framework positions children as key informants of their experiences with computers in their daily lives; and illuminates the discourses in which children, parents and teachers engage as key indicators of the practices, beliefs and relations that shape and are shaped by children as they interact with computers in their homes and schools.

This chapter explores the discourses in which children (their parents and teachers) participated as they described their interactions with computers in their daily lives at home and at school. It draws together data from several of the author's projects (Downes 1998b; Downes, Arthur and Beecher 2001; Groundwater-Smith, Downes and Gibbons 2000). All three studies were informed by the above framework. In total, these projects involved around 1,000 children across various age groups (preschool, primary and high school) who had access to computers and related technologies in their homes. Parents and teachers were also informants: in the first study, the parents and teachers of 13 high-using children were interviewed, and in the second study, which took place within a single school, about 25 teachers (a quarter of all teachers in the school) took part in focus groups. Details of actual samples and methodologies can be found in the author's previous publications.

Children's discourses and interactions with computers in their homes

The key discourses that children participated in when discussing the importance and place of computers and computing in their homes were 'computers as entertainment', 'computers as the future', and 'computers as personal productivity tools'. Parents and teachers also engaged in these discourses to varying degrees but, because of their conceptions of childhood, technology and education, at times had differing concerns and beliefs about what was allowable or desirable practice and behaviour. The home was the site where children were more able to negotiate meaning and practices around conflicting concerns and beliefs. At school, children had little opportunity, if any, to negotiate.

Computers as entertainment

Computers 'as entertainment' was a key discourse for most children. Many spoke at length about the importance of computers as a source of entertainment within their homes. Using the computer was seen as an active form of leisure where the process of trying to win or of winning at games (for younger children) or the process of 'surfing the net' and 'chatting online' (for older children) was pleasurable. This sense of pleasure has been reported in a wide range of other studies as well (Ba, Tally and Tsikalas 2002; Becker 2002; Capella 2002; Furlong et al. 2000; Land 1999; Mumtaz 2001; Sutherland et al. 2000).

As in other studies (Subrahmanyam et al. 2000), children in our study believed that game playing could develop useful computing skills and that there was educational value in games that involved them learning basic skills such as reading, maths, spelling and general knowledge. When asked about parental concern about the content of some games, the children expressed the belief that they could separate game playing from the real world. In general, while parents did not see the use of the computer for leisure as important, they were reasonably comfortable about it being so, provided there was some educational or recreational value in the activity and they were not used excessively or in preference to homework being completed. In the 1998 study, only two parents of the thirteen families in the study commented negatively about game playing. Interestingly, both parents linked their objections to concerns about the role of the computer, implying by their comments that they wanted the computer to be viewed by the children as a 'tool' rather than a 'toy':

> I do not want them to use it as a toy. I do not believe in sticking kids in front of the computer to play games…that's not really a positive use of the computer. (Downes 2002a, p.4)

The parents who were comfortable with their children playing games at home, were also comfortable with the computer being used as both 'toy' and 'tool'.

The Internet and chat/email facilities were also thought of as entertainment with an element of educational value (learning to search, finding out useful things, 'talking' about homework with their school friends). Many studies report parental fears about online relationships and about how using the Internet for ICQ, chat, etc., negatively affected social development and a child's personal relationships in the real world (Colwell Grady and Rhaiti 1995; Kraut *et al.*1998; Shields and Behrman 2000). When asked about parental concern about the content of some of the websites and/or stranger-danger in chat rooms or on ICQ, the older children in our Groundwater *et al.* (2000) study expressed the belief that they could manage the appropriate use of these. Livingstone and Bovill (2001) also found that

> …students were not interested in the wider issues that preoccupy adults…nor are they fazed by adult fears about the anarchic nature of the internet or how it may be used for criminal or exploitive purposes. They tend to see it as offering them new freedoms and opportunities for control and self-expression. (p.8)

The issues of gender are complex. While there is clear evidence of the gendered nature of computer use in homes (AAUW Educational Foundation 2000; National Center for Education Statistics 2000) there is a surprising lack of awareness or talk about gender in the children's conversations about games or Internet use (Becker 2002; Mumtaz 2001). In our studies, this lack of gendering of the discourses was in contrast to the actual uses of the children in terms of the time spent and the choices of games played and choice of sites and activities when connected to the Internet (Downes 2002b). In most homes, the practices were strongly gendered, albeit in complex ways. The absence of the gendered discourses more closely allied with the notion that while parents gave 'permission' for girls as well as boys to participate in game playing and use of the Internet for leisure on the family computer, they neither encouraged nor demanded boys or girls to do so. Similarly, boys and girls both believed that within the constraints of family rules, children who wanted to did play games or 'surf the net' and others chose not to do so. In this sense 'who' played games or 'surfed the net' in the family was not a discursive issue for parents and children. In the main, both believed that children who wanted to do so, did; others chose not to do so. Parents generally put priority on the computer as an educational tool and as such those kinds of activities had priority over games and entertainment. Furlong *et al.* (2000, pp.137 and 234) found that this often redressed the supposed gender imbalance of access, as female activities were seen as 'serious'.

Computers as the future

Another key discourse for most children was 'computers as the future'. They considered being able to operate a computer essential for their future functioning as adults, particularly as workers (Caron, Giroux and Douzou 1989; Facer *et al.* 2001; Furlong *et al.* 2000). As one child said:

> so when you grow up and you have a job you know how to use the computer. If you get into a situation where you have to use a computer you know how to work the controls and that. (Downes 1998b, p.148)

This view seemed to be universal in that boys and girls spoke of this belief. It was also universal in the sense that it was not linked to particular types of computer uses or to particular types of work. Both parents and children used 'the child as learner' and 'the adult as worker' as their main constructions for linking computers, the future and children; children had to learn about computers now to prepare for their role as adult workers.

Computers as a tool

A third discourse in which children engaged was the computer as a tool. When talking about the computer as a tool children referred to two main tasks: writing and accessing information. They explained that the computer's main advantage was that it makes the tasks easier: easier to write and present written work well and easier to find 'more' information. When talking about word-processing, children spoke about the speed of task completion, the quality of the final product's appearance and the ease of correcting and editing. The issue of improving the quality of the writing was not so clear-cut. Some children believed that it made their writing 'better' because they could get all their ideas down first, then worry about the fixing up later, others only spoke in terms of making it 'easier'.

One area of disagreement that emerged between parents and children related to the possible negative impact on children's handwriting. Parents' concerns were focused on the 'child as learner' – a learner of handwriting – using tools that in some ways eliminated the need to write by hand, or at least reduced the opportunities to practise handwriting. The parents believed that handwriting was still an essential skill, while word-processing was only advantageous. They wanted their children to be 'literate' in both: handwriting for the present and word-processing for the future.

The children took a different view. They argued that both handwriting and word-processing were essential skills for the present. Word-processing was essential because it made writing so much easier. They did not think that continual word-processing reduced their handwriting skills. Many of the upper primary children thought that they were already established as a good or a poor hand writer and those that identified as poor hand writers, mainly boys, praised the ability of the computer to create presentable versions of their writing. These differences in views did provide for points of contest between some parents and children. Where parents were concerned, they exercised power through rules that were used to set limits. As one mother said:

> I say 'Why are you using the computer like this? I want you to write'. I say 'You'll forget how to write soon if we don't stop this.' So we now set aside some things, they don't do on the computer. (Downes 1998b, p.155)

Another area where children and their parents believed that the computer was a productivity tool was accessing information either from a CD-Rom or the Internet. Children spoke about the ease of use compared with books and libraries and about how much more interesting electronic forms of information were than print. While parents generally shared these views they did identify a down-side to the use of such sources. This time, however, parents were not so much concerned with the matter of losing more traditional library and book skills, but rather of losing an appreciation of the older technologies and of losing the preparedness to put in the effort that the older technologies demanded.

Overall, the main difference between children and their parents stemmed from the differences in the conceptions that they hold about childhood. Parents, while agreeing with children on the wide range of benefits of using computers, worried about their children losing or not fully developing the traditional skills, or losing interest and motivation in using them. Their notions of 'the child as learner' and 'the vulnerable child' were particularly strong in the sense that children, as learners, were more vulnerable to skill-loss than adults who have already mastered the skills. These notions created tensions with their own strongly held views of the importance of learning to use the computer 'for the future'. In contrast, children positioned themselves as 'workers' as well as learners, and saw the use of the computer for 'work', writing and 'looking up information' for school as essential. For this reason they did not suffer from the same reservations (Groundwater *et al.* 2000).

Overall, the analysis of the socio-cultural contexts of children's computing highlights the tension between structure and agency and discourses and practices. Through media presentations of advertising, government policy and local school practices and parental experiences in the workplace and in commercial activity, discourses about 'computers as the future' and 'computers for education' entered the home. These discourses were inclusive of gender and community type. Patterns of access, which were strongly influenced by parental expertise developed in the workplace and patterns of use within the home, were gendered and unequal in terms of community affluence. But overall the tension/relationship between discourses and uses was reciprocal, with both influencing each other. Family rules about computer use provided a particularly strong conduit for discourses to influence practices. For example, at points of competition around use, rules gave priority to older family members and to 'work' above 'leisure'. Importantly, for girls (who more often than boys engaged in productive work) rules about priority uses facilitated their access to computers at times of competition with male siblings.

The discourses and patterns of use combined to reinforce the potential affordances stemming from the functional identity of the computer. The affordance as 'tool' was strengthened through the dominant discourses, the rules regarding priority use and the actual patterns of use of parents and older siblings. The affordance of 'toy' was legitimated by parental approval, if not active participation in the use of computers for entertainment. However, it is important to note that this approval in some families is somewhat restricted by concerns about the time-consuming nature of game playing and Internet use. The legitimation process was also supported by parental and sibling use for leisure, though such use (game playing and Internet use) was both gendered and, in the case of parents, strongly related to community affluence.

The above analyses clearly indicate that the affordances of 'toy' and 'tool' can co-exist for children in the home. This notion of co-existence is a significant finding. Much of the early literature in the discourses surrounding domestic computing spoke in terms of competing discourses. This study has found that while the affordances have been shaped differently through the interactions of the discourses and patterns of use, children (and their parents) perceive both as legitimate conceptions of the multifunctional domestic computer.

Conclusion

The above results affirm one of the central tenets of the childhood studies paradigm: childhood, as a social construction, provides an interpretive frame for contextualizing the lives and experiences of the young. In particular, within this study, it provided a key part of the theoretical framework to better understand the social contexts within which children interact with computers in their homes. Furthermore, children themselves socially construct childhood and computing in ways that help shape their daily interactions with the technology. These interactions are, in turn, shaped by the affordances of the computer as perceived by the children and adults around them. This reciprocity of agency between the child and the technology is embedded within the social environment shaped by dominant discourses about the technology and childhood. These discourses create concerns within the minds of adults which, in turn, support or conflict with children's discourses. It is within this framework that children conceive of the computer as an essential and playable tool.

Note

1   Throughout this chapter, unless otherwise stated, children refers to 3–18-year-olds, and educational settings to early childhood settings (for 3–5-year olds) and schools and colleges (for 5–18-year-olds).

CHAPTER THIRTEEN

Preschool Girls, Conflict and Repair

Susan Danby

Introduction

In recent sociological investigations of taking children seriously, we have come to recognize the importance of three interrelated observations. One such understanding is that childhood is a social construction, and not just a biological phase of development (James *et al.* 1998; Mayall 1999; 2003; Prout and James 1997; Waksler 1991b). Children are seen to be active in constructing and determining their own lives. When children are positioned as social constructs, they are described as social actors rather than as natural phenomena (Mayall 1994).

A second observation is that theoretical understandings derived from the sociologies of childhood construct children as being socially competent in their everyday social interactions. The construction of the child can be only a local and particular description, as description is critically linked to the situatedness of the activity. Childhood, then, is understood as local, particular, and socially consti- tuted. As Hutchby and Moran-Ellis (1998b) point out, 'competence has...to do with children's ability to manage their social surroundings, to engage in meaning- ful social interaction within given interactional contexts' (p.16). The work of children, then, is described as a practical accomplishment where children organize and manage their everyday activities in ways that show their compe- tence. One way that children do this is by managing conflict in their everyday activities. Arguments and conflict, which suggest disagreement, are also co- constructed activities as children test their social positions within their social worlds (Goodwin 1995; Jacoby and Ochs 1995; Maynard 1985). Children work to repair and rebuild their own social orders, and this often happens outside the audible and visible scrutiny of the adult.

A third observation, then, is that studies of children and childhood are best addressed when the research methodology recognizes the children's worlds and cultures (Christensen and James 2000; Prout and James 1997; Waksler 1991b). These observations lead to the recommendation that children's social relationships should be studied in their own right. Within this domain, studies investigating 'the concrete features of competent interaction is nothing more or less than a study of what children normally and routinely do in their everyday activities' (Speier 1982, p.82).

This chapter elaborates the serious business of play by showing how children as young as three- and four-years-old are already competent practitioners of their social worlds. The analyses presented describe the complicated resources of language and non-verbal interaction on which they drew in order to interact as competent members of the classroom, and build their social orders alongside those of adults. In this way, children can be understood as '"doing the business" of childhood' (James *et al.* 1998, p.34).

Talk-in-interaction: Accounting for social interaction

The analysis uses an approach known as talk-in-interaction (Psathas 1995), working from the premise that talk, in its details, should be examined as a topic in its own right (Sacks 1984). This approach explicates first how talk is accomplished among participants by scrutinizing each member's situated use of language or performance, 'for it is the interaction of competence and performance that is essential for understanding everyday activities' (Cicourel 1970, p.138). Consequently, studying the development of language is not 'essential for deriving measures of everyday social organization' (Cicourel 1970, p.137). These measures can be derived from the talk itself.

This chapter draws on understandings and applications of ethnomethodology to show how people make sense of everyday activities and interactions (Baker 1997; Cicourel 1970). Analysis shows how members accomplish their orderly and accountable practices by studying actual, singular sequences of social interaction from which descriptions and accounts emerge (Baker 1997; Pomerantz and Fehr 1997; Sacks 1984). Talk-in-interaction is more than an analysis of talk because it takes into account all aspects of interaction, both verbal and non-verbal. In this way, talk-in-interaction has an ethnomethodological orientation. The overriding feature of talk-in-interaction is its emphasis on actual data: 'analysis is strongly "data-driven"' (Heritage 1984, p.243). The value of using this approach to explicate sequences of talk-in-interaction by children in their everyday interactions in a preschool room 'is that it can uncover and formulate functions which practices facilitate, yet which are, or were, unrecognized or unappreciated by members' (Heap 1990, p.47). In order to do this, Sacks (1984) emphasizes 'using observation as a basis for theorizing' (p.25). He explains,

> we can start with things that are not currently imaginable, by showing that they happened. We can then come to see that a base for using close looking at the world for theorizing about it is that from close looking at the world we can find things that we could not, by imagination, assert were there. We would not know that they were 'typical' (lecture 1, fall 1971). Indeed, we might not have noticed that they happen. (p.25)

Evident in the examples of data shown in this chapter is the complex social interactional work of the children. Indeed, in one episode I was unaware of the powerful non-verbal interaction taking place among the three girls until I had viewed and reviewed the video recorded data several times. What I discovered was a carefully sequenced series of moves that involved the girls walking close to each other, but without touching. This intricate non-verbal repair seemed to repair the girls' problem in a way that the teacher's intervention did not.

Data and methodology

The play activities of children aged three to five years were observed and video-recorded in a preschool classroom. There were two teachers and up to sixteen children in the room, located in a childcare centre in an Australian inner-city area. Data collection consisted initially of a period of participant observation one morning a week over a year and then a period of videotaped observations of the play experiences of the children over a three-week period at the beginning of the school year. I video-recorded episodes of play that occurred within the classroom as well as outside in the playground. Video recording captured the complexity and interconnectedness of the talk and action in the classroom (Mehan 1979; 1993), allowing for an examination of natural talk and non-verbal behaviour in everyday life and preserving the data in a way that most closely resembles the original form (Baker 1998).

It is from the video-recorded data that episodes of talk-in-interaction were selected for transcription and analysis. Selected episodes chosen for analysis were transcribed using conventions of conversation analysis (Psathas 1995; Sacks 1992/95). (An explanation of the transcript notation used is given in the Appendix at the end of this book.) I transcribed the actual talk of the participants in fine-grained detail to show such features of talk as the pauses, overlaps and intonations. In addition, I described in the transcript the participants' non-verbal behaviour, which included facial expressions, gestures, orientations to each other and to objects and other actions. In this way, transcripts can focus 'squarely on the microgenesis of co-construction over the span of interactional time...to reveal realms of interactional work that take place even in fractions of a second' (Jacoby and Ochs 1995, p.174).

This type of approach allowed for careful observation and re-examination of the data, which facilitated detailed interpretations. Close examination of the transcripts of children's play found themes of accomplishment and competence that could have been overlooked in an analysis that was less concerned with examining the moment-by-moment utterances and non-verbal actions.

The girls' talk-in-interaction

This chapter uses an episode of play involving three girls interacting with each other to show that they were powerful in organizing their social worlds in ways that are not always easy to see from adult perspectives. It shows how the young girls competently organized and maintained their everyday interactional activities. In this way, play was treated as serious business, used as an interactional resource to construct their social order. These analyses name what the children had been seen to do and are analysts' themes and not themes identified or labelled by the children.

Interactional competence entails children's learning how to develop social skills and build friendships. As Speier (1982) points out, it may be used to refer to a developmental learning process where children learn how to enter and participate in their social organizations. Such a developmental perspective posits children as 'precompetent' (Speier 1976, p.98), 'incomplete' (Mackay 1974, p.181), 'underdeveloped' (Waksler 1991b, p.63) and, consequently, lacking power and knowledge (Mayall 2003; Waksler 1991b). This perspective also derives from an adult perspective that ascribes children's competence, or lack of it (Mayall 2003; Waksler 1991b).

Waksler (1991b) provides an example to illustrate how adults ascribe interactional competence. When children are playing a game with rules, adults are sometimes upset and complain when the children change the rules. Waksler argues that adults do so in order to preserve and teach the social order of the adults and thus keep the advantage for the adults. Such adult biases keep the status quo. She claims that it is in the interests of the adult to deny children their present accomplishments in order to preserve this belief about children as being incompetent. Waksler (1996) says that adults even go so far as to ignore adult memories of their own childhood 'trials' (e.g. having to eat your vegetables, going to bed) so that they do not have to recognize or take into account the child's perspective.

The construction of children as being competent only in certain adult-prescribed ways or as *developing* competence is common in both early childhood research and teaching practices. In such descriptions of children, the child is reduced to being a vessel partially filled, not complete until adulthood. Much research has shown what children can't do (in terms of language development, cognitive development, and so on), which is taken to show that children know less than adults. As Waksler (1991b) says, 'children are viewed as in their very nature not grown up and thus *not something* rather than *something*' (p.63). The concept of children's incompetence suggests that adults can make judgements for and over children without regard to their value systems (Goode 1994).

Contrast the approach that describes children as developing into adults with one that views children as already competent. The latter is the position that this chapter takes. Competence, here, refers to the notion that children *are* 'competent interpreters in the world' (Mackay 1974, p.184) and describes children as understanding the social structures in which they operate (Cicourel 1970). This perspective, using the understandings of the field known as studies in sociology of childhood, describes the work of childhood not as an unfolding of developmental potentials but as a practical accomplishment of children themselves. As Hutchby and Moran-Ellis (1998a) argue,

> Competence cannot be separated from the structural contexts in which it is displayed or negotiated. Neither can social competence ultimately be understood simply as a property of individuals: whether it is with other children or with adults, in everyday situations of peer group play or in more formal, adult-framed settings, children's manipulation of culturally available resources to manage the trajectories of interaction, as well as the social impact of others' actions in the setting, represents the true grounding for claims about children's social competence. (p.16)

One way to recognize young children's competence is to give them a place to speak for themselves. For example, in *Frogs and Snails and Feminist Tales*, Davies (1989) describes talking to preschool-aged children and taking seriously their views. She saw the children as competent to discuss issues of gender and moral order in relation to the stories that were read to them and in her study disclosed that very competence.

I now offer an example from my research, drawing upon the argument set out in Danby and Baker (1998b), that children are socially competent in their interactions with each other. In this instance, conflict became evident in the interactions of three girls (Elana, Portia, and Amelia). The three girls had been playing for approximately ten minutes in an open space in the classroom, using three chairs joined together as a prop representing a car. As part of the play, Portia told Elana to remain at the 'car.' Elana resisted this instruction and moved across to the dramatic-play area known as home corner. Amelia and Portia entered the home-corner area and pretended to lock Elana in 'jail'. With a great flourish, Elana, refusing to accept this incarceration, pretended to unlock the imaginary door with her imaginary key and she strode out of home corner. When Portia grabbed her arm to pull her back into home corner, Elana cried out and the teacher immediately intervened. The teacher first called out, and then moved to stand beside the three girls. She attempted first to find out why Elana was crying. She then asked Portia and Amelia to find a solution to make Elana 'feel better'. She used a model of care and consolation to enact what she considered a repair of Elana's hurt feelings. However, she seemed either unsure or unaware of what Portia and Amelia might have seen as Elana's infraction. Thus, she did not attend to this matter. The transcript begins below when the teacher entered the scene. Another child, John, stood nearby during this interaction with the teacher, and was a witness to the scene involving the three girls.

Part A

11. T'er: ((Teacher is now at the scene.)) No Amelia Portia back here and you talk to Elana please ((Amelia and Portia turn around and come back. John is now standing as part of the group. Elana remains silent.)) what's the problem (1.0) why is she crying (1.0) why is she she crying? ((softer voice)) (1.0) Did you hurt her feeling

12. Portia: No? ((Amelia looks at Portia.))

13. T'er: Who hurt her feelings then Amelia did you hurt Elana's feelings then

14. ((Amelia shakes her head and Portia looks at her.))

15. John: [She did] ((pointing to Portia))

16. T'er: [Then why] is she sad Portia why is she sad?

17. John: She did she she she pulled her hand ((pointing to Portia and then Elana))

18. T'er: Did you pull her hand Portia <u>but</u> why is Elana crying yu' you have to tell me so we can solve the problem (2.0) Do you think you can talk to Elana and make her feel better? (1.0) Can you make her feel better? because she's feeling a bit sad at the moment. ((Elana remains silent.))

19. ((Portia starts to walk away, turns, goes to Elana and gives her a hug; Elana looks down and remains silent; Amelia watches.))

20. T'er: Thank you Portia I think that makes her feel much better

21.   ((Portia, Amelia and John walk away towards book corner.
              Portia looks at the book display; Amelia, still clutching a book,
              stands and looks at the teacher and Elana.))

Elana's cries immediately brought the teacher into the scene. At first, the teacher tried to find out why Elana is crying, linking the crying with the possibility that Elana's feelings were hurt (turns 11 and 13). When Amelia and Portia disagreed with the teacher's formulation of the problem (turns 12 and 14), John came forward with a reason, suggesting that Portia pulled Elana's hand (turns 15 and 17). This explanation seemed acceptable to the teacher, who took this up in her next question to Portia (turns 18). After a two-second pause, the teacher shifted her interest from trying to find what caused the problem to asking Portia and Amelia to find a number of possible solutions to help Elana feel better (turn 18). Finally, she accepted Portia's hug (turn 19) as an accepted and appropriate solution to fix Elana's crying and hurt feelings. The teacher left, appearing to believe that she has repaired the conflict.

Immediately upon the teacher's departure, Portia and Amelia discussed what to do next. Portia charged Amelia with having to make Elana feel better. Amelia at first resisted this idea, initially accusing Portia of causing the problem, but eventually Amelia walked towards Elana, who was now in the far side of the classroom. As I continued to videotape what then occurred, I did not realize the significance of what was happening until I viewed and reviewed the videotaped episode. It was then that I saw with much surprise that the girls themselves repaired their problem of the breached social order after the teacher departure through an intricate non-verbal choreography of walking and standing close to each other (Danby and Baker 1998).

Part B

29. Portia: (   ) ((in a very quiet voice))

30.   ((Amelia immediately walks over to the puzzle table, the other
              side of the room, where Elana is standing with a book. Amelia
              sits down and glances briefly as Elana walks away.))

31.   ((Elana walks away looking at the book until she stands in
              front of book corner, but facing away from Portia, looks up,
              and swings arms and book from side to side, looks briefly at
              researcher.))

32.   ((Portia walks out of book corner, past Elana on her way to her locker, and pulls out something from her locker and then replaces it.))

33.   ((Amelia leaves the puzzle table and brushes past Elana towards the preparation room.)) whe whe whe (in a rhythmic fashion)

34.   ((John brushes past Elana)) (   ) ((says something to Amelia))

35.   ((Portia brushes past Elana, giving her a brief glance, and goes to the preparation room, meeting the teacher as she comes out)) (   )

36.   ((Teacher acknowledges Portia by a look and weaves around her as she keeps walking; Portia stops and holds her dress.))

37.   ((Amelia and Elana talk briefly to each other. Amelia then walks into home corner and Elana follows.))

38.   ((Portia goes to sit beside the teacher assistant in construction area.))

The girls began to fix their own problem non-verbally as they brushed past each other and weave in and out of the preschool spaces. They showed an 'art of walking' (Ryave and Schenkein 1974, p.265) in that they were acutely aware of each other's movements and oriented towards them. Amelia and Elana finally repaired their interrupted relationship as they began first to talk quietly to each other (turn 37), and then they returned to home corner. Portia, however, was not part of this interaction. Her repair and acceptance was not yet complete. After Amelia and Elana returned to home corner, Portia walked across the preschool classroom to sit beside the teacher assistant in another part of the preschool classroom (turn 38).

What is most evident from this transcript is the intricate choreography showing how Amelia, Portia and Elana worked to repair their relationship. It was accomplished outside the teacher's direction and intervention. However, the teacher's presence cannot be discounted as the teacher appeared to provide the moral work of care and consolation that the girls used to then effect their own repair. In this way, the girls appeared converted to this moral order that she imposed (Danby and Baker 1998; Mayall 2002). While the teacher did not actually fix the problem, she provided a moral discourse within which the girls found their own solution, although the solution seems only partial for Portia.

This episode shows that the girls were able to operate within their own social orders and also within that of the teacher, an operation not reciprocated by the teacher. Yet, the teacher's actions in this episode could never be dismissed. In the first place, the teacher assumed the girls' competence in finding solutions in order to fix the problem of the crying child and hurt feelings. But at the same time, she assumed that they were incompetent in dealing with the situation and so needed her help. This transcript shows that the girls were indeed competent to deal with the situation as they used their own interactional resources (the intricate walking) to enact the repair that the teacher's version (the hug) could not. This shows the paradox that adults and teachers assume children's competence in certain tasks while, at the same time, denying them their competence (Mackay 1974). As Baker and Freebody (1989) note, children 'must know how to do something they are not credited with being able to do in order to participate in the adults' agenda for learning how to do it' (p.84).

This example illustrates that by looking very closely, it was possible to see the competence of the young girls in their everyday actions. This lens was used to look at their everyday actions, not to see daily experiences as important only for some future development but to celebrate their daily experiences in the present moment. As Leavitt (1994) says, 'young children's daily experiences are as important as the outcomes of these experiences'(p.92). The work of the young girls here shows the social orders to which they orient on a daily basis.

Conclusion

Studies of the social practices of children first require analysis of 'the concrete features of interactional competence' (Speier 1982, p.182). This approach treats talk as a topic, and recognizes its importance in organizing everyday life. Talk-in-interaction offers an approach to looking very closely at the children's social episodes to show how they use their talk and action to build and maintain the social scenes. By looking at the visible (and audible) structures of the participants' talk and action, these analyses can provide an account of how the children themselves could have made sense of the situations. As Mayall (1999) notes, 'from the researcher's perspective, study of processes, including bodily and verbal interactions, is a key way of getting at how children construct their social identities' (p.15).

This chapter has explicated how three preschool-aged girls organized and articulated their everyday activities to build social orders. The analyses of these transcripts show that the girls were indeed active in constructing and determining their own social lives. Examples of everyday activities shown throughout this chapter contradict the popular notion described by Waksler (1991b) that 'children *as a category* know *less* than adults, have *less* experience, are *less* serious, and are less important than adults in the ongoing work of everyday life' (p.63).

What became evident in this analysis was the seriousness of the children's activity and interaction. Children's free activity has often been defined as play, and described as a necessary component of early childhood classrooms (cf. Ailwood 2003). Often, these descriptions have described play as an enjoyable and voluntary activity (Garvey 1990; Mayall 2002). However, what is not always evident in such descriptions is the serious nature, *the work*, of play. In what adults may view as play situations, the children's work is the very serious business of constructing social order. As Denzin (1982) notes:

> when they are left on their own, young children do not play, they work at constructing social orders. 'Play' is a fiction from the adult world. Children's work involves such serious matters as developing languages for communications; defining and processing deviance; and construction rules of entry and exit into emergent social groups. Children see these as serious concerns and often make a clear distinction between their play and their work. This fact is best grasped by entering those situations where children are naturally thrown together and forced to take account of one another. (p.192)

Perhaps because play encounters are so fleeting, especially the free-play activities studied here, it is difficult for adults to observe them and therefore to understand them. Making use of videotape data, as this study has done, has provided an analytic tool to slow down the moment so that fleeting moments of interaction can be examined more closely.

The lack of distinction that adults make when talking about children's activities makes invisible to adults the serious nature and significance of what young children actually do in their encounters with each other as they build their social orders. This understanding has led me to explore the social distance between children and adults that is thought to exist by many. In maintaining a distance between the worlds of adults and children, it is easy to trivialize what children do, or to describe within adult perspectives what they are doing. To deny children the seriousness of their everyday activities is to deny them the serious nature of the work that they do in building and maintaining their social orders in everyday interactional encounters.

CHAPTER FOURTEEN

Children's Perceptions of School

Neriman Osman

Introduction

Children spend the majority of their childhood lives at school, yet the way they view school is not often investigated. At the time the research presented in this chapter was conducted there was little Australian research available on children's perspectives on school, although, as Hammersley (2000) has remarked, qualitative work in schools is valuable because of the way in which it highlights problems. In the 1998 study discussed here, a small number of primary school-aged children were asked about their views of school.

Researchers on childhood, writing from the alternative, or 'new' childhood studies, paradigm (De Winter 1997; Freeman 1987; Flekkoy and Kaufman 1997; John 1996; Mayall 1994; Mayall 1996; Prout and James 1997; Qvortrup 1994) have highlighted the importance of research approaches with children that view children as agents, knowers and competent informants. This paradigm informed the study reported on here where children discussed their experiences of school.

Research on children's experiences of school

The relative lack of research specifically on children's experiences of school can be attributed to adult perceptions of children as immature and not knowledgeable about school matters, due to their status as children. Stafford, Laybourn and Hill (2003) notes that the majority of the research about student voice is driven by adults' agendas. Results from Stafford et al.'s (2003) exploratory study of the views of school children and young people in Scottish schools concluded that young people felt devalued and excluded from matters in school because adults did not give them recognition or consult with them about school issues.

Similar findings were reported in research conducted by Wyse (2001) in two primary schools and two secondary schools in England. This research demonstrated an absence of awareness of rights by both children and teachers, and found that schools provided limited opportunities for children to express their views, and that fair treatment in school was based on conditions rather than being a right. At the same time, primary-school children demonstrated an ability to think seriously about complex issues.

At the time of the study reported on here, the limited amount of research available in Australia on children's perspectives of school, generally used quantitative methodoldogy in its approach (ACER 1987; Ainley 1995; Ainley and Bourke 1982; Batten 1981; Cranston 1988). This research tended to report on children's positive attitudes towards school. In contrast, the findings of the few qualitative Australian studies (Danaher 1995; Foggart 1986; Hatton 1995; Williamson 1995), while focusing on educational aspects of schooling, highlighted children's negative views of school.

The limited qualitative research in schools in Australia, and more generally in the literature, has placed little emphasis on the context in which students' schooling occurs. Rudduck and Flutter (2000) has noted that schools do not give the attention needed to regimes, relationships, structures, intellectual challenge, and students' values and commitment to school, which can all play an important role in policy making.

A description of this study

The 1998 research used in this chapter was a small study (Osman 1999) that used qualitative methods to gain an understanding of some primary-school children's experiences of and views on school. In the study, six children from a Sydney suburban, state government, primary school participated in two focus group discussions. Four boys and two girls aged between nine and eleven participated in the study.

Focus groups were viewed as the most appropriate method to meet the aims of this research, providing scope for participants to react to and build on the responses of others (Minichiello *et al.* 1990). Two focus-group discussions of one hour and forty-five minutes duration, were held over a three-week period. In attending to power imbalances that can impact negatively on research (Oakley 1994), the research sought more equal relations between herself and the children by seating herself with the children in a circle, on a chair or on the floor, in order to be at a similar physical height.

Techniques used to build rapport and initiate conversation included an 'imaginary' task. Hill (1997) recommends using creative activities as appropriate applications for exploratory research. In commencing the research, children were asked to imagine the researcher to be an alien from outer space who required knowledge about their views of school with the possibility of constructing a similar institution on her planet. Children were invited to draw on large sheets of cardboard the way they viewed school and to write comments in speech bubbles above their drawings. The children seemed to enjoy this task and in the second focus-group discussion, the female children asked to repeat the task. Drawing assisted the children to explore their views and elaborate on them in the discussions.

Initially the female participants appeared shy and uncomfortable in initiating conversation. This may have been due to the fact that there were fewer girls than boys in the study. However, further into the discussion the girls became more engaged, as topics of interest were discussed. The children generally determined the direction of the discussion and expressed their thoughts openly in the focus groups.

Analysing the data required a number of steps. Both focus groups were taped and each tape was transcribed word for word. Each unit of data was coded and categorized into themes. Several themes were identified within the data and provided a framework for the analysis.

Findings from the study

The three major themes emerging from analysis of the focus group data are discussed here: control and authority, rules and structures, and gender and favouritism.

Control and authority

The children discussed in their drawings negative characteristics they attributed to teachers. Their drawings depicted teachers in classroom settings, displaying a considerable degree of frustration. The children wrote in speech bubbles above the teachers. 'Do your work!'; 'Why you…, you're on a level' (a measurement of punishment administered to children dependent on their behaviour); 'Stop'; and 'Go to the corner'. One child drew a large, monstrous, frightening-looking teacher, shouting 'Sing louder, children'. Interestingly, the pupils were drawn considerably smaller than teachers were. When asked, why the huge difference in size, one boy replied, 'Because that is how we feel.' The difference in size symbolized how powerless the children felt at school. The children depicted 'yelling' by teachers as part of the school culture.

All the children, on many occasions, described teachers' actions as being 'unfair'. Children often felt that they were not given the opportunity to be heard, to tell their side of the story. Punishment given to pupils was described as harsh, contributing to the children feeling devalued and not respected by teachers.

> ...There was an ambulance one day because someone fainted or...something...and I went to look and I was like a few centimetres out of bounds and Mrs I came down and said 'Get to my room right now', so I went down to her room and she said that I had to pick up 200 papers in the next day...like the next day...and so I had to do it. (Billy)

> Once Mrs K dropped a piece of paper on the ground and she said, 'Pick that up for me' and she just walked away. (Jerry)

Use of the lavatory was an area where control by adults was experienced particularly forcibly. Children expressed concern that teachers did not allow them to use the lavatory during class time. The children were angry at teachers' attitudes regarding the use of the lavatory. Of greatest concern to the children were the physiological consequences. One child commented:

> And the teachers will say NO!!... And if you're busting what can you do!! Wee in your pants!! Be constipated!! You don't really have a choice!! ...and they think they have control that they can't let you go to the toilet 'cause your going to run off or something... I don't know!! (Drew)

Waksler (1996) argues that:

> Adult's control of children's use of bathroom facilities highlights adults' routine assumption that they know better than children, what children's inner states are. Adults' assumptions about how much control children have over their bodily functions may be at odds with children's experiences. (p.2)

Mayall (1996, p.111) states that, 'schools seem to instruct children to regulate their bodies in the interests of adult timetables and agendas and not self care'.

The children highlighted inconsistent rules and expectations as they were applied to children and adults' use of the lavatory, giving an example that teachers use the lavatory discreetly during class time. The children perceived this as an unjust advantage for the teachers and were upset at their powerlessness in that teachers did not take their physiological needs seriously. This seemed to reduce the children's trust of the teachers.

> And teachers go whenever they want. (Katherine)

> Yeah they just walk out of the room! (Drew)

And go to the library toilet. (Billy)

Or just say 'I'm going to Mrs M to see something' and they just go down to the toilet…I have seen teachers do that. (Drew)

And they lie. (Katherine)

Children wanted some control, by contributing to formulating school policies and being part of the decision-making process. Here they wanted more equal relations with, and respect by, teachers. One child devised a strategy for dealing with everyday issues in school but felt defeated by the lack of change in the school system with traditional authoritarian structures.

Yeah, just like…just say tick your name off on the door, like if your teacher is wondering where you are, if you just tick your name if you're going somewhere…and tick like if you're going to get your hat from a room or going to the toilet or on a message board or something like that instead of going up to the teacher and getting (*imitates teacher's voice*) 'NOOOO!! Get and do your work!!' That's the attitude towards it all. (Drew)

One of the children described how punishment was more threatening at school than at home.

You kind of feel that if you don't obey the teachers, like you don't know what they are going to do…it's kind of a surprise…but if you do something bad with your parents it's just like you know what is going to happen, you'll either get grounded or you'll get a smack or something. (Billy)

Children resented that teachers had a degree of control over their activities similar to that of their parents.

Yeah, it's like they're our parents, they have control and when teachers shout at me, I just think, God they're not my parents, they can't really do that!! (Drew)

In this study children were echoing a finding of Mayall's study (2002, p.77) in two UK primary schools in the 90s, where primary school students indicated a clear awareness that schools are controlled by adults and they have little choice but to do as they are told. Mayall's (2002, p.14) research, also identified that parents' power encourages children's control and autonomy whereas teacher's power is directed at conformity. Children in the study reported here felt disempowered by their teachers and were wanting respect within the educational institution.

Rules and structures

Rules in schools were a complex matter for the children. They found it difficult to make sense of the rules at school, emphasizing that there were no formal guidelines on what they could and could not do in school. They felt the type of punishment administered was dependent on teachers' interpretation of their behaviour. In the children's eyes the punishment was often inappropriate and demeaning. One example given was:

> There's a blue seat (children have to sit on this when they get into trouble) and these kids were making this rock thing on the ground, they weren't throwing them or anything...and they got into trouble...and I was watching them while they were doing this rock thing...and they had to sit on the blue seat and I was only watching them but I had to sit on the blue seat as well. (George)

Children referred frequently in their discussions to 'levels' – a disciplining mechanism used in their school with the aim of correcting inappropriate behaviour. The children viewed these strategies negatively, arguing that punishment did not correct what teachers described as 'bad' behaviour at school as 'kids continued doing the wrong thing'. In some situations being placed on a 'level' was viewed as extremely unreasonable, in that little regard was shown for the child's account of the circumstances.

> She was just standing up in the weather shed. (Pamela)

> ...I stood up before the bell. (Katherine)

> Well, just say if you just came walking to sit under the shade shelter; you'd go on a level. (Jerry)

> Well, she put 20 people on a level for walking up to the shade shelter...they just put their bags down and they walked up and Mrs L put them on a level but that is stupid. (Billy)

> I was playing at the wrong time and put on a level. (Katherine)

> I was coming to school one day last year and I said 'hello' to my friends as soon as I arrived, then we stayed down there...for like 10 seconds...and then Mrs Q comes out and said 'OK all you people up to my room right now!' and then um... We went up there and then we missed out on all our second half lunch and she...there were at least forty people and this girl said 'Are we going to go on a level?' and she said (*the teacher*) 'You'd better be quiet or else you will be!!' They are just really mean, Mrs!...she's one of the...!!! (*sighed with frustration*). (Drew)

Children in this study felt detached from their school by their experiences of unfair, punitive measures taken by teachers that were non-negotiable. Their experiences contrasted with that of students who experience a 'caring school environment', as highlighted by the NSW Commission for Children and Young People Inquiry Report (2000, p.73). Such environments have been shown to have positive effects on students' health, well-being, social and personal development. The Report refers to findings from a national US longitudinal study that found 'school connectiveness' was related to students' perception of fair treatment of them by teachers; their relationship with people in the school and a sense of belonging to the school community.

Children's experiences of oppression in school, through lack of opportunities to have their voices heard, is consistent with John's (2003, p.53) use of the term 'unpeople', in describing children and young people as powerless, unrecognized and anonymous and comprising a minority group. In her exploration of power she states:

> one could argue that being totally ignored is the ultimate in powerlessness; it means one does not count, that one's existence is immaterial – it is as if you were not just a 'lower' but not even a person. (John 2003, p.52)

John maintains that conventional educational practices in schools exclude children from any sense of power, as they limit the development of children's ability to negotiate their own conception of reality (John 2003, p.49 and p.216).

Gender and favouritism

Children identified differential treatment between females and males and attributed it to gender bias. The boys perceived that the teachers gave girls favourable treatment at school. There was a consensus amongst the boys that 'female teachers don't understand what it is like to be a boy because they are females'. They felt that female teachers lacked empathy and understanding of males, with emotional consequences for the boys.

The boys stated that they received harsher and more frequent penalties than girls for doing the 'same things' and they also felt they were not praised by teachers for good work.

> ...And like we have this boy named Michael and a girl named Bronwyn and like if Bronwyn, she is always like talking loudly and she doesn't get on any level, and if Michael speaks a couple of times, he'll get on a level and Bronwyn won't. (Jerry)

> ...And they are just giving the attention to the girls like they get a chance but the boys don't because they should know better or something. (Drew)

Yeah, when we were in Mrs T's class, we all had to be quiet because she had a headache...and Mrs T got somebody to stand up for talking...and when that person saw somebody else talking they had to stand up...and if it was your second time standing up, you had to pick up fifty papers...and there was this girl, Melissa, she stood up a second time and Mrs T said [after the children had verified to the teacher that it was the second time Melissa stood up] 'um...oh...you don't...ooh...nah...that's not true' and so Melissa doesn't have to pick up the fifty papers!! (George)

You always see boys picking up the papers, never girls! (Jerry)

Tough versus soft approaches can contribute to the gender division felt by students in schools. Thorne (1993) considers differences in values between genders are developed by cultural feminine and masculine ideals that are encouraged and maintained in school, perpetuated by stereotypes and ideologies. In this study, both the boys and girls considered female teachers discriminatory in their attitudes towards boys, in that they treated girls more favourably. This was not the case in relation to male teachers, who were more likely to be seen by children as not basing their treatment of boys and girls on gender differences. Mayall (1996) suggests that a high proportion of female teachers in school nurture a sympathetic environment for girls.

Gender was not the only criterion that was described as eliciting different responses from teachers. The children considered that children who were labelled as 'goody goodies' or 'smart' were highly regarded and given preferential treatment by teachers. The children felt undermined and devalued when teachers consistently rewarded the same children over and over again for achievement and described this as unfair treatment.

But it is like saying cause you're not as smart, you don't know all those things, you don't get white cards and stuff and it's unfair. (Drew)

The smartest girl gets all the white cards and house points. (Billy)

Yeah she gets everything... 10 out of 10 and everything. (Pamela)

Goody goodies get all the attention because of the teachers. (George)

One child indicated that some teachers made it obvious that they have 'teachers pets'.

Yeah, Mrs L. she was saying that she doesn't have any teacher's pet and um once she goes um... She looked straight at Stewart, like he is always getting into trouble...she goes 'ohh he'll never be my teacher's pet!!!...like thinking of him. (Katherine)

Conclusion

In exploring their views about their schooling, children in this study demonstrated a capacity to reflect on and contribute ideas about their school.

Findings indicated that some children feel oppressed by their teachers' use of their greater power, and the ways in which this impinges on their autonomy and well-being. Their experiences in their interactions with teachers indicate to them that they are not taken seriously in school and consequently they feel oppressed and detached from their schooling. This study has implications for strategies for developing school policies in Australia that are more responsive to children's needs for autonomy and justice.

CHAPTER FIFTEEN

Organizational Morality and Children's Engagement in Early Childhood Programmes

Donna Berthelsen

Introduction

This chapter reports three case studies of early-childhood teachers and their beliefs and practices in supporting young children's moral and social learning. Morality, in this chapter, is broadly defined as a social orientation: self-control, empathy, conscience, altruism, and moral reasoning (Berkowitz and Grych 1998).

Buzzelli (1992, 1995, and 1996) proposed that schooling in any form is a cultural process and, inherently, a moral activity, in that children are exposed to social values and are learning how they are expected to be, and act, as students and citizens. This applies to early childhood programmes as much as to school settings. In any classrooms, an organizational morality is promoted. Teachers' practices emphasize the importance of conformity and adherence to the rules and routines. By their choice of pedagogy, teachers communicate to children their personal and professional teaching values (Olson and Bruner 1996) and these values are conveyed to children implicitly as well as explicitly (Daniels, Kalkman, and McCombs 2001).

According to McCadden (1998), moral education is less likely to occur through the specific content of the curriculum and is more likely to be evident in the everyday interactions between teachers and children. McCadden developed an ethnography of an early-childhood classroom (a kindergarten programme) in the public-education system in the United States. He raised a raft of issues about the moral dynamics in the teaching–learning process. He posits that children are moral beings from a young age:

> ...who develop over time to a more and more nuanced ability to understand and navigate the codes and 'recipe knowledge' of moral interaction. They develop only in so much as they learn through experience and observation what it means in their social group to 'be a good girl' or 'be a good boy and learn how to utilize this meaning for various (some good, some not so good) purposes. (1998, pp.10–11)

McCadden notes that it is ironic that in developing the ability to navigate moral rules in the institution of school young children are led to a less moral stance. They move away from simple precepts of accepting themselves and others, to conform to the institutional morality. Children enter school with a *relational morality* with desires to be loved and accepted and to find ways to connect to other people. At the same time, teachers are focused on an agenda based on *organizational morality* in which they sincerely work 'to do the right thing' by the children, as they endeavour to instil a sense of self-discipline, attentiveness to tasks, independent work, and attendance to the rules (p.15).

Early-childhood programmes currently espouse the value of a constructivist model for practice. According to Palincsar (1998, p.355), the challenge of social constructivist practice is about achieving an intersubjective attitude. This is about the joint construction of meaning through dialogue, by which participants in the learning process achieve a shared understanding. However, in most classrooms dialogues between teachers and children are primarily based on a static IRE pattern (Initiation–Response–Evaluation). Teachers pose questions, children respond and teachers provide evaluative statements (Buzzelli 1996). While the value of this approach may be appropriate for many learning situations, it is not one in which children's voices are heard.

A greater acknowledgement of children's perspectives would be apparent if the frequency of children's contributions increased, so that there were more conversational turns. The 'initiations' would be in the service of requesting explanations (that is, 'responses'), and these would be followed by 'reconceptualizations' that included restatements, rephrasing, expansion and evaluations (Palincsar 1998, p.362). The crucial role of the teacher would be in discussion orchestration. Instead of evaluating children's responses, teachers would elicit children's opinions, ask clarifying questions and reflect children's statements in order to support children's sense of mastery and to legitimize children's contributions. These ideas provide a means for understanding classroom discourses.

Buzzelli (1996, p.527), developing the ideas of Maher and Tetreault (1994), proposed that the dialogue between teachers and children reveals how power is shared (or *not* shared) in the classroom. He introduced concepts of:

- 'mastery' (What knowledge and mediational means are given to children to master tasks as a result of their participation in classroom activities?)

- 'voice' (How are children's interests, questions, and concerns and issues incorporated in teacher–child interactions?)

- 'authority' (How is authority on knowledge and ways of learning in the classroom communicated?); and

- 'positionality' (What is the teacher's position relative to children as learners and what is to be learned?).

This perspective provides a means for examining just how teacher power is shared with children in early childhood classrooms.

Within this study, the beliefs and practices of early-childhood teachers are explored with a focus on how teachers instil an understanding of the organizational morality inherent in the culture of schooling. It is focused on teachers' understanding and their values about their role in the development of children's moral behaviour.

Research approach

The research process comprised three case studies. Data were collected through observations in three early-childhood programmes, serving four- to five-year-old children, and through interviews with the teachers in those programmes. The research involved video-taping the teacher reading a story centred on a moral principle to the class and the subsequent teacher–group discussion. This context was selected because it was assumed that storytime is a primary situation in which moral messages are explicitly conveyed and discussed. This session was for a period of 15 to 20 minutes. The purpose of the video observation was partly for analyses of what occurred during the group session but also as a stimulus for the teacher interview focused on beliefs and practices that support social and moral responsibility. The interview was conducted about one week after the observation session and lasted for approximately 40 minutes. The interview involved structured questions and the viewing of the video as a stimulus for reflection by the teacher.

The teachers came from three different educational systems – from a state public-education preschool, from a Catholic Education preschool, and from an early-childhood classroom in an Anglican College. This diversity was explicitly sought. The teachers approached were not known to the researchers, nor was there any prior knowledge about their practices or background. Members of the research team knew the principals of the schools in which the subsequent participating preschool classes were located and their permissions were obtained to contact the preschool teachers to invite participation in the research. After agreement was obtained from the teachers, an initial familiarization visit was made to the preschool classroom by a member of the research team to provide information about the research project. The teacher was asked to select one storybook to read in the video session from a number of books supplied by the researchers.

In the interview, teachers were asked to reflect on the video story session. The video was used as a stimulus for reflection that would help make explicit the values and beliefs which the teachers held. There were five initial questions in the interview presented to each teacher:

1. What are the most important things that you think that children should learn during the time they are in your class?

2. What do you think are the best ways to guide and manage children's behaviour?

3. What are important rules in your classroom for children's behaviour?

4. What situations commonly lead to conflict between children in the classroom and how do you prefer to handle such conflicts?

5. What are the strategies you use to support social and moral responsibility?

A research assistant spent two one-hour sessions in each classroom and after completing the videotaping of the story session, made anecdotal records about the physical and interpersonal environment of the classrooms. The research assistant was an experienced early-childhood teacher. Observations of the classroom were focused on the nature of teachers' directions; choices available to children; the general quality of teacher–child interactions; nature of child–child interactions; and the nature of teacher feedback to children.

The interview and observational data are descriptively analysed to develop representations of the teachers' beliefs and practices. In developing a profile of each teacher, reference is also made to the content and processes in the video session, as well as the observations made by the research assistant in the classrooms. The names of the participating teachers have been altered. Here, the teachers are called Ruth, Louise and Ann.

Findings

Ruth's classroom

Ruth has been teaching for eighteen years. She has a Diploma of Teaching and has completed her Bachelor of Education degree. She is currently working towards her Master's degree. She has taught in public and private school systems, in primary and preschool classrooms. This was her first year at this school, an Anglican private school. Ruth was teaching a 'prep' class of four- and five-year-olds. The 'prep' programme incorporated an early-childhood play-based approach but children were also introduced to formal literacy and numeracy activities.

OBSERVATIONS OF THE CLASSROOM

The classroom was spacious. There was a large carpeted area on the floor where group times were held. Children's artwork was displayed throughout the room. Nativity scenes were evident as it was Christmas time. Directions by the teacher to the children were verbalized in a positive manner: 'Michael, can you find a spot to sit where you can see'; 'We're ready to start now, David'; 'Would you like to join us now, Rebecca?' The children appeared to have a warm and friendly rapport with the teacher. On one occasion, a child was removed from the group for what the teacher considered to be inappropriate behaviour. She told the child several times to sit up properly, but the child continued to wriggle and lay down. She told the child he needed to sit on the thinking chair (only a small distance away), and why she had chosen this for him. After approximately ten minutes the child was asked if he'd thought about his behaviour and how to improve it, and was invited to rejoin the group.

RUTH'S INTERVIEW

Ruth described the most important things that children should learn during the year:

> As far as their work skills within the classroom, they need to be reflective thinkers, and not to rely totally on the teacher's directions; …to think for themselves; …I encourage them to cooperate with each other so that they don't have to feel like, 'I'm stuck and don't know what to do.' They can negotiate and discuss it with their friends.

An important rule in Ruth's classroom was 'respect for each other'. For example,

> We need to speak one at a time and listen to everybody, because everybody wants to hear what you have to say, but they can't hear if other people are talking. If you want other people to listen to you, then you need to listen to them.

On moral situations, Ruth identifies the following issues as important: sharing, kindness, being respectful. She described a specific situation and her approach for dealing with it:

> We've had one we had to deal with today, actually. There's a child that has come into the class late in the year. There was a group of three, who were friends, and then this child came in and became friendly with one of those children, and one of the other little girls felt that her friend was being taken. Well, she just started behaving like, 'I want to be top dog.' And set up a pecking order, ostracizing the new girl, and done in such a way that another of the little girls starting behaving in the same way, and the third little girl was just uncertain. She wasn't sure what to do. 'How should I behave?' So I got the four of them in and we talked about it, and we talked about sharing our friends, 'Is there really anything to be afraid of, when we share friends?' And when we share, we end up with more friends than when we started. We'll see how it goes tomorrow.

What was evident to the observer in Ruth's classroom was the explicit religious philosophy:

> First of all, I see my responsibility as a teacher but my teaching is not just a career, it's a ministry. I see my responsibility in the classroom is not just to educate children in academic stuff, but to lead the children into a relationship, into exploring a relationship with God. It's up to them. It's their decision what they do with that, but to give them the opportunity to explore and develop from a Christian perspective. Moral issues obviously are very high on the agenda. I start every morning with a devotional time with the children. We discuss a lot of moral issues that come up within that time.

VIDEO SESSION

The book that Ruth read for the video story session was *John Brown, Rose, and the Midnight Cat*, and in her approach to the story and in her questioning and discussion with the children the focus was very much on feelings:

> They are responsive at this age to get in touch with themselves; they have to start thinking about feelings. To start to control their behaviour they have to think about what they feel, and why they do what they do, which at this age, isn't based so much on a reasoning level. So it's more, 'How do I feel about it?' And sometimes it can be difficult for them. They know they're feeling something but they're not sure how to express it. Sometimes when we're talking about feelings, because this comes up quite frequently, and if they can't articulate it then I say, 'Well, what do you feel like doing?'; 'What do you want to do?'. And they might demonstrate to me or tell me what they want to do, and then we get around it that way. I'd probably try and express the word at their

level of understanding, to try and explain so that they can connect with the feeling.

The dialogue in which Ruth engaged the children before, during and at the end of the story was primarily characterized by the Initiation–Response–Evaluation (IRE) pattern, common to early-childhood classrooms (Buzzelli 1996). Ruth (T) confined the children (C) to short responses that did not allow them to expand and co-construct meaning with her but limited them to the 'known answer' (p.519). While this is appropriate in a range of learning situations, Buzzelli noted that children will take on more understanding if the E turn in the IRE is used to expand children's responses, so encouraging their ideas and enhancing learning. Ruth did not expand on the children's responses nor allow them to offer ideas into the dialogue.

T: I wonder what she was sick from?

C: The Midnight Cat.

T: Why would that make her feel sick?

C: It might have scratched her or something like, or bit her or something. (inaudible)

T: Perhaps… What do you think Nicholas?

C: (laughing) I dunno.

C: (another child) Sometimes you can get sick when you get bitten.

T: You can, but we know that John Brown would never go near the cat, would he? I wonder why she's feeling sick like that.

Louise's classroom

Louise teaches a preschool class in the Catholic Education system. She has been at the school for one year. She has a Diploma of Teaching in Early Childhood and is presently studying for her Bachelor of Education. She qualified twenty-two years ago and has spent sixteen years teaching in community kindergartens with three- to five-year-old children.

Observations of the classroom

The classroom was open-planned and there was a large carpeted area on the floor where group times were held. A Nativity scene was set up, as it was Christmas time, and there were other religious artworks. The teacher gave children notice about transitions, and encouraged them to finish what they were doing and join her on the carpet. The teacher involved the children in decision-making about activities in which they wished to engage. All requests to children were verbalized in a positive manner: 'Do you think we should read our story now?' There was a lot of physical affection between the teacher and children, expressed through gestures, smiles, and hugs. The children were encouraged, but not necessarily 'expected' to listen at group times, but generally they sat still, with their hands in their laps. One child during the video session appeared to become restless, and she wriggled away and lay down. Louise asked her to move closer to the group and she did.

Louise's interview

The most important things that Louise believes that children should learn during their preschool year are:

> To develop self-confidence; a belief that, 'Yes, I can do, within my limits, anything I want to do.' Then, of course, we have to develop all the skills that would go with that. If they have a belief in themselves and self-confidence, they can tackle the other hurdles that they will need to cross.

Important rules of Louise's classroom:

> We practise listening. We practise being quiet. You can't just say to kids, 'Be quiet'. There's a lot of role play on that at the beginning of the year. We role-play good listening skills, 'How do I know that you're listening?' If I sit down in front of a group, I want to make sure they're all listening. I use a key like, 'How will I know you're listening to me?' And that's the sign for them to turn and look, and we also expect them to do that with each other. If they're talking to each other, then they're expected to look at each other.

Louise is a practising Catholic:

> This is my first year as a preschool teacher in a Catholic school. Things that I tried to promote in a secular centre, I now have the freedom to relate to our faith. So now I can relate the reasons to the children; 'Why do I want us all to be caring and sharing people? Because you want to be like God, and that's what God wants us to be.' In the preschool, I think it's more a personal thing. It's lived by the whole school but I think with children of this age, it has to come from the way you live with them, rather than anything more general.

Video session

In the video session, Louise selected *John Brown, Rose and the Midnight Cat* to read to the children. The children were familiar with the story. Within the dialogue that she had with the children Louise particularly focused on the expression of emotions. Louise's comments on these issues:

I think that to be caring people, we have to be aware of other people's feelings, and that doesn't come naturally – that's something that you develop an awareness of, and that's something we try to do here, is to be aware of when we're happy, when we're sad…and I want them to feel that they can express their feelings too. Seeing it through books is an outlet. It's a safe way sometimes of showing your emotions without being overwhelmed. You can be sad about something that's happening to others and it also lets you know that you can be sad about things, too. We talk about that.

The dialogue in which Louise engaged the children before, during and at the end of the story was primarily characterized by the IRE pattern (Buzzelli 1996). Louise (T) confined the children (C) to short responses without expansions. Closed questions were asked and the children gave single-word response. Teacher control and direction was evident. Drawing on the ideas of Maher and Tetreault (1994) and Buzzelli (1996), it is clear that the dialogue between the teachers and children reflects the power held by the teacher. Children's voices (ideas and opinions) were not incorporated in interactions. The authority was that of the teacher.

T: How do you think she felt when her husband died?

C: Sad. (chorus)

T: How else would she feel?

C: Lonely.

T: You could feel lonely too. But do you think she still felt lonely and sad?

C: Yes. (chorus)

C: No, 'cause she had the dog. (chorus)

T: But would living with a dog be the same as living with your husband?

C: No. (chorus)

T: Not quite…she probably isn't as lonely; but I think sometimes she'd still get a bit lonely.

Ann's classroom

Ann has been teaching in a preschool setting in the public-education system for ten years. She graduated with a Diploma of Teaching in Early Childhood twenty years ago and has held various educational roles, including being an early-childhood advisory teacher. She also holds a Graduate Diploma in Multicultural Education.

Observation of the classroom

The classroom was spacious and there was a large carpeted area on the floor where group times were held. As it was Christmas time, most artwork reflected this theme but other examples of children's illustrated storywriting was evident. Children were expected to conform to directions given to them about moving between activities, particularly at transition times. At group times, the children generally gathered in a circle formation in front of the teacher, on the carpet. The teacher used a relatively quiet, but positive tone when speaking with children, and most of the children were compliant. When children who became restless, wriggled, or began to talk to peers, the teacher quickly spoke to them or reminded them of her expectations. There was a strong focus on appropriate behaviour. The teacher gave reasons to children if she commented on inappropriate behaviour.

Ann's interview

The most important things that Ann wants the children to learn in her classroom:

> I want them to have an inquiring mind about a whole host of things, and I want them to learn that what others do is valued. I think that is a difficult thing for some of the children in this area [an upper-middle class suburb]. Many of the children are very bright, have very inquiring minds, and are very motivated, but not all the children are like that and they also must be valued. It's a big thing that children should value each other, and value what others do.

Ann emphasizes that there are situations when follow-up and discussion are warranted in order to ensure children develop a clear understanding about appropriate actions:

> What's right and what's wrong; what's fair and what's not. I use discussion on many issues and if I have already tried a discussion strategy, then I go on to use a book or puppets, and create the theme again. Recreate the issue and work through it, 'What do you think we could have done?' Very often, I would use a book but for some children the book isn't stimulating enough, which is why I'd move to props. I also use drama. There are many very complex issues in our society. There are bigger gaps between those who have and those who have not, and that concerns me. It concerns me that sometimes the children don't think enough about the needs of others in a significant way. It's difficult for

some of the children to think outside their experiences and this is a tricky issue to deal with.

On her personal values and beliefs, Ann says:

> I'm careful about how I approach certain things. I wouldn't approach something with a religious attitude. I think there are lots of things, as a Christian, that morally and socially are very important but I don't think you necessarily need a specific Christian base for that. I don't know the impact of my own spirituality on my teaching but I am aware of it. I was aware of it recently when we had our end-of-year party lunch. We wouldn't usually say a prayer before we have our lunch, but I did have the children stop and think about all the other children in the world. Those who aren't as fortunate as they are. I didn't take a religious perspective, but I did give consideration to it. I don't think you need a specific religion view to do that.

Video session

For the video-story session, Ann read *The Little Red Hen*. In the session, she drew out real-life issues from the children on the moral principles in the story of cooperation and helping. The children talked about feelings, such as being angry, happy and sad, helping and sharing but the interaction was primarily shaped by the IRE pattern – as was evident in the story sessions of Ruth and Louise, which did not expand on children's ideas. The following excerpt is framed around the IRE pattern.

T:	Do you think she should have explained to them that if they wanted to eat it, then they had to help? Is that what you do when you're playing?
C:	Yes.
T:	What sort of things do you say, Madeleine?
C:	I say stop that I don't like it.
T:	But if you're trying to get somebody to cooperate with you?
C:	Could you please help me?
T:	And do you give them a reason? Do you always need a reason to cooperate with each other?
C:	Yes. (chorus)

Discussion

This research involved three experienced early-childhood teachers. The teachers espoused a strong moral agenda for the children in their classrooms focused on personal responsibility and independence. The teachers indicated that a major focus in their actions was to ensure that children had respect for others. This research provided a number of insights. While a constructivist and child-centred perspective may be advocated, it was apparent that the teacher remains at the centre, the single individual in every classroom whose beliefs, decisions and outlook count most in giving shape to what happens in that environment.

Children's participation in early childhood programmes is a preparation for formal schooling. Their attendance marks a significant transition in their lives. Any group programme has high expectations of responsibility and independence. New and high demands are placed on children's social and emotional competence. As young children make the transitions between home and educational settings, they learn to understand the organizational morality underpinning the manner in which education operates. McCadden (1998) proposed that there are different moral domains for teachers (organizational) (p.35) and children (relational) (p.81). As children make this transition it is important that the relational morality of children is acknowledged. While the organizational morality may be emblematic of the role of the teacher there must also be room to take account of young children's relational morality. If teachers' organizational and children's relational morality are legitimate positions, then greater understanding of their distinctive domains may locate areas of conflict that can be addressed. McCadden (1998) admits that there is a tendency to assume that the relational domain, focused on connections between individuals, is a more desirable outcome but this is a biased representation that does not account for societal and community expectations about schools and education. This begs the question as to how schools also can change and be more democratic in their organization. Educational institutions also need to foster moral values that enable active civic engagement, characterized by fairness, reasonableness, tolerance and mutual respect (Okin and Reich 1999).

Teachers need to reconsider their own agendas with respect to the values that young children are likely to hold, especially those children who have a different cultural and social background. The issue is one of finding the connections between the organization and relational domains. Children's perspectives of the world are different from, and more complex, than it is likely that adults give them credit for. Children from different social backgrounds to those of the teacher are less likely to hold the organizational values that the teacher holds and, as a result, receive less acceptance.

In considering the similarities and differences in the teachers' approaches in this study, it is important not to generalize too broadly and to see differences as systemic. However, two of the teaching contexts allowed the expression of religiosity. The teachers' religious beliefs arose naturally in their interviews as an influence on how these teachers considered their role in the relation to children's development of moral and social behaviours. The contexts in which Ruth and Louise taught supported the expression of personal religious values. Ann, while describing herself as a Christian and a religious person, practised in a secular context that would not be likely to accept explicit articulation of teachers' personal beliefs about religion. Clearly, the expression of explicit religious beliefs is not essential to how children learn to be socially and morally responsible. Australia is a multicultural society and, therefore, there is multiplicity of religious beliefs. It is also a strongly secular society. How teachers account for the values of children with different social, cultural and religious background in their practices is not well understood. Jackson, Boostrom and Hansen (1993) noted that the nature of teachers' responsibilities make it appropriate to speak of teaching as a moral enterprise, and Sockett and LePage (2002) also called for teachers to understand that their classrooms are moral spaces rather than technical areas.

There is a need for more attention to the nature of teacher authority and how it is used in classrooms. Buzzelli's (1996) concepts of mastery, voice, authority, and positionality permit analysis of how children's voices are heard in early-childhood classrooms. It is a useful framework for studying the relative power exerted by teachers in all classrooms. With respect to classroom dialogue in the story sessions, these teachers primarily used the pattern of IRE. They clearly held a position of authority and positioned themselves as expert. Buzzelli's perspective is that greater acknowledgement of children's views is necessary and this is possible when teachers use an expanded form of the IRE pattern in interactions. Teachers need to reflect on how their espoused values of a child-centred or social constructivist approach may not be evident in their actual interactional behaviours with children.

Conclusion

A more explicit discussion about the various domains of moral understanding is necessary. This seems to be suppressed in current discussion about early-childhood teaching, and this non-attention begs questions concerning connections between teachers' values and how teachers connect with children's morality. The findings reported here indicate a need for greater attention to the specifics of children's relational morality and the connections it has with the organizational morality of schooling, especially in the early years of education.

This exploratory research has provided some interesting findings that lead to other research questions about the linkages between personal beliefs and teaching practices. While there is rhetoric about constructivist practices in the early-childhood education literature, respect and consideration of children's views may not necessarily be present. In order to truly engage children in education from the outset, there needs to be a community in the classrooms that values the qualities of the child as a collaborator and contributor. How can early-childhood teachers become more attuned to the 'moral' significance of their actions and the quality of the classroom environments that their interactions create?

CHAPTER SIXTEEN

Today I Discovered...

Helen Woodward

Introduction

'Today I discovered how to write poetry.' 'Today I discovered the pattern inside an apple.' How often do we listen to the children in our care? How often do we really give them the opportunity to tell us what they know, what they understand or what they have discovered? When we take children seriously and when we involve them in their own learning we not only have to listen to them but we must also ensure that the assessments we construct allow the children to be active partners in their learning. We have to create situations whereby they can say, 'Today I discovered...' knowing that it is important and that someone will be listening.

Assessment is one of the most controversial topics in any learning institution and the role of the relative players in assessment is challenging. This chapter presents three key strategies that recognize not only the value of involving children in their own assessment but the essentialness of this involvement if accurate, just and complete assessment of children's educational growth is going to be made and if children are going to be 'allowed' to discover pathways through the learning spectrum that best suits them. These strategies are based on research emanating from schools and prior to school settings and the resulting programmes designed to cater for the needs of the children, the teachers and the parents.

The three key strategies are; negotiated assessment, child self-assessment and child-led conferences. Negotiated assessment is an assessment programme that insists on an active partnership between the child, the teacher and the parent. Child self-assessment has evolved out of negotiated assessment and not only develops reflection strategies for the children but values the children's knowledge and understanding of themselves and their learning. Child-led conferences – again emanating from negotiated assessment – are a method of reporting to parents that puts the children in the 'driving seat'. In this process they are given opportunity to show their parents what they know, what they have discovered, what they can do and what they are like as learners. All three strategies demonstrate that unless we take children seriously by including them in the process when we are assessing them, and unless we allow them to make discoveries about their own learning, we are forfeiting their right to a just and equitable education.

Assessment has long been thought of as the domain of the teacher. With increased expectations of educators within schooling systems, reduced timeframes and the demands for greater accountability, schools and prior-to-school settings are beginning to realize that they have a ready source of expertise and information at their fingertips: the children they are assessing.

Children as active partners

The belief that children have the right and the ability to take an active part in both their learning and the assessment of that learning, although not new, is not necessarily taken seriously by those who influence the learning of these children. Downes (1998a) recognized that rarely, if at all, were children actually accorded the role and status of stakeholders, and therefore valuable participants, in their schooling. With specific reference to assessment, inclusion of children in the development of portfolio assessment was supported by many educationalists (Brady 2000; Danielson and Abrutyn 1997; McMackin *et al.* 1998; Skawinski and Thibodeau 2002; Woodward 1993). The reality, however, was that many children's portfolios were teacher's collections of children's work, with only nominal involvement of the children. They were, in fact, the teachers' portfolios about the children, not the child's portfolio that demonstrated what that child had discovered about his/her learning. The key issue here is that of acknowledging children as stakeholders in their own learning and taking seriously their right to secure a dynamic role in their own development.

To fully enable children to participate actively in their learning and the assessment of that learning, assessment must be negotiated with each of the stakeholders involved. Such negotiation means that children are given the opportunity not only to assist in the planning but also to share what they have discovered with the various stakeholders. These key factors are discussed under the following main headings: 'negotiated assessment', 'child self-assessment' and 'child-led conferences'.

Negotiated assessment

Negotiated Assessment[1] is a programme that insists on an active partnership between the child, the teacher and the parent (Woodward 1993). It is a programme characterized by continuing negotiation between all stakeholders in the assessment process, in order to determine the focus, the procedures, the inter pretations and the proposals for action that guide decisions and inform learning. In addition to the teacher, these stakeholders include the *children* and their *parents or caregivers.*

In a research project that investigated literacy assessment in primary schools (Woodward 1989) the teachers indicated that interaction between teachers and children was limited because the teachers were the main assessors and recorders of that assessment. It is my belief that we cannot hope accurately to assess the children in our care if we do not ask them what they are thinking, what they have discovered, what they understand and what they know. Similarly, what we find out about children and their learning, and the goals we have for them, should be shared with the children. There have been many secrets kept from children in the classroom (for example, the teacher's expectations, and the results of observations made of the child's developmental progress) with little or no credence being given to the child's ideas. Again, assessment and planning for learning had been decidedly one-sided. I also, at this time, gave some thought to the idea that the parents were another source of information, yet untapped, that could yield another perspective about the child's progress and development.

The idea of negotiated assessment began to evolve to overcome the problem of teachers as the only assessors. A model was formulated that included both parents and children in the assessment process, and that was intended to make better use of both the time spent and the data collected.

The important issues that were essential to model were:

- the continual interaction between the primary stakeholders, which consisted of: focused observation by the teacher followed by discussions between the child and the teacher; input from the child through discussion and self-assessment; and interaction between the teacher and the parents by way of parent observation or profile sheets

- the collection of data from a variety of sources and perspectives, which consisted of data from parents, teacher and child observations over time and in a variety of situations and products of work selected by both the child and the teacher

- the analysis of data through the writing of reports that inform each of the stakeholders, which was achieved through making decisions about the merit and worth of both the processes and products observed and collating analysis into a descriptive report. (Woodward 1993, p.18)

Negotiated assessment, then, primarily involves the collection, interpretation and reporting of qualitative information about the child's learning. It focuses on the individual quality of each child's learning processes and products, so that all those involved in the child's progress understand the child better and are more able to assist him or her in the learning processes required for future development.

For negotiated assessment to take place, the role of the stakeholders needs to be explored. The stakeholders are those who share the load of assessment – in this case, the teacher, the parents and the children.

The teacher

The role of the teacher in negotiated assessment, though discussed first here, is not necessarily that of major stakeholder. The teacher is, however, pivotal to the process. By exploring the teacher's role in this programme first it is hoped that a better understanding of what negotiated assessment is will be developed. This role includes data collection and analysis, and initiating, encouraging and negotiating the involvement of the other stakeholders. The key procedures to be discussed here are: focused observation, product collection and analysis, and reporting progress.

FOCUSED OBSERVATION

One of the key procedures in any classroom assessment programme is observation (Woodward 1997). In negotiated assessment it is even more vital for all the stakeholders to be keen and perceptive observers. My initial research on the recording of observations in anecdotal records, however, made it clear that there had to be a more systematic way to organize the observation of the children in the classroom that would ensure that each child's behaviours were adequately and regularly recorded. Every child in the class must be observed, not just the attention-seekers or the children whose performance is in some way outstanding. Care must be taken to observe and record the *learning* that occurred, not the expected behaviour or compliance with roles and routines. After much deliberation and consultation with colleagues and teachers the notion of 'focused observation' was born.

Focused observation means that instead of trying to observe all the children in a class at one time, the teacher selects five or six children to be the focus of his or her observations for a particular period of time – say, over one or two weeks. This small group of children is observed closely and anecdotal records are written on the learning that is observed. After the designated period of time, the focus shifts to another group of five or six, and so on, until all the children have been systematically observed. In this way, every child is the focus of careful observation for four to six periods a year (in addition to the ongoing incidental observation that normally occurs within any classroom).

Most probably, the children will be randomly selected for observation so will range in ability and needs, but selection could be on the basis of a previously established class grouping. Observation in itself, however, is not sufficient. These observations must be accurately recorded. An important factor here is that the closer to the time of observation the recording is done, the more accurate the data will be.

PRODUCT COLLECTION AND ANALYSIS

In negotiated assessment, the teacher's role is to observe not only the learning processes and behaviours of the children being focused on, but also to look closely at the 'products' of their work. Collecting work samples from the group of children being focused on gives an extra dimension to both the data and its organization. Every sample that is collected must be dated, with comments written on it highlighting the progress that has been made and the outcomes demonstrated.

In addition to the process/product observations, observations should be made of the child's understandings and beliefs. These observations can only be substantiated through consultation with the child. The children should be asked how they feel about various areas of schooling, what they have discovered or what they would like to learn. Sometimes this interaction takes the form of a discussion, or the child may be asked to complete a self-assessment item. Wherever possible, the child should have knowledge of any observations made as a result of the consultation.

REPORTING PROGRESS

At the end of each data-collection period a descriptive summary is written on each focus child. The reason for this summary is two-fold: first, to draw together all the information accrued and, second, to report the child's progress to the other stakeholders. The reporting procedure is continuous, with parents receiving reports throughout the year. The distinctive features of these reports are that they have several parts to them. The first part highlights the child's achievements since the last report. The second part shows the child's needs, couched in positive and productive terms, and the third part indicates how the parents can help the child at home. The back of the report in divided into two sections: one each for the parents' and for the child's response. These reports are accumulated in a folder that travels back and forth from school to home as each report is added.

The parents

Traditionally, the important role that parents might play in the assessment of a child's progress has been ignored by the education system. In negotiated assessment the role of parents is not only recognized but also greatly valued and seen as vital to the success of the programme. To create the necessary connections between the parents and the teachers, and to strengthen the links between the parents and their children, a variety of procedures need to become part of the framework of the classroom-assessment programme. These procedures include descriptive reports to which both parent and child are asked to respond, parent-observation profiles, parent reports, assessment and communication books, portfolios and child-led conferences. Parent reports will be discussed next in this section and child-led conferences will be discussed in detail later in the chapter.

PARENT REPORTS

After several focused observation rotations, resulting in several reports, the parents are sent an open report sheet accompanied by their child's report folder. They are asked to read back through the reports, theirs and the child's comments, and write about the progress that they see their child has made. Emphasis is placed on the collaborative nature of the reporting with the child being part of this process.

The main issues when involving parents in their children's assessment is to assure them that what they know is valued and that they will be supported in the development and understanding of their child's learning processes. The response from the parents will serve the needs of both the teachers and the children. When parents have a better understanding of their children's learning, they are more able to help them. Stronger links between the parents and their children are forged as they collaborate about the child's learning. Surely education and society will only benefit from such a process.

The children

One of the most important features of negotiated assessment is the involvement of the children who are being assessed. It is brought about in several ways: the teachers continually interacting with each child during the focused observation periods and the children learning how to set goals, be reflective, and how to assess themselves. We look at goal-setting below and self-assessment and reflection will be discussed in detail later in the chapter.

GOAL-SETTING

Goal-setting is carried out in many ways and will develop over time. Children cannot be expected to become expert goal setters overnight. Demonstration of the process is essential and should begin with discussions about what the children want to learn as a class. Time needs to be set aside for these processes to be learned and practised (see Woodward 2001, p.12).

When working with children in goal-setting, initially set the goal (which can be refined if necessary), then look with the child at what they are going to have to do to achieve that goal. Discussion then needs to centre on the idea of 'How will I know when I have achieved the goal and an ongoing record of progress?'

As more of the work is carried out, children will become better at being more precise with their goals, which, in turn, will become more refined.

Child self-assessment

The idea of children as self-assessors is growing in popularity within education. It sometimes appears to be tokenistic by only being records of work done and not records of the learning achieved. Child self-assessment, as noted here, has evolved out of negotiated assessment. It not only develops sound reflective strategies for the children but also values the children's knowledge and understanding of themselves and their learning. Given time and support, children will develop the capacity to assess themselves as they know many things about themselves that will supplement the parents' and teachers' knowledge about the child. In fact, there are some things that *only* the children know about themselves. They know what they believe and what they feel. They know what they understand and what they want to learn.

There are four primary reasons why self-assessment is important. These are that:

- only the learner knows the full extent of the enjoyment, understanding and the interaction experienced during the activity
- children have the right to contribute to knowledge gathered about their progress and to have access to the expectations held by other interested parties
- giving children more control and responsibility for what they do through self-assessment fosters the development of the skills of independent life-long learning
- it also makes them aware of their own learning processes and progress.

Teachers are always conscious of the time constraints placed on them in the classroom and should therefore be prepared to transfer to the children as many assessment tasks as possible.

There also are four dimensions to self-assessment that need to be taken into consideration. These dimensions are: reflection, expectation, acceptance and valuing.

Reflection

Reflection enables the child to look back on their learning and to think about the next steps that they need to take. This process assists them in analysing and better understanding the processes and the practices that aid their learning, while encouraging them to deliberate on possible ways forward. Children cannot be *made* to be reflective but need to be given opportunity and time to learn the variety of skills needed.

Expectation

Children will 'deliver' to the level of diligence and expertise that is expected of them. If the expectations are low then their response will be low. Similarly, if the expectations are high the output will be high. If it is expected that they will self-assess their work, and if the necessary skills and time are made available to them, the process of self-assessment will improve. Time has to be allocated and the purpose made obvious before worthwhile self-assessment procedures are put in place. There is also an expectation on the part of the child. They should expect to be part of their own learning and assessment. To be able to take part in this process they need to know what the teacher expects of them in regard to learning experiences and outcomes. In consultation with others they should begin to understand and recognize what their learning will look like and how to improve their learning opportunities.

Acceptance

For children to be truly part of the learning and assessing cycle their input must be accepted as genuine. Their ideas and knowledge must be seen as worth while and included in the planning and reporting process. Children are very quick to pick up on surface acceptance and will withdraw their input on future occasions if this dimension is not genuinely attended to.

Valuing

It is commonly understood that self-assessment is a valuable tool, but it also must be valued for its worth and what it can tell us about children's learning. It is more than just accepting what they have to offer. Time, space and energy must be expended if true self-assessment is to occur and if the children are to become reflective, life-long learners.

Strategies for encouraging child self-assessment

There are a number of strategies that will encourage children to participate in their own assessment. These strategies include: logs, learning journals, portfolios, assessment books, self-assessment sheets and child-conferences. Logs, journals and portfolios are discussed below in this section and child-led conferences being discussed later.

RECORD-KEEPING LOGS

Journals or logs are where the children keep records of the work they have carried out. These records are characterized by reading logs, writing logs, and reading and writing summaries but also by records of, for example, science activities, groupwork completed or homework carried out. This form of recording is not new to the children when it comes to self-assessment (Woodward 1993) and is extremely valuable, particularly when charting progress and understanding what is important to them. These logs take a variety of forms but they are most commonly either printed formats (as used in reading logs) or diary entries. To make the best use of these records, summaries of the logs or diaries should be made as evidence of progress in learning. A simple summary format is used from time to time but in doing so there must be an assurance that the accumulated evidence will be valued and used. These summaries consist of questions that précis these records. Initial recording of, for example, how many and what type of books were read gives an overview of predominating genre, of uncompleted readings and the nature of the texts. Further reflections on these books would reveal specific interests, level of reading and the child's understanding of the reading process. The issue to remember here is to demonstrate how each procedure works and to then allocate time for the records to be attended to. This allowing of time establishes that the teacher values the process; without it some children will do the required recording, but most will not.

JOURNAL WRITING

There are several differing thoughts on journal writing. Some people confuse it with diary writing, while others use it to describe log records as explained above; here the focus is on reflective journal writing. Much has been written about the value of reflection and how it promotes learning by encouraging the children to think about their development, assisting them to become deeper learners and to learn about their own learning. The difficulty lies in just how to assist children to become reflective. Being reflective is not an innate ability. It must be taught and it must be valued. To teach reflection to young children means initial time must be given to the process so that worthwhile time is experienced later.

The process will need to be taken in slow steps and should not be ritualized to the point of being boring for the children. Once they understand what being reflective is then the process can be varied. Primarily, being reflective means thinking about learning and looking forward to new learning possibilities.

PORTFOLIOS

The idea of portfolios has been with us for some time and in many different guises. Before deciding how to use portfolios some decisions need to be made: who is the audience and what is the purpose of the portfolio as an assessment item?

I believe there is a dual audience for portfolios. Initially, a portfolio is for the owner/author (in this case the child) and then it is for the community that the owner/author selects. In the school setting the audiences are primarily the teacher, friends and the parents or caregivers. The purpose of portfolio assessment is to record and reflect on the owner's learning. These beliefs stem from the view that a portfolio is:

> a collection of work that best illustrates the achievements and learning of its owner as selected and reflected on by the owner. (Woodward 1993, p.34)

For many teachers, though, the collection of work is either the responsibility of the teacher themselves or a combination of teacher and child. As discussed earlier, however, it is the teacher who selects the majority of data for school portfolios. The purpose of these portfolios is usually to inform the teacher of the child's learning, with little thought being given to the child's role in the process. However, for every item included in the portfolio a short reflection by the child (oral or written) should accompany the item. These reflections must show the importance of the item or what has been learnt from the activity resulting in the item. Reflection helps the child to focus on a deeper level of thinking and encourages them to reason and analyse their work.

From time to time, each child will need to sit with a friend, mentor or teacher to talk about the items in their portfolio and reflect on why they are there. After this interaction the portfolios are taken home and discussed with the parent or caregiver, or become part of a child-led conference. Portfolios give a view of the child's learning that is unobtainable through the average classroom activities.

There are many other self-assessment processes but the main issue to remember with them all is the need to value these processes by not only developing the necessary skills with the children but also by valuing the children's voices as they tell us about their learning.

Child-led conferences

Child-led conferences – again, emanating from negotiated assessment – are a method of reporting to parents that puts the children in the 'driving seat'. In this process the children are given opportunities to show their parents, through their portfolios, what they know, what they have discovered, what they can do and what they are like as learners – with the purpose of celebrating the children's learning and give direction for improvement.

There are several goals for child-led conferences. The most important of these are:

- to provide children with an authentic context for self-assessment, with an opportunity to assume some responsibility for informing their parents about their learning

- to increase the children's involvement, ownership and control of their learning, and

- for the children to be accountable for their own learning.

Child-led conferences are growing in popularity in the education forum and as a result many formats have emerged. Whichever format is used, however, there are several prerequisites to be considered when designing these conferences. These prerequisites ensure children, parents and teacher are informed and involved. It is important to be aware of the rationale for handing the leadership role to children and to recognize opportunities for children's reflection, judgements, decision-making, organization and genuine communication.

Once the decision has been made to use child-led conferences, preparation for the conference, the actual conducting of the conference and the post-conference procedures need to be considered. In this particular process, four or five conferences between parents and children run simultaneously at stations around the room. Each conference should take about 30 minutes, with the child being the instigator and the teacher moving quickly from station to station to ensure everything is as it should be.

Preparation for child-led conferences

Initially, contact has to be made with the parents to inform them of the process and the expectations of the conference and to set a schedule. Where possible, allow the children to do the letters and proformas required. Meanwhile, the children's portfolios need to be refined and presented to a 'friend' (peers and/or other children) as a rehearsal for their parents' visit.

Conducting child-led conferences

As each parent comes into the room the child introduces him or her to the teacher (it is better if the conference start times are staggered in order to allow these introduction to be done). The child then takes their parents to their station to talk them through their portfolio. Parents are asked to respond to their child's learning and to sign and comment in the 'guest book'.

Post the child-led conference

Ensuring that the children debrief after this event is very important. They can debrief by talking to each other and the teacher about their experience during the child-led conference. They should also write or draw a thank you letter to their parents.

Many schools and settings use this form of reporting as their sole reporting system while others use it in conjunction with the more formal report cards. Whichever way it is used, the child-led conference gives the children the opportunity to further understand and demonstrate their learning.

Conclusion

The forms of assessment discussed here have been trialled in many educational settings. Their key strengths are that by involving the stakeholders, particularly the children, in assessment, the children become more involved in their own learning and motivated in their learning processes. Difficulties do occur in multi-language situations and in early years of schooling as it is often seen that children within these areas are not capable of carrying out these processes. Creative teachers, however, have worked around some of these barriers and have proven that expectation and motivation serve as cornerstones to the children learning about their own learning.

Involving all those with a specific and vested interest in each child's progress in the learning and assessment cycle shows we are beginning to share the load of assessment and to recognize the children's rights as stakeholders. By discussing progress, making explicit our expectations and by tapping into the child's personal learning framework we are beginning to negotiate better assessment procedures. It is imperative, if assessment is to become useful, manageable and valid – and if we are to become responsible educators – that we learn to share the load by negotiating assessment and valuing the role the children have in the process. All three strategies discussed above demonstrate that unless we take children seriously when we are assessing them, by including them in the process, we are forfeiting their right to a just and equitable education. We need to give them opportunity to celebrate their learning and discoveries with those close to them, giving them voice and ownership in their quest for knowledge and enabling them to take their place in the learning continuum.

Current research (Woodward and Munns 2004; forthcoming) is investigating the connection between children's engagement in their own learning and self-assessment. A framework that enables explorations of this connection at different levels is being developed, so that the children's discoveries about their learning can be more adequately demonstrated and higher intellectual quality can be achieved.

Note

1   In the Woodward 1993 publication the term 'evaluation' was used. In light of the changing understandings about this terminology, the term 'assessment' is currently replacing the previous concept of evaluation.

CHAPTER SEVENTEEN

The Voice of the Child in the Family Group Conferencing Model

Patricia Kiely

Introduction

Child-inclusive practice is relatively new to the welfare sector. It provides an opportunity for improved decision-making and safer and more responsive services for children and their families. It is unsafe to assume that adults will 'do the right thing' for children. We cannot allow ourselves to turn back the pages of history in search of a past where adults made all the decisions, based on the belief that children's feelings and knowledge were seen as somehow inferior. This would ignore the experience of systems abuse and broken promises to children when they are at their most vulnerable after suffering abuse, neglect or major life-changing events.

Since 1989 the right of the child to participate in decisions about their life has been enshrined in Article 12 of the UN Convention on the Rights of the Child (UN 1990). It suggests that 'children's own views and voices have to be heard and taken into account' (John 1996, p.4). Children should be treated as consumers and therefore have certain basic civil rights in their dealings with statutory services, community agencies and treatment centres (Cloke and Davies 1997). There is considerable debate, however, about how to hear the voices of children, whether children should be invited to case-planning conferences and whether they should be asked to participate in decision-making.

Children have been generally kept out of case-planning meetings, on the assumption that they are incapable of participating in the process and of making viable decisions due to their lack of experience and their developmental stage. This belief focuses on some limitations of the current ways of operating and ignores the child's competence to express their concerns and opinions under advantageous and fair conditions. Expecting children to perform like adults in adult processes will only emphasize the differences between adults and children and not address the needs of the child or create the best and most appropriate conditions for the child's full participation. Just attending a meeting does not ensure participation (Farnfield 1997; Shemmings 1996). The process must be accessible and comprehensible. This obliges adults to design methods with which children feel comfortable in order to truly include the voice of the child.

The fear that conferences could be abusive for some children, especially if they attend when not equal in the process, has resulted in exclusion of children or an extremely cautious and limited involvement. However, when children's views were canvassed Farnfield (1997) found that 'they believed they had the right to hear what people were saying about them regardless of whether they found the conference distressing' (p.11). Children want their needs and wishes taken into consideration when plans are being made about them (Hart, Zeidner and Pavlovic 1996). Their ideas should be given equal weight in any process that claims to take children seriously. Farnfield (1997) found that 'children not only want adults to listen to them, and try and understand their problems, they also want them to make something happen' (p.9).

Lansdown (1997, pp.19–20) notes three critical factors that influence the current thinking about children. These are the facts that:

- children are not always protected by their families

- families need support to care for their children, and

- the nature of families has changed because of the high rate of single parenthood and divorce.

These factors have increased the number of plans required about the support needs of children and their families.

Rationale for including children's voices

In line with growing public demand for openness and accountability in their dealings with professionals, it is our belief that children should be included in decision-making about their care plans because of a number of important reasons.

Children have basic civil and natural-justice rights, which dictate that they should hear what professionals have to say about them and that they should be able to have their opinions and needs heard and taken seriously. They need to be aware of their rights in order to have a say. Children may require assistance to understand the process and their options and freely to make informed choices (Schofield and Thorburn 1996). This view follows a particular construction of childhood that does not accept the idea that children are somehow 'lesser beings'.

Most children who have experienced neglect or abuse will remain living with, or want contact with, their family (Cashmore and Paxman 1996). How this should happen safely needs to include the child's point of view, otherwise the abuse, which already has happened, may continue in another form by the system. Decisions about the care of children will affect them profoundly.

Children have valuable knowledge and insight, which can assist in ensuring that there is complete and accurate information available upon which to base plans. This is one way to guarantee that care plans meet their needs. Children are often confronting in their honesty with the adults around them. On the other hand, some children are reluctant to have their say if it is likely to hurt or upset someone else. They may require assistance to negotiate these conflicting needs. For children and young people to cooperate with an action plan, they need to agree that it addresses their requirements and is viable.

By involving children in decision-making, a sense of trust between the children, authorities and other agencies can be developed, so that in the future a more supportive and positive relationship may be generated to keep the children safe.

One model of case-planning meetings that attempts to address some of the barriers to children having a voice and a part in decision-making about their future care plans is family group conferencing. The Family Group Conference model changes the role of professionals from decision-makers to supporters, in-formation-givers, and conference facilitators. It is the family and children who are central to the proceedings and make the decisions:

> It encourages a shift of power in family decision making and can allow chil-dren's voices to be heard within a family situation, even in families where children are not routinely listened to. (Holland *et al.* 2003, p.12)

It can give children a sense of powerfulness when they are at their most vulnerable (Holland *et al.* 2003).

Since 1995, UnitingCare Burnside, a non-government organization, in part-nership with the Australian New South Wales Department of Community Services (Cumberland/Prospect Area), has been offering Family Group Confer-ences to families where plans are needed for the future care and protection of their children. This model of working with families has, as its core, the participation of as many family members as possible who are willing and able to support the child/young person. The process is crafted in such a way that family members are provided with supports to assist them to have their say at the planning meetings. It is the family who creates the case plan ('action plan').

Children/young people are part of this process. A great deal of work goes into the preparation of children/young people and their families for each of these Family Group Conferences. This chapter is an attempt to distil Burnside's experience with Family Group Conferences and the difficulties we have encountered while attempting to provide a better way for children/young people to have their say about their future.

The Family Group Conferencing model

Family Group Conferencing is a way of working with families that began in New Zealand and is based on the Maori inclusion of the extended family networks for the care of their children. It was found to be equally effective with non-Maori families in assisting them to make safe plans for the care and protection of their children.

In New Zealand, Family Group Conferences are mandated by the New Zealand Children and Young Persons and Their Families Act 1989, when there are serious concerns for the child's welfare resulting in state intervention in the child's life. The plans from these conferences go to Court and become the basis of undertakings that the families make for the care and protection of their children.

This is not the case in New South Wales, Australia. Here, the new Children and Young Person's (Care and Protection) Act 1998 allows for a range of alternative dispute-resolution processes but does not specifically mandate any one model. Family Group Conferencing – which allows for greater accountability from professionals than previous case-planning models, transparency in procedures and consumer participation in collaborative decision-making – is consistent with international trends in child-welfare legislation and practice.

Family group conferences comprise the following four processes.

- Pre-conference preparation: this may involve the facilitator spending up to 20 hours working with the family and professional services to prepare for the Family Group Conference. This work is key for the success of the Family Group Conference.

- The conference itself is made up of three stages: Stage One (information-sharing) – information is shared by the statutory officers and other professionals about the care and protection concerns, assessments, the family strengths and supports available, and any questions asked by the family are answered; Stage Two (private family time) – private time for the family alone to work on an 'action plan' that will keep the child safe; Stage Three (discussion and ratification of the action plan) – the statutory officers and conference facilitator return to discuss the family's plan and to ensure all the care and protection issues have been covered.

- After the conference the facilitator meets with key family members with their action plan to ensure the typed plan is an accurate representation of the plans made on the day of the conference, and to make sure that everyone understands what has been agreed.

- Review meetings are arranged at times that the family request and are organized by the facilitator. These meetings, which frequently occur three months post-conference and at similar intervals as required, allow an assessment of the action plan and any changes needed.

The success of Family Group Conferencing depends on the extent to which family members are involved in the process of decision-making and come up with a workable plan that is accepted by the statutory authority and that will keep the child adequately safe and cared for.

The question arises as to how the child/young person can have a real say in this process. As we have worked with this model, we have been challenged by the need to find ways that the voice of the child is heard, respected and included.

How are children's voices currently being heard in Family Group Conferencing?

Prior to the Family Group Conference

In New South Wales the statutory officers work as advocates for the child in their investigation of notifications and in their contact with the child. There are some limitations to this dual role of investigation and support, as bias and neutrality could become an issue. There may also be some difficulties in working with the family or the child in the future, if either party believes that the statutory officer has not been supportive of them.

Assessments are carried out by various professionals in order to record the child's needs and to evaluate the functioning of the family. It is believed that further work is required to develop a framework that more adequately enables the child's voice and ideas to be heard in the preparation of these reports. Methods that allow adequate time and strategies that are sensitive to children's developmental stages are more likely to provide the best opportunity for children to feel safe in having a say about their concerns and needs. Professionals working with children should have an extensive understanding of the effects of abuse and neglect and the impact of family relationships.

In the preparation stage of the family group conference process, the facilitator visits all key members of the family including the children, making clear the purpose of the Family Group Conference and the statutory authority's bottom line. The bottom line is the point where some decisions, that are not available for the family to make and are not negotiable, have been made by the Courts or Statutory Authority. An example is that the children cannot live with their parents at this time because of the risk of continuing abuse. Other issues above the bottom line can be decided by the family such as: where the child will live while they are unable to live with their parents; who in the family will have contact with the child while they are not permitted to live with their parents, etc. In some cases there is no bottom line as the authorities have no restrictions on the matters to be decided by the family as long as they address the community concerns about the care and welfare of the children. It is an opportunity to discuss the issues and questions that need to be answered in order to create the action plan. It is at this time that the vulnerabilities of the child in relation to having a say at the Family Group Conference or in any other forum are assessed, and strategies to accommodate them are put into place. At this time it is helpful for the child to get to know the facilitator (Farnfield 1997), who develops the supports that the child requires to participate in the Family Group Conference. This may take the form of an advocate who can help children cope with their sense of isolation and powerlessness within the family and anxieties about the conference. It is felt that the child should be included from the beginning of the process and informed about what is going to happen and how they can be involved. They need to be prepared for this involvement, encouraged to explore their anxieties about the process and helped to understand how the supports available to them can be used. They should also be prepared for what information they are likely to hear at the Family Group Conference and what this might mean for future plans. Adequate time is necessary to do this well. It could also be useful to develop illustrated written material that is attractive to children, age-appropriate and that complements the discussions that the facilitator has with the child.

Understanding the family system is of vital importance. This can inform the facilitator about possible blocks in the way of the child's participation. It is also the responsibility of the facilitator to manage any structural constraints, for example, arranging a suitable venue for the conference where the family feels comfortable (Houston 2003). This may be in the family home. Food is arranged to suit the culture and ages of the participants. For children, videos or toys might also be supplied in a separate room to give them a break in the proceedings. Farnfield (1997) and Wilson and Bell (2003) found that children appreciated this flexibility.

A barrier to attendance may be the time at which the family meeting is held (Treseder 1997). After school might be more acceptable to some children. This requires flexibility on the part of the professionals to work outside their normal hours.

To ensure it is clear that the focus of the conference is the child, one idea would be for invitations to the conference to be designed and sent out, with the involvement of the child. This could give a sense of ownership of the conference to the child.

During the Family Group Conference

The child, from the age of ten, is usually invited and offered support to be present for the whole or part of the Family Group Conference. By having the child present it is more likely that the focus of the conference will be about the child's needs.

After being informed about what supports are available, the child may request an advocate who can accompany them to the Family Group Conference to help them understand what is happening and assist them in having a say. Farnfield (1997, pp.17, 20) and Scutt (1995, pp.239–240) found that children do not want to feel 'invisible' and do not want their experience or interests interpreted by professionals. An extra Burnside staff member who attends the Family Group Conference and can assist on the day has sometimes taken on this role in the Burnside project. At other times the child may prefer a counsellor or friend to be their advocate.

In the Family Group Conference model the conference facilitator is independent of the presenting case. This allows for a clear delineation of roles and responsibilities, thereby avoiding confusion between the traditional mix of risk assessment, information provision, statutory duties, acting as support or advocate for the child and responsibility for the implementation of the care plan.

The Family Group Conference facilitator also has the responsibility to ensure that everyone is heard and protected at the Family Group Conference. Managing the emotional context, encouraging questions and comments, pacing the discussion, insisting on plain, jargon-free language and checking that both the family and child understand what is being said, are essential components of an inclusive meeting. This emphasizes the obligation for those named in the plan to follow through on their promises. It is important to ensure that the professionals do not 'hijack' the meeting and turn it into a workers' forum. A checklist of ideas given to workers during the preparation stage of the conference outlines how they can best participate in the conference and support the family.

Children do not enjoy meetings that are too inflexible and formal. They want 'to concentrate on the issues rather than worry about procedural rules' (NSW

Commission for Children and Young People 2001, p.21). Farnfield (1997) found that some children want a specific time set aside for them to speak in meetings. Family Group Conferences can provide for these needs.

The statutory officers are expected to work as advocates for the child by sharing information about the child's needs for care and protection in Stage One of the Family Group Conferences. Professionals who have made assessments, or who have been offering services to the family or child, will share what they know about the child's requirements and are able to be advocates for the child at this point.

Post the Family Group Conference

Soon after the Family Group Conference has been completed the facilitator meets with the family and the child to discuss the action plan to ensure its accuracy. Where possible, the child is seen by themselves. This debriefing is important to assist children make sense of the meeting and to understand implications of the plan.

All participants receive a copy of the action plan. It is important that it is written in such a way that the child can understand and relate to it. The child's views should be clearly articulated on the plan.

Review meetings are another opportunity for the family and child to have a say about how the plan is going and what changes are needed. Again, the Family Group Conference facilitator is able to visit the child and prepare them for this meeting, arrange an advocate, and ascertain any needs the child has to enable them to have a say. Children need to understand any changes to the plan with clear explanations about the reasons. The revised action plan is distributed to all who attended.

Quite often action plans are presented at Court for ratification. This is an effective way for the child's views to be presented at Court and emphasizes the obligation for those named in the plan to follow through on their promises.

Remaining dilemmas

Having children participate fully in Family Group Conferences is rather complex and we have not found solutions to all the dilemmas this presents.

At what age should children attend a Family Group Conference? Currently we invite them when they are ten years old, or younger if they seem capable of participating. 'Ability' is judged by those who know the child. An assessment of the child's ability to understand and to cope with the conference is required. There is a belief (Farnfield 1997) that each child should be assessed as an individual instead of relying on checklists or arbitrary age restrictions. Who should make this determination and on what grounds is a point of debate.

Whether the child attends a conference or not, the question arises about who should work with the child – the Family Group Conference facilitator or a neutral advocate? An advocate is there to ensure that the child's rights and needs are represented at the conference and in the action plan. They do not offer counselling, mediation or negotiation.

Who should select the advocate and what training do they need? Herbert and Mould (1992) found that advocates require a high level of skill. Adequate resources for appropriate recruitment of workers, and specific training and supervision to develop the competencies to work with children to enable them to have a voice, is essential (Mackay 2001). Advocates external to the family will need to establish a high level of trust with the parents in order to have access to the children. Farmer and Owen (1995) found that a good relationship with the parents was essential to work successfully with the child. If advocates were paid by the statutory authority, there may be a perception of collusion. The question of how much time is required to ensure that the advocate has established trust and a working relationship with the child is an important one. Advocacy is not therapy and different methods and tools to assist children to have a voice need to be designed. On the other hand, if the advocate is a member of the family, this may cause a conflict of interest and damage to future family relationships.

How can power imbalances be managed in Family Time, Stage 2 of the Family Group Conference, so that the child is not vulnerable? Should the advocate be invited into Family Time and what role would they play during this decision-making stage? What happens if the family is not accepting of the advocate's attendance? Finally, how long does the advocate continue to offer services to the child after the Family Group Conference is completed?

Another issue arises if parents do not want their children at the Family Group Conference. Some families do not believe that children should have a say. This may be the family culture. Under these circumstances it is important to consider what methods are available to assist children have a say when they do not attend the conference, and also who will represent the child's views.

On the other hand, how are the rights of the parents protected when they do not want their children to hear some of the family history, e.g. about certain adult relationships? In some of the conferences we have facilitated, children have attended only part of the proceedings. As the process is not mandated in the jurisdiction of New South Wales in Australia, the facilitator has no power to insist that the child or anyone else be present. The only recourse the facilitator has is to refuse to convene the Family Group Conference.

Should alleged perpetrators of child abuse be at the conference with the child or is sexual abuse a category of abuse that requires a different approach? Research undertaken by Meyer (2001) suggests that families can get together and make safe plans with their children in cases where there has been sexual abuse. However, 'the overall trend was for the perpetrator to be excluded from the conference' (Meyer 2001, p.14).

Research suggests (Farnfield 1997) that children who have dysfunctional attachments to their parents (for example, enmeshment) have difficulty expressing their own opinions and participating in decision-making. Farnfield (1997) noted that 'children do not always tell adults what is going on...nor can their view of events be taken as the only version of events' (p.9). What processes are available to assist these children and how can they be kept safe after they have had their say when it is upsetting for others in the family?

Whose decisions make up the action plan when there is a conflict between the adult and child? This is a broader issue, which highlights the importance of listening and understanding children so that decisions are child-centred even if the child cannot always craft them.

The practices of welfare agencies can assist children to have a voice. Continuity of professionals could make meetings less stressful for children. It would be beneficial to children if agencies could ensure that the same conference facilitator or advocate is available to support the child in review meetings. The design of children's case files should capture their voices and ensure that decisions and actions centre around their needs. Case files should be 'child friendly', as in many jurisdictions children and their families can access them.

Systemic issues can arise when organizations that follow child-inclusive practices work in an environment where many do not follow this approach inside and outside the sector. Marketing and promoting an awareness of child-inclusive practices is an important role in supporting children. Agencies that are serious about child-inclusive practices need to consider how children can have a real say about service planning, delivery, operation and evaluation and what provision there is for complaints to be addressed. Openness on the part of service providers allows for the development of better quality and more effective programmes (Davies and Dotchin 1997; Mackay 2001). A 'whole-of-agency' approach to child-inclusive practice is required to ensure that on all levels there is congruency.

Conclusion

Case planning is clearly a very important area of child protection. Family Group Conferencing has much to offer families and children to enable them to have a voice in decision-making about the future care and welfare of their children. The model takes into account many current community expectations about participation, transparency and accountability of process, and attempts to address a number of issues highlighted by the inclusion of children in decision-making forums.

However, for those professionals committed to ensuring that children really participate in the development of their life plans, the questions raised in this chapter urgently require answers. While these questions remain outstanding it is impossible to guarantee that children will be heard or included as full participants in decision-making. For this reason it is imperative that new processes be developed and researched in consultation with children to explore more creative options for safe expression of their opinions and needs and a true-role in decision-making.

Transcript Notation

Data are transcribed using a system created by Gail Jefferson and described in Psathas (1995). The following are the features used in these transcripts.

( )	word(s) spoken but not audible
(was)	best guess for word(s) spoken
(( ))	transcriber's description
voice	normal speaking voice
voice	increased volume
VOICE	volume is extremely loud
[ ]	two speakers' turns overlap at this point
=	no interval between turns
do:on't	sound extended
(2.0)	pause timed in seconds

Punctuation marks describe characteristics of speech production. They do not refer to grammatical units.

?	a question mark indicates a rising intonation
him-	a dash indicates a cut-off of the prior word
four.	a period indicates a stopping fall in tone
!	an exclamation mark indicates an animated tone
out	an underlined word signifies emphasis

References

AAP (Australian Associated Press) (2004) 'Mother convicted but community split on smacking kids.' *Sydney Morning Herald*. 2 April.

AAUW Educational Foundation (American Association of University Women Educational Foundation) (2000) *Techsavvy: Educating Girls in the New Computer Age*. Washington D.C.: American Association of University Women Educational Foundation. Available from www.aauw.org/2000/techsavvy.html

ABS (Australian Bureau of Statistics) (2003) 'Household use of information technology.' In *Australia Catalogue No 1301* Canberra, Australia: Commonwealth of Australia.

ACCA (Association of Child Caring Agencies) (1980) *Young People in Care Speak Out*. North Parramatta: NSW Association of Child Caring Agencies.

ACEE and AYRC (Australian Centre for Equity through Education (ACEE) and Australian Youth Research Centre (AYRC)) (2001) *Building Relationships: Making Education Work – A Report on the Perspectives of Young People*. Canberra: Commonwealth of Australia.

ACER (Australian Council of Education Research) (1987) *School Life Questionnaires*.

Adams, D. (2003) 'Severe blow probably killed boy, court told.' *The Age*. 12 March.

Ailwood, J. (2003) 'Governing early childhood education through play.' *Contemporary Issues in Early Childhood 4*, 3, 286–299.

Ainley, J. (1995) 'Students' views of their school.' *Journal of the Australian College of Education 21*, 3, 5–15.

Ainley, J. and Bourke, S. (1982) 'Student views of primary schooling.' *Research Papers in Education 7*, 2, 107–128.

Alanen, L. (1988) 'Rethinking childhood.' *Acta Sociologica 31*, 1, 53–67.

Alanen, L. (1992) *Modern Childhood? Exploring the 'Child Question' in Sociology*. University of Jyväskylä, Institute for Educational Research. Publication Series A, 50.

Alanen, L. (1994) 'Gender and generation. Feminism and the "child question".' In J. Qvortrup, M. Bardy, G. Sgritta and H. Wintersberger (eds) *Childhood Matters. Social Theory, Practice and Politics*. Aldershot, UK: Avebury.

Alanen, L. (2000) 'Women's studies/childhood studies: parallels, links and perspectives.' In J. Mason and M. Wilkinson (eds) *Taking Children Seriously: Proceedings of A National Workshop, Childhood and Youth Policy Research Unit*. University of Western Sydney, Sydney.

Alanen, L. (2001) 'Childhood as a generational condition: Children's daily lives in a central Finland town.' In L. Alanen and B. Mayall (eds) *Conceptualizing Child–Adult Relations*. London and New York: RoutledgeFalmer.

Alanen, L. and Mayall, B. (2001) *Conceptualizing Child–Adult Relationships*. London: RoutledgeFalmer.

Albrow, M. (1990) 'Introduction.' In M. Albrow and E. King (eds) *Globalisation, Knowledge and Society*. Newbury Park – Beverly Hills – New York: Sage.

Alderson, P. (2000) *Young Children's Rights: Exploring Beliefs, Principles and Practice*. London: Jessica Kingsley Publishers.

Alldred, P., David, M. and Edwards, R. (2002) 'Minding the gap: Children and young people negotiating relations between home and school.' In R. Edwards (ed.) *Children, Home and School: Regulation, Autonomy Or Connection?* London: RoutledgeFalmer.

Allport, G.W. (1954) *The Nature of Prejudice*. Reading, MA: Addison-Wesley.

Ambert, A.M. (1986) 'Sociology of sociology: The place of children in North American sociology.' In P.A. Adler and P. Adler (eds) *Sociological Studies of Child Development: A Research Annual*. Greenwich: JAI Press.

Australian Curriculum Studies Association (ACSA) (1996) *From Alienation to Engagement: Opportunities for Reform in the Middle Years of Schooling*. ACT: ACSA.

Ba, H., Tally, W. and Tsikalas, K. (2002) 'Investigating children's emerging digital literacies.' *The Journal of Technology, Learning and Assessment 1*, 4, 4–47.

Baker, C. (1997) 'Ethno methodological studies of talk in educational settings.' In B. Davies and D. Corson (eds) *Encyclopedia of Language and Education. Volume 3: Oral Discourse and Education*. Dordrecht: Kluwer Academic.

Baker, C. (1998) 'Transcription and representation in literacy research.' In J. Flood, S.B. Heath and D. Lapp (eds) *A Handbook for Literacy Educators: Research on Teaching the Communicative and Visual Arts*. New York: Macmillan.

Baker, C.D. and Freebody, P. (1989) *Children's First School Books: Introductions to the Culture of Literacy*. Oxford: Basil Blackwell.

Baker, C.D. and Campbell, R. (1999) 'Children, language and power.' In R. Campbell and D. Green (eds) *Literacies and Learners: Current Perspectives*. Sydney: Prentice-Hall.

Baker, C.D. and Keogh, J. (1995) 'Accounting for achievement in parent–teacher interviews.' *Human Studies 18*, 2 and 3, 263–300.

Batten, M. (1981) *Perceptions of the quality of school life: Case study of schools and students*. Australian Council for Education Research, monograph no.13.

Beane, J. (1993) 'Curriculum integration and the search for self and social meaning.' Paper for the *Alliance for Curriculum Reform Conference*, October, Chicago.

Becker, H.J. (2002) 'Who's wired and who's not: Children's access to and use of computer technology.' *The Future of Children 10*, 2, 44–75.

Benhabib, S. (1992) 'Models of public space: Hannah Arendt, the liberal tradition, and Jürgen Habermas.' In C. Calhoun (ed.) *Habermas and the Public Sphere*. Cambridge, Massachusetts: MIT Press.

Berkowitz, M.W. and Grych, J.H. (1998) 'Fostering goodness: Teaching parents to facilitate children's moral development.' *Journal of Moral Education 27*, 371–391.

Binning, E. (2003) 'Space games in morning and death in the afternoon for three-year-old.' *The New Zealand Herald*. 27 November.

Bolzan, N. (2003) *Kids are like that! Community Attitudes to Young People.* National Youth Affairs Research Scheme. [online] Available from: www.dfacs.publications [Accessed on 13 November 2003].

Boss, P. (1995) 'Physical punishment in child rearing.' *Children Australia 20,* 3, 27–32.

Bradshaw, J. (2002) 'Child poverty and child outcomes.' *Children and Society 16,* 2, 131–40.

Brady, L. (2000) 'Portfolio for assessment and reporting.' In *Australian Association for Research in Education Conference,* 4–7 December, Sydney.

Bremner, R. (ed.) (1970) *Children and Youth in America. A Documentary History. Volume 1* (600–1865). Massachusetts: Harvard University Press.

Brous, D., Green, D. and Jaggs, D. (1980) 'Children and the state.' In R.G. Brown (ed.) *Children Australia.* Sydney: Allen and Unwin in association with the Morialta Trust of South Australia.

Burman, E. (1994) *Deconstructing Developmental Psychology.* London and New York: Routledge.

Butler, I. and Williamson, H. (1994) *Children Speak. Children, Trauma and Social Work.* Essex: Longman.

Butler, J. (1990) *Gender Trouble: Feminism and the Subversion of Identity.* New York: Routledge.

Buzzelli, C.A. (1992) 'Young children's moral understandings: Learning about right and wrong.' *Young Children 47,* 47–53.

Buzzelli, C.A. (1995) 'Teacher–child discourse in the early childhood classroom: A dialogic model of self-regulation and moral development.' *Advances in Early Education and Day Care 7,* 271–294.

Buzzelli, C.A. (1996) 'The moral implications of teacher–child discourse in early childhood classrooms.' *Early Childhood Research Quarterly 11,* 515–534.

Calvert, J. (2001) 'Dad fined for beating.' *Herald Sun.* 1 November.

Cant, S. (1999) 'Accused "hit baby 10 times".' *The Age.* 26 April.

Cappella, E. (compiled) (2002) 'Appendix B: What children think about computers.' *The Future of Children 10,* 2, 186–191.

Carney, T. (1985b) 'The interface between juvenile corrections and child welfare.' In A. Borowski and J.M. Murray (eds) *Juvenile Delinquency in Australia.* Sydney: Methuen.

Caron, A.H., Giroux, L. and Douzou, S. (1989) 'Uses and impacts of home computers in Canada: A process of reappropriation.' In J.L. Salvaggio and J. Bryant (eds) *Media Use In The Information Age.* Hillsdale, NJ: Lawrence Erlbaum and Associates.

Carter, J. (2002) *Towards Better Foster Care: Reducing the Risks in Caring for Other People's Children.* West Melbourne: The Children's Foundation.

Cashmore, J. (1997) 'Systems Abuse.' In M. John, (ed) *A Charge Against Society. The Child's Right to Protection.* Children in Charge 3. London: Jessica Kingsley Publishers.

Cashmore, J. and de Haas, N. (1995) *Discussion Paper: Legal and Social Aspects of the Physical Punishment of Children.* Commonwealth Department of Human Services and Health, Australia.

Cashmore, J. and Paxman, M. (1996) *Longitudinal Study of Wards Leaving Care.* Sydney: University of New South Wales, Social Policy Research Centre.

Cashmore, J., Dolby, R. and Brennan, R. (1994) *Systems Abuse: Problems and Solutions.* Sydney: New South Wales Child Protection Council.

Chisholm, R. (1979) 'When should the State take over?' *Legal Service Bulletin.* August.

Chisholm, R. (1980) 'Children and the law.' In R.G. Brown (ed.) *Children Australia.* Sydney: Allen and Unwin.

Christensen, P. and James, A. (2000) 'Childhood diversity and commonality: some methodological insights.' In P. Christensen and A. James (eds) *Research With Children: Perspectives and Practices.* London: Falmer Press.

Christensen, P. and O'Brien, M. (eds) (2003) *Children in the City: Home, Neighbourhood and Community.* London and New York: RoutledgeFalmer.

Cicourel, A.V. (1970) 'The acquisition of social structure: Toward a developmental sociology of language and meaning.' In J.D. Douglas (ed.) *Understanding Everyday Life: Toward The Reconstruction of Sociological Knowledge.* London: Routledge and Kegan Paul.

Clark, L. (2001) 'Legal cruelty or every parent's right?' *The Daily Telegraph.* 12 July.

Cloke, C. and Davies, M. (eds) (1997) 'Introduction.' In C. Cloke and M. Davies (eds) *Participation and Empowerment in Child Protection.* Wiltshire, Chichester: John Wiley and Sons.

Cloke, C. and Davies, M. (eds) (1997) *Participation and Empowerment in Child Protection.* Wiltshire, Chichester: John Wiley and Sons.

Cockburn, T. (1998) 'Children and citizenship in Britain. A case for a socially interdependent model of citizenship.' *Childhood 5*, 1, 99–117.

Coffey, M. and Dent, S. (1999) 'Child experts plead for curbs on parents who spank: Ban the smack.' *Herald Sun.* 8 June.

Cohen, S. (1972) *Folk Devils and Moral Panics.* London: University of London Press.

Coleman, J. (1972) *How Do the Young Become Adults? Report No. 130.* Baltimore: Center for Social Organization of Schools, Johns Hopkins University.

Colwell, J., Grady, C. and Rhaiti, S. (1995) 'Computer games, self esteem, and gratification of needs in adolescents.' *Journal of Community and Applied Social Psychology 14*, 195–206.

Connell, R.E. (1987) *Gender and Power. Society, the Person and Sexual Politics.* Cambridge: Polity Press.

Connell, R.W. and Dowsett, G.W. (1992) *Rethinking Sex: Social Theory and Sexuality Research.* Melbourne: Melbourne University Press.

Conway, D. (2004) 'NSW: Damned if you smack, and damned if you don't.' *AAP Newsfeed.* 2 April.

Cook-Gumperz, Jenny (1991) 'Children's construction of "childness".' In B. Scales, M. Almy, A. Nicolopoulu and S. Ervin-Tripp (eds) *Play and The Social Context of Development in Early Care and Education.* New York: Teachers College Press.

Cooter, Roger (ed.) (1992) *In the Name of The Child. Health and Welfare 1880–1940.* London and New York: Routledge.

Corsaro, W.A. (1997) *The Sociology of Childhood*. London: Pine Forge.

Corteen, K. and Scraton, P. (1997) 'Prolonging "childhood", manufacturing "innocence" and regulating sexuality.' In P. Scraton (ed.) *'Childhood' in 'Crisis'*. London: University College London Press.

Cousens, P. and Stevens M. (1997) 'The Rights of the Child in a Paediatric Oncology Unit.' In M. John (ed) *A Charge Against Society. The Child's Right to Protection*. Children in Charge 3. London: Jessica Kingsley Publishers.

Cranston, N. (1988) *A Report of Students' and Teachers' Pereeptions and Attitudes and Other Aspects to Emerge During the First Year*. Alexander Hills College, Research Services Branch Department of Education, Brisbane.

Creighton, S. and Russell, N. (1995) *Voices from Childhood*. London: NSPCC.

Crossley, N. (1996) *Intersubjectivity: The Fabric of Social Becoming*. London: Sage.

Crimes Act 1900 (NSW) S.61AA (2) (b). See: http://www.austlii.edu.au/au/legis/nsw/consol_act/ca190082/s61aa.html

Cullen, M. and Whiteford, H. (2001) *The Interrelations of Social Capital with Health and Mental Health*. Canberra: National Mental Health Strategy Discussion Paper, Commonwealth of Australia.

Cussianovich, A. (1997) 'The "out of place": paradigm of a new society.' Paper presented at *Urban Childhood Conference*, 9–12 June, Trondheim, Norway.

Dakar Declaration (1998) Adopted by Representatives of the Movements of Working Children and Youth of Africa, Latin America and Asia at their Meeting in Dakar, Senegal, March 1998.

Dakar Working Children's Association (1998) Report on the Child Labour Section, Urban Childhood Conference, Trondheim, 9–12 June 1997. *A Letter from the Street*. West African Movement of Working Children and Youth.

Danaher, P. (1995) 'Show children's perceptions of their schooling experiences.' *Journal of the Australian College of Education 21*, 3, 43–50.

Danby, S. and Baker, C. (1998) '"What's the problem?" Restoring social order in the preschool classroom.' In I. Hutchby and J. Moran-Ellis (eds) *Children and Social Competence: Arenas of Action*. London: Falmer.

Daniels, D., Kalkman, D. and McCombs, B. (2001) 'Young children's perspectives on learning and teaching practices in different classroom contexts.' *Early Education and Development 12*, 253–273.

Danielson, C. and Abrutyn, L. (1997) *An Introduction to Using Portfolios in the Classroom*. Virginia: Association for Supervision and Curriculum Development.

Davidson, A. and Spegele, R. (1991) *Rights, Justice and Democracy in Australia*. Melbourne: Longman Cheshire.

Davidson, J. (1984) 'Subsequent versions of invitations, offers, requests, and proposals dealing with potential or actual rejection.' In J.M. Atkinson (ed.) *Structures of Social Action: Studies in Conversation Analysis*. Cambridge: Cambridge University Press.

Davies, B. (1989) *Frogs and Snails and Feminist Tales: Preschool Children and Gender*. Sydney: Allen and Unwin.

Davies, M. and Dotchin, J. (1997) 'Improving quality through participation: An approach to measuring children's expectations and perceptions of services.' In E. Farmer and M. Owen (1995) *Child Protection Practice: Private Risks and Public Remedies.* London: HMSO.

Davis, H. and Bourhill, M. (1997) '"Crisis": The demonization of children and young people.' In P. Scraton (ed.) *'Childhood' in Crisis.* London: UCL Press.

Davis, K., Leijenaar, M. and Oldersma, J. (eds) (1992) *The Gender of Power.* London – Newbury Park – Beverly Hills – New York: Sage.

de Kretser, L. (2002) 'Top judge's swipe on child smacking.' *The Advertiser.* 5 July.

De Lauretis, T. (1987) *Technologies of Gender: Essays on Theory, Film, and Fiction.* Bloomington: Indiana University Press.

De Swaan, A. (1988) *In Care of the State: Health Care, Education and Welfare in Europe and the USA in the Modern Era.* Cambridge: Polity Press.

De Winter, M. (1997) *Children as Fellow Citizens, Participation and Commitment.* Oxford: Radcliffe Medical Press.

Dean, M. and Hindess, B. (eds) (1998) *Governing Australia: Studies in Contemporary Rationalities of Government.* Cambridge: Cambridge University Press.

Denborough, D. (1996) 'Power and partnership? Challenging the sexual construction of schooling.' In L. Laskey and C. Beavis (eds) *Schooling and Sexualities: Teaching for a Positive Sexuality.* Victoria: Deakin Centre for Education and Change, Deakin University.

Dencik, L. (1995) 'Modern childhood in the Nordic countries: "dual socialisation" and its implications.' In L. Chisholm, P. Buchner, H.H. Kruger and M. de Bois-Raymond (eds) *Growing up in Europe: Contemporary Horizons in Childhood and Youth Studies.* Berlin: Walter de Gruyter.

Denzin, N.K. (1982) 'The work of little children.' In C. Jenks (ed.) *The Sociology of Childhood: Essential Readings.* Aldershot: Gregg Revivals.

Department of Health (2000) *Protecting Children, Supporting Parents: A Consultation Document on the Physical Punishment of Children.* London: Department of Health.

Dewey, J. (1966) *Democracy and Education.* New York: Free Press. (Original work published 1916.)

Dickey, B. (1980) *No Charity There: A Short History of Social Welfare in Australia.* West Melbourne: Thomas Nelson.

Dietz, T.L. (1998) 'An examination of violence and gender role portrayals in video games: Implications for gender socialization and aggressive behaviour.' *Sex Roles 38,* 425–442.

Downes, T. (1998a) 'Children's participation in evaluating the role of new information and communication technologies in schools.' *Education and Information Technologies 4,* 3, 331–341.

Downes, T. (1998b) *Children's Use of Computers in Their Homes.* Thesis (PhD). University of Western Sydney.

Downes, T. (2002a) 'Blending play practice and performance. Children's use of computer at home.' *Journal of Educational Enquiry 3,* 2, 21–34.

Downes, T., Arthur, L. and Beecher, B. (2001) 'Effective learning environments for young children using digital resources: An Australian perspective.' *Information Technology in Childhood Education 1,* 129–143.

Duke, R. and Aitkinson, J. (1992) 'Adults' and children's perceptions of smacking: Student report.' Cited in J. Cashmore and N. de Haas (1995) *Discussion Paper: Legal and Social Aspects of the Physical Punishment of Children.* Commonwealth Department of Human Services and Health, Australia.

Durrant, J. (1999) 'Evaluating the success of Sweden's corporal punishment ban.' *Child Abuse and Neglect 21,* 5, 435–448.

Dusseldorp Skills Forum (2003) *How Young people are Faring: Key Indicators 2003.* [online] Available from: www.dsf.org.au [Accessed on 11 January 2001].

Dwyer, P., Stokes, H., Tyler, D. and Holdsworth, R. (1998) *Negotiating Staying and Returning: Young People's Perspectives on Schooling and the Youth Allowance.* Victoria: Department of Education.

Editorial (1999) *Herald Sun.* 10 June.

Editorial (2001) 'Ban on smacking is hitting too hard.' *The New Zealand Herald.* 10 May.

Editorial Opinion (1995) 'A smack for smacking.' *Sydney Morning Herald.* 5 February.

Edwards, R. (ed.) (2002) 'Introduction: Conceptualizing relationships between home and school in children's lives.' *Children, Home and School: Regulation, Autonomy or Connection?* London: RoutledgeFalmer.

Edwards, R. and Alldred, P. (2000) 'A typology of parental involvement in education centring on children and young people: Negotiating familialisation, institutionalisation and individualisation.' *British Journal of Sociology of Education 23,* 3, 435–455.

Edwards, R. and David, M. (1997) 'Where are the children in home–school relations? Towards a research agenda.' *Children and Society 11,* 194–200.

Ellicott, T. (2000) 'Law to spank parents who smack.' *The Australian.* 26 October.

Elliott, M. (1992) 'Images of children in the media: "Soft kiddie porn".' In I. Itzin (ed.) *Pornography: Women, Violence and Civil Liberties. A Radical New View.* New York: Oxford University Press.

Elshtain, J.B. (1982) '"Thank heaven for little girls": The dialectics of development.' In J.B. Elshtain (ed.) *The Family in Political Thought.* Amherst: University of Massachusetts Press.

Ericsson, K. and Larsen, G. (2002) 'Adults as resources and adults as burdens: The strategies of children in the age of school–home collaboration.' In R. Edwards (ed.) *Children, Home and School: Regulation, Autonomy or Connection?* London: RoutledgeFalmer.

Face, C. (1995) 'Human costs: A view from within.' In S. Rees and G. Rodley (eds) *The Human Costs of Managerialism: Advocating the Recovery of Humanity.* Sydney: Pluto Press.

Facer, K., Furlong, J., Furlong, R. and Sutherland, R. (2001) 'Constructing the child computer user: From public policy to private practices.' *British Journal of Sociology of Education 22,* 1, 91–108.

Fairclough, N. (1998) *Discourse and Social Change.* Oxford: Polity Press.

Farmer, E. and Owen, M. (1995) *Child Protection Practice: Private Risks and Public Remedies.* London: HMSO.

Farnfield, S. (1997) *The Involvement of Children in Child Protection Conferences – Summary of Findings.* University of Reading.

Fattore, T., Galloway-Smith, M. and Turnbull, N. (2000) 'Managerialism meets human rights: The consequences for children.' In S. Rees and S. Wright (eds) *Human rights and Corporate Responsibility: A Dialogue.* Sydney: Pluto Press.

Faye, D. (1998) Report on the International Conference on Child Labour, Oslo, 27–30 October 1997. *A Letter from the Street.* West African Movement of Working Children and Youth.

Fine, G.A. and Sandstrom, K.L. (1988) *Knowing Children. Participant Observation with Minors.* Newbury Park – Beverly Hills – New York: Sage.

Flekkøy, M.G. and Kaufman, N.H. (1997) *The Participation Rights of the Child: Rights and Responsibilities in Family and Society, 'Children in Charge' Series.* London: Jessica Kingsley Publishers.

Fling, S., Smith, L., Rodriguez, T., Atkins, E. and Nixon, K. (1992) 'Videogames, aggression, and self-esteem: A survey.' *Social Behaviour and Personality 20,* 1, 39–46.

Foggart, A.C.S. (1986) *How Children View Schooling.* Master thesis, Canberra College of Advanced Education, Canberra.

Foucault, M. (1977a) *Discipline and Punish: The Birth of the Prison.* London: Allen Lane.

Foucault, M. (1977b) *The History of Sexuality: An Introduction. Vol.1.* English Translation. London: Random House.

Franklin, B. (1986) 'Introduction.' In B. Franklin (ed.) *The Rights of Children.* Oxford: Basil Blackwell.

Franklin, B. (1998) 'Children's Political Rights.' In E. Verhellen (ed.) *Understanding Children's Rights. Ghent Papers on Children's Rights – No 3.* Ghent: Children's Rights Centre, University of Ghent.

Franklin, B. (2002) 'Children's rights and media wrongs: Changing representations of children and the developing children's rights agenda.' In B. Franklin (ed.) *The New Handbook of Children's Rights: Comparative Policy and Practice.* London and New York: Routledge.

Fraser, N. (1989) *Unruly Practices: Power, Discourse and Gender in Contemporary Social Theory.* Minneapolis: University of Minnesota Press.

Fraser, N. (1992) 'Rethinking the Public Sphere: A contribution to the critique of actually existing democracy.' In C. Calhoun (ed.) *Habermas and the Public Sphere.* Cambridge, Massachusetts: MIT Press.

Freeman, M. (1987) 'Taking children's rights seriously.' *Children and Society 1,* 4.

Freeman, M. (2000) 'The future of children's rights.' *Children and Society 14,* 4, 277–93.

Friere, P. (1973) *Pedagogy of the Oppressed.* New York: The Seabury Press.

Frost, N. and Stein, M. (1989) *The Politics of Child Welfare. Inequality, Power and Change.* Hertfordshire: Harvester and Wheatsheaf.

Furlong, J., Furlong, R., Facer, K. and Sutherland, R. (2000) 'The national grid for learning: A curriculum without walls?' *Cambridge Journal of Education 30,* 1, 91–110.

Garfinkel, H. (1984) *Studies in Ethnomethodology*. Cambridge: Polity Press.

Garton, S. (1990) *Out of Luck: Poor Australians and Social Welfare 1788–1988*. Sydney: Allen and Unwin.

Garvey, C. (1990) *Play*. Cambridge, MA: Harvard University Press.

Gawlik, J., Henning, T. and Warner, K. (2002) 'Physical Punishment of Children.' *Issues Paper No. 3*, Tasmania Law Reform Institute, http://www.law.utas.edu.au/reform

Ghandi, L. (1998) *Postcolonial Theory: A Critical Introduction*. Sydney: Allen and Unwin.

Giles, D. (2001) 'Gentle spanking can hit the spot.' *Herald Sun*. 26 August.

Gittins, D. (1998) *The Child in Question*. London: Macmillan.

Goddard, C. (2002) *In the Firing Line*. Sussex: John Wiley and Sons.

Goddard, C. (2003) 'Look into the eyes of Ali Ismail Abbas: What do you see?' *The Age*. 30 April.

Goddard, C. and Carew, R. (1993) *Responding to Children, Child Welfare Practice*. Melbourne: Longman Cheshire.

Goddard, C. and Liddell, M. (1995) 'Child abuse fatalities and the media: Lessons from a case study.' *Child Abuse Review 4*, 355–364.

Goddard, C.R. (1994) 'Lessons from the life and death of Daniel Valerio.' *Montage* 12, June 12.

Goddard, C.R. (1996) *Child Abuse and Child Protection*. Melbourne: Churchill Livingstone.

Goddard, C.R and Saunders.B.J. (2000) 'The gender neglect and textual abuse of children in the print media.' *Child Abuse Review 9*, 1, 37–48.

Goddard, C.R. and Saunders, B.J. (2001a) *Child Abuse and the Media 14*. Melbourne: Australian Institute of Family Studies and National Child Protection Clearinghouse House.

Goddard, C.R and Saunders, B.J (2001b) 'Journalists as agents and language as an instrument of social control: A child protection case study.' *Children Australia 26*, 2, 26–30.

Goldner, V. (2004) 'Three slaps made this mother a criminal – I did smack him but not hard.' *The Daily Telegraph*. 2 April.

Goldner, V. and Taylor, Z. (2004) 'Helpless mum hit toddler.' *Herald Sun*. 3 April.

Goldson, B. (2001) 'The demonization of children: From symbolic to the institutional.' In P. Foley, J. Roche and S. Tucker (eds) *Children in Society. Contemporary Theory, Policy and Practice*. London: Palgrave.

Gomes da Costa, A.C. and Schmidt-Rahmer, B. (1991) 'Brazil: Children spearhead a movement for change.' In *The Convention: Child Rights and the UNICEF Experience at the Country Level*. Florence: UNICEF International Child Development Centre (Innocenti Studies).

Goode, D. (1994) *A World Without Words: The Social Construction of Children Born Deaf and Blind*. Philadelphia: Temple University Press.

Goode, D.A. (1986) 'Kids, culture and innocents.' *Human Studies 9*, 1.

Goodnow, J. and Burns, A. (1985) *Home and School: A Child's-Eye View*. Sydney: Allen and Unwin.

Goodwin, M. (1995) 'Co-construction in girls' hopscotch.' *Research on Language and Social Interaction 28*, 3, 261–281.

Gordon, L. (1988) *Heroes of Their Own Lives: The Politics and History of Family Violence: Boston 1880–1960*. London: Virago.

Gough, B. and Reavey, P. (1997) 'Parental accounts regarding the physical punishment of children: Discourses of dis/empowerment.' *Child Abuse and Neglect 21*, 5, 417–430.

Gower, P. (2001) 'Cruel "disciplinarian" goes to jail.' *The New Zealand Herald*. 3 May.

Gray, P. (2002) 'Judges must stick to judging: Family Court Chief Justice Alastair Nicholson deserves a smack himself.' *Herald Sun*. 9 July.

Greber, J. (2000) 'Appeal lodged on child belting.' *The Courier Mail*. 31 October.

Greene, S. (1999) 'Child development: Old themes, new directions.' In M. Woodhead, D. Faulkner and K. Littleton (eds) *Making Sense of Social Development*. London and New York: Routledge in association with the Open University.

Griffith, A. and Smith, D. (1987) 'Constructing cultural knowledge: Mothering as discourse.' In J.S. Gaskell and A.T. McLaren (eds) *Women and Education. A Canadian Perspective*. Calgary: Detselig.

Grimshaw, J. (1986) *Feminist Philosophers: Women's Perspectives on Philosophical Traditions*. London: Harvester Wheatsheaf.

Groundwater, S., Downes, T. and Gibbons, P. (2000) 'Information technology in teaching and learning.' *Evaluation Report for SECGGS Darlinghurst*. Unpublished report.

Gubrium, J.F. and Holstein, J.A. (1997) *The New Language of Qualitative Method*. Oxford: Oxford University Press.

Habermas, J. (1987) *The Theory of Communicative Action, Volume Two: System and Lifeworld*. Cambridge: Polity Press.

Habermas, J. (1989) *The Structural Transformation of the Public Sphere*. Cambridge, Massachusetts: MIT Press.

Habermas, J. (1990) *Moral Consciousness and Communicative Action*. Cambridge, Massachusetts: MIT Press.

Habermas, J. (1992) 'Further Reflections on the Public Sphere.' In C. Calhoun (ed.) *Habermas and the Public Sphere*. Cambridge, Massachusetts: MIT Press.

Habermas, J. (1996) *Between Facts and Norms: Contributions to a Discourse Theory of Law and Democracy*. Cambridge: Polity Press.

Haddock, G. and Zanna, N. (1998) 'On the use of open-ended measures to assess attitudinal components.' *British Journal of Social Psychology* 37, 129–149.

Hall, S. and Ward, J. (2000) 'British to get to bottom of child discipline.' *The Age*. 19 January.

Hammersley, M. (2000) *The Relevance of Education*. UK: Oxford Review of Education.

Hannam, D. (1999) 'Schools for democracy – from rhetoric to reality.' Paper at *10 Years of the Convention on the Rights of the Child*, 26–27 February, Dublin. In *Connect 118*, August, p.5.

Harding, S. (1986) *The Science Question in Feminism*. Ithaca: University Press.

Harding, S. (1987) 'Introduction: Is there a feminist method?' In S. Harding (ed.) *Feminism and Methodology*. Bloomington: Indiana University Press.

Harding, S. (1991) *Whose Science? Whose Knowledge? Thinking from Women's Lives*. Milton Keynes: Open University Press.

Hardman, C. (1973) 'Can there be an anthropology of children?' *Journal of the Anthropology Society of Oxford 1*, 2.

Hart, R. (1992) *Children's Participation: From Tokenism to Citizenship: Inocenti Essay No 4*. Florence: UNICEF, International Child Development Centre.

Hart, R. (1998) 'Children's right to participate: Some tools to stimulate discussion on the issue in different cultures.' In E. Verhellen (ed.) *Understanding Children's Rights. Ghent Papers on Children's Rights – No 3*. Ghent: Children's Rights Centre, University of Ghent.

Hart, S., Zeidner, M. and Pavlovic, Z. (1996) 'Children's rights: Cross-national research on perspectives of children and their teachers.' In M. John (ed.) (1996) *Children in Charge: The Child's Right to a Fair Hearing*. London: Jessica Kingsley Publishers.

Harvey, L. (1990) *Critical Social Research*. London: Unwin Hyman.

Hastings, A. (1998) 'Connecting linguistic structures and social practices: A discursive approach to social policy analysis.' *Journal of Social Policy 27*, 2, 191–211.

Hatton, E. (1995) 'Middle school students' perceptions of school organization.' *Journal of the Australian College of Education 21*, 3, 17–27.

Haydon, D. (2002) 'Children's rights to sex and sexuality education.' In B. Franklin (ed.) *The New Handbook of Children's Rights. Comparative Policy and Practice*. London: Routledge.

Heap, J.L. (1990) 'Applied ethnomethodology: Looking for the local rationality of reading activities.' *Human Studies 13*, 39–72.

Hearn, J. (1990) 'Child abuse and men's violence.' In The Violence Against Children Study Group. *Taking Child Abuse Seriously*. London: Unwin Hyman.

Heilio, P., Lauronen, E. and Bardy, M. (1993) *Politics of Childhood and Children at Risk*. Vienna: European Centre for Social Welfare Policy and Research.

Hendrick, H. (1990) 'Constructions and reconstructions of British childhood: An interpretive survey, 1800 to the present.' In J. Allison and A. Prout (eds) *Constructing and Reconstructing Childhood: Contemporary Issues in the Sociological Study of Childhood*. London – New York – Philadelphia: Falmer Press.

Hendrick, H. (1994) *Child Welfare: England 1872–1989*. London and New York: Routledge.

Hendrick, H. (1997) 'Constructions and reconstructions of British Childhood: An interpretive survey, 1800 to the present.' In A. James and A. Prout (eds) *Constructing and Reconstructing childhood: Contemporary Issues in the Sociological Study of Childhood*. London: Falmer Press.

Hendrick, H. (2003) *Child Welfare: Historical Dimensions, Contemporary Debate*. London and New York: Routledge.

Herbert, M.D. and Mould, J.W. (1992) 'The advocacy role in public child welfare.' *Child Welfare LXXI*, 2, March–April, 115–130.

Hester, S. and Eglin, P. (eds) (1997) *Culture in action: Studies in membership categorization analysis.* Lanham: University Press of America.

Hickley, M. (2001) 'Smacks take a beating in UK.' *Herald Sun.* 8 September.

Hill, M. (1997) 'Participatory research with children.' University of Glasgow, UK. Centre for the Child and Society. *Child and Family Social Work 2*, 171–183.

Hodgkin, R. (1997) 'Why the "gentle smack" should go.' *Children and Society 11*, 201–204.

Hogan, D. (1997) 'Valuing the child in research: Historical and current influences on research methodology with children.' In D. Hogan and R. Gilligan (eds) *Researching Children's Experiences: Qualitative Approaches.* Dublin: Children's Research Centre, Trinity College.

Holdsworth, R. (1986) *Student Participation and the Participation and Equity Programme, PEP Discussion Paper No 2*, Canberra: Commonwealth Schools Commission.

Holdsworth, R. (1988) 'An anecdotal history of student participation.' In R. Slee (ed.) *Discipline and Schools: A Curriculum Perspective.* South Melbourne: Macmillan.

Holdsworth, R. (1997) 'Student participation, connectedness and citizenship.' *Connect* April, 104.

Holdsworth, R. (1998) 'Two challenges.' *Connect* April, 110.

Holdsworth, R. (1999) 'Enhancing effective student participation: 33 curriculum approaches.' *Connect* April, 116.

Holdsworth, R. (2000) 'Schools that create real roles of value for young people.' *Prospects 30*, 3, 349–362.

Holdsworth, R. (2002) 'Remembering STC.' *Connect* March, 133–134.

Holdsworth, R., Cahill, H. and Smith, G. (2003) *Student Action Teams: Phase 2 – 2001–2002: An Evaluation of Implementation and Impact.* Melbourne: Australian Youth Research Centre Research Report 22.

Holdsworth, R., Stafford, J., Stokes, H. and Tyler, D. (2001) *Student Action Teams: An Evaluation: 1999–2000.* Melbourne: Australian Youth Research Centre Working Paper 21.

Holland, S., O'Neill, S., Scourfield, J. and Pithouse, A. (2003) *Outcomes In Family Group Conferences for Children on the Brink of Care: A Study of Child and Family Participation. Draft Final Report, March 2003.* UK: Cardiff University School of Social Sciences.

Holloway, S.L. and Valentine, G. (eds) (2000) *Children's Geographies: Playing, Living, Learning.* London and New York: Routledge.

Honneth, A. (1995) *The Struggle for Recognition: The Moral Grammar of Social Conflicts.* Cambridge: Polity Press.

Honneth, A. and Farrell, J. (1997) 'Recognition and Moral Obligation.' *Social Research 64*, 1, 16–26.

Horne, M. (1990) 'Is it social work?' In The Violence Against Children Study Group. *Taking Child Abuse Seriously.* London: Unwin Hyman.

House of Commons (2003) *Health – Minutes of Evidence Taken Before the Health Committee.* 27 March. Available from: http://www.publications.parliament.uk/

Houston, S. (2003) 'A method from the "life world".' Some possibilities for person-centred planning for children in care.' *Children and Society* 17, 57–70.

Howell, W. (2003) 'Toddler basher guilty.' *Herald Sun.* 15 March.

Huizinga, J. (1949) *Homo Ludens: A Study of the Play-element in Culture.* London: Routledge and Kegan Paul.

Hume, M. (2003) 'Give the NSPCC a clip around the ear, somebody.' *The Times.* 5 May.

Hutchby, I. and Moran-Ellis, J. (1998a) 'Situating children's competence.' In Ian Hutchby and Jo Moran-Ellis (eds) (1998b) *Children and Social Competence: Arenas of Action.* London: Falmer Press.

Hutchby, I. and Moran-Ellis, J. (ed.) (1998b) *Children and Social Competence: Arenas of Action.* London: Falmer Press.

ILO (1999) *Convention No. 182 Concerning the Prohibition and Immediate Action for the Elimination of the Worst Forms of Child Labour.*

Jackson, P.W., Boostrom, R.E. and Hansen, D.T. (1993) *The Moral Life of Schools.* San Francisco: Jossey-Bass.

Jacoby, S. and Ochs, E. (1995) 'Co-construction: An introduction.' *Research on Language and Social Interaction 28,* 3, 171–183.

James, A. (1993) *Childhood Identities. Self and Social Relationships in the Experience of the Child.* Edinburgh: Edinburgh University Press.

James, A. (1998) 'Foreword.' In I. Hutchby and J. Moran-Ellis (eds) *Children and Social Competence: Arenas of Action.* London: Falmer Press.

James, A. and Prout, A. (1990) 'A new paradigm for the sociology of childhood: provenance, promise and problems.' In A. James and A. Prout (eds) *Constructing and Reconstructing Childhood: Contemporary Issues in the Sociological Study of Childhood.* London: Falmer Press.

James, A. and Prout, A. (1997) *Constructing and Reconstructing Childhood.* (2nd edn). London: Falmer Press.

James, A., Jenks, C. and Prout, A. (1998) *Theorizing Childhood.* London: Polity Press.

Jenkins, H. (ed.) (1998) *The Children's Culture Reader.* New York: New York University Press.

Jenks, C. (1982) 'Introduction.' In C. Jenks (ed.) *The Sociology of Childhood: Essential Readings.* Hampshire: Gregg Revivals; London: Batsford Academic and Educational Ltd.

Jenks, C. (1996) *Childhood.* London: Routledge.

John, M. (1996) 'Voicing: research and practice with the "silenced".' In M. John (ed.) *Children in Charge: The Child's Right to a Fair Hearing.* London: Jessica Kingsley Publishers.

John, M. (ed.) (1996) *Children in Charge: The Child's Right to a Fair Hearing.* London: Jessica Kingsley Publishers.

John, M. (2003) *Children's Rights and Power: Charging Up for a New Century.* Children in Charge 9. London: Jessica Kingsley Publishers.

Johnson, V., Smith, E. Ivan., Gordon, G., Pridmore, P. and Scott, P. (eds) (1998) *Stepping Forward. Children and Young People's Participation in the Development Process.* London: Intermediate Technology Publications.

Jordanova, L. (1989) 'Children in history: concepts of nature and society.' In Scarre, Geoffrey (ed.) *Children, Parents and Politics.* Cambridge: Cambridge University Press.

Kelley, P., Mayall, B. and Hood, S. (1997) 'Children's accounts of risk.' *Childhood 4,* 3, 305–24.

Kempe, H. (August 1975) 'Keynote Address.' In *The Battered Child: Proceedings of the First National Australian Conference.* Perth.

Key, E. (1909) *The Century of the Child.* New York: G.P. Putnam.

King, M. (1997) *A Better World for Children: Explorations in Morality and Authority.* London: Routledge.

Kitzinger, J. (1988) 'Defending innocence: ideologies of childhood.' *Feminist Review,* Spring 28.

Kitzinger, J. (1990) 'Who are you kidding? Children, power and the struggle against sexual abuse.' In A. James and A. Prout (eds) *Constructing and Reconstructing Childhood: Contemporary Issues in the Sociological Study of Childhood.* London: Falmer Press.

Kjørholt, A.T. (1998) Children as active citizens: Perspectives on Norwegian Child Policy and the implementation of the UN Convention on the Rights of the Child. Paper presented at *Children's Rights and Wrongs Conference,* 5–6 November, Nicosia, Cyprus.

Kohlberg, L. (1984) *Essays on Moral Development.* San Francisco: Harper and Row.

Kraut, R., Patterson, M., Lundmark, V., Kiesler, S., Mukopadhyay, T. and Scherlis, W. (1998) 'Internet paradox: A social technology that reduces social involvement and psychological well-being?' *American Psychologist 53,* 9, 1017–1031.

Krivacska, J.J. (1992) 'Child sexual abuse prevention programmes: The prevention of childhood sexuality?' *Journal of Child Sexual Abuse 1,* 4, 83–112.

Krüger, M. (1987) 'Überlegungen und Thesen zu einer feministischen (Sozial-)Wissenschaft.' In U. Beer (Hrsg.) *Klasse Geschlecht. Feministische Gesellschaftsanalyse und Wissenschaftskritik.* Bielefeld: AJZ-Verlag.

Kundapur Declaration (1996) *First International Meeting of Working Children,* 27 November–9 December, Kundapur, India.

La Fontaine, J.S. (1999) 'Are children people?' In J.S. La Fontaine and H. Rydstrøm (eds) *The Invisibility of Children.* Papers from a conference on *Anthropology and Children,* May. Sweden: Department of Child Studies, Linköping University.

Land, M.J. (1999) 'Evidence of gender disparity in children's computer use and activities.' Paper presented at the *Annual Meeting of the Association for Education in Journalism and Mass Communication,* 4–7 August, New Orleans, LA.

Lansdown, G. (1994) 'Children's Rights.' In B. Mayall (ed.) *Children's Childhoods: Observed and Experienced.* London: Falmer Press.

Lansdown, G. (1997) 'Children's rights to participation and protection: A critique.' In C. Cloke and M. Davies (eds) *Participation and Empowerment in Child Protection.* Wiltshire: John Wiley and Sons.

Leavitt, R.L. (1994) *Power and Emotion in Infant–Toddler Day Care.* Albany: State University of New York Press.

Lefort, C. (1990) 'Flesh and Otherness.' In G. Johnson and M. Smith (eds) *Ontology and Alterity in Merleau-Ponty.* Illinois: Northwestern University Press.

Leiminer, M.J. and Baker, C.D. (2000) 'A child's say in parent–teacher talk at the preschool: Doing conversation analytic research in early childhood settings.' [online] *Contemporary Issues in Early Childhood 1*, 2, 135–152. Available from: http://www.triangle.co.uk

Letter (1999) 'Smacking controls kids.' *Herald Sun.* 11 June.

Letter (1999) 'Parents must control kids.' *Herald Sun.* 15 June.

Letter (1999) 'Be sensible on smacking.' *Herald Sun.* 16 June.

Letter (1999) 'A lesson in discipline.' *Herald Sun.* 19 June a.

Letter (1999) 'Undermining parent's rights.' *Herald Sun.* 19 June b.

Letter (1999) 'Smacks not necessary.' *Herald Sun.* 21 June.

Lindsey, D. (1994) *The Welfare of Children.* New York: Oxford University Press.

Lipari, K. (2000) 'Rules spell out how to smack a child.' *The Daily Telegraph.* 26 October.

Little, G. (1999) 'Student forum provides ownership.' *Connect,* June, 117.

Livingstone, S. and Bovill, M. (2001) 'Families and the internet: An observational study of children and young people's internet use.' *Report for R Texact Technologies.* Suffolk, UK.

Luhmann, N. (1998) *Essays on Self-reference.* New York: Columbia University Press.

Mac An Ghaill, M. (1994) *The Making of Men: Masculinities, Sexualities and Schooling.* Buckingham: Open University Press.

Mackay, M. (2001) *Through a Child's Eyes. Child-inclusive Practice in Family Relationship Services. A Report from the Child-inclusive Practice Forums.* Canberra: Human Development Consulting.

Mackay, R.W. (1974) 'Conceptions of children and models of socialization.' In R. Turner (ed.) *Ethnomethodology: Selected Readings.* Harmondsworth: Penguin Education.

MacKinnon, L. (1998) *Trust and Betrayal in the Treatment of Child Abuse.* New York: Guildford Press.

Macnaughten, P. (1993) 'Discourses of nature: argumentation and power.' In E. Burman and I. Parker *Discourse Analytic Research.* London: Routledge.

Maher, F.A. and Tetreault, M.K. (1994) *The Feminist Classroom.* New York: Basic Books.

Makrinotti, D. (1994) 'Conceptualization of childhood in a welfare state: A critical reappraisal.' In J. Qvortrup, M. Bardy, G. Sgritta and H. Wintersberger (eds) *Childhood Matters. Social Theory, Practice and Politics.* England: Avebury.

Marshall, B.L. (1994) *Engendering Modernity. Feminism, Social Theory and Social Change.* Cambridge: Polity Press.

Mason, J. (ed.) (1993) *Child Welfare Policy: Critical Australian Perspectives.* Sydney: Hale and Iremonger.

Mason, J. and Falloon, J. (1999) 'A children's perspective on child abuse.' *Children Australia 24*, 3, 9–13.

Mason, J. and Falloon, J. (2001) 'Some children define abuse: Implications for agency in childhood.' In L. Alanen and B. Mayall (eds) *Conceptualizing Child–Adult Relations.* London: RoutledgeFalmer.

Mason, J. and Gibson, C. (2004) *The Needs of Children in Care. A Report on a Research Project.* Sydney: SJSC, University of Western Sydney and Uniting Care, Burnside. Available from www.uws.edu.au/sjse

Mason, J. and Noble-Spruell, C. (1993) 'Child protection policy in New South Wales: A critical analysis.' In J. Mason (ed.) *Child Welfare Policy: Critical Australian Perspectives.* Sydney: Hale and Iremonger.

Mason, J. and Wilkinson, M. (eds) (1999) *Taking Children Seriously, Proceedings of a National Workshop.* Campbelltown, University of Western Sydney: CYPRU.

Matthews, J.J. (1984) *Good and Mad Women.* London – Sydney – Boston: George Allen and Unwin.

Mayall, B. (1994a) 'Children in action at home and at school.' In B. Mayall (ed) *Children's Childhoods: Observed and Experienced.* London: Falmer Press.

Mayall, B. (1994b) 'Introduction.' In B. Mayall (ed.) *Children's Childhoods: Observed and Experienced.* London: Falmer Press.

Mayall, B. (1996) *Children, Health and the Social Order.* Buckingham: Open University Press.

Mayall, B. (1999) 'Children and childhood.' In S. Hood, B. Mayall and S. Oliver (eds) *Critical Issues in Social Research.* Buckingham: Open University Press.

Mayall, B. (2002) *Towards a Sociology for Childhood: Thinking from Children's Lives.* Buckingham and Philadelphia: Open University Press.

Mayall, B. (2003) *Sociologies of Childhood and Educational Thinking.* London: Institute of Education, University of London.

Maynard, D. (1985) 'On the functions of social conflict among children.' *American Sociological Review 50,* April, 207–223.

Maynard, M. (1998) 'Feminists' knowledge and the knowledge of feminisms: epistemology, theory, methodology and method.' In T. May and M. Williams (eds) *Knowing the Social World.* Buckingham: Open University Press.

McCadden, B.M. (1998) *It's Hard to be Good: Moral Complexity, Construction, and Connection in a Kindergarten Classroom.* New York: Peter Lang.

McGillivray, A. (ed.) (1997) *Governing Childhood.* Aldershot: Dartmouth Publishing Co.

McIlveen, L. (2001) 'Rod not spared in discipline rethink.' *The Australian.* 4 April.

McMackin, M.C., DeCola, C., Galligani, G. and Foley, J. (1998) 'Learning deliberately about portfolio assessment.' *Educational Action Research 6,* 3, 413–426.

McNeish, D. and Newman, T. (2002) 'Last words: the views of young people.' In D. McNeish, T. Newman and H. Roberts (eds) *What Works for Children? Effective Services for Children and Families.* Buckingham: Open University Press.

Mehan, H. (1979) *Learning Lessons: Social Organization in the Classroom.* Cambridge, MA: Harvard University Press.

Mehan, H. (1993) 'Why I like to look: On the use of videotape as an instrument in educational research.' In M. Schratz (ed.) *Qualitative Voices in Educational Research.* London: Falmer Press.

Mellor, S. (1998a) *'What's the Point?'* *Political Attitudes of Victorian Year 11 Students, Research Monograph No 53.* Melbourne: ACER Press.

Mellor, S. (1998b) 'Student cynicism about political participation: "What's the point?" – What can schools do?' *Connect.* June, 111.

Meltzoff, A. and Moore, M. (1991) 'Cognitive foundations and social foundations of imitation, and intermodal representation in infancy.' In M. Woodhead, R. Carr and P. Light (eds) *Becoming a Person.* London: Routledge.

Merleau-Ponty, M. (1962) *Phenomenology of Perception.* London: Routledge and Kegan Paul.

Merleau-Ponty, M. (1964) *The Primacy of Perception, and Other Essays on Phenomenological Psychology, The Philosophy of Art, History and Politics.* Evanston: Northwestern University Press.

Meyer, M. (2001) Family decision making and its application to child sexual abuse. Paper presented at the *8th Australian Conference on Child Abuse and Neglect,* 19–22 November, Melbourne.

Miljeteig(-Olssen), P. (1992) 'Children's participation: Giving children the opportunity to develop into active and responsible members of society.' *Social Education 56,* 4, 4.

Miljeteig, P. (1994) Children's involvement in the implementation of their own rights – present and future perspectives. Paper presented at *International Society for the Study of Behavioral Development; XIIIth Biennial Meetings,* 28 June–2 July, Amsterdam, The Netherlands.

Miljeteig, P. (1999) 'Understanding child labour.' *Childhood 6,* 1, 5–12.

Miljeteig, P. (2000) 'Creating partnerships with working children and youth.' *Social Protection Discussion Paper No. 21.* Washington, DC: The World Bank.

Miller, A. (1997) *Breaking down the Wall of Silence to Join the Waiting Child.* (Revised edn). London: Virago Press.

Minichiello, V., Aroni, R., Timewell, E. and Alexander, L. (1990) *In Depth Interviewing, Researching People.* Melbourne: Longman Cheshire.

Mission Australia (2003) Mission Australia Youth Survey Results [online]. Available from: www.mission.com.au/cm/Resources/SocialPolicyDocs/SPR02_Youth%20Survey [Accessed 13 January 2004].

Mizen, P., Pole, C. and Bolton, A. (eds) (2001) *Hidden Hands: International Perspectives on Children's Work and Labour.* London and New York: RoutledgeFalmer.

Moir, J. (1993) 'Occupational career choice: Accounts and contradictions.' In E. Burman and I. Parker *Discourse Analytic Research.* London: Routledge.

Montandon, C. (2001) 'The negotiation of influence: Children's experience of parental education practices in Geneva.' In L. Alanen and B. Mayall (eds) *Conceptualizing Child–adult Relations.* London and New York: RoutledgeFalmer.

Moore, H. (1994) *A Passion for Difference.* Cambridge: Polity Press.

Morrell, S. (1999) 'No more smacking.' *Herald Sun.* 14 June.

Morrow, V. (1994) 'Responsible children? Aspects of children's work and employment outside school in contemporary UK.' In B. Mayall (ed.) *Children's Childhoods: Observed and Experienced.* London: Falmer Press.

Mukherjee, D., Stokes, H. and Holdsworth, R. (1997) *The Nature of Health Service–School Links in Australia.* Sydney: Australian Health Promoting Schools Association.

Mumtaz, S. (2001) 'Children's enjoyment and perception of computer use in the home and the school.' *Computers and Education 36,* 347–362.

National Center for Education Statistics (2000) *Trends in Educational Equity of Girls and Women.* Washington, DC: US Department of Education, Office of Educational Research and Improvement.

New South Wales Commission for Children and Young People (2000) *A Report of an Inquiry into the Best Means of Assisting Children and Young People with No One to Turn to.* [online] Sydney: NSW Commission for Children and Young People. Available from: www.kids.nsw.gov.au/files/inquiryreportchap5.pdf

New South Wales Commission for Children and Young People (2001) *Taking Participation Seriously. A Practical Guide to Helping Children and Young People Take Part in Decision Making.* Sydney: New South Wales Commission for Children and Young People.

Newell, P. (1994) 'Putting an end to physical punishment.' *Children Australia 19,* 4, 44–48.

Nicholson, L. (1990) 'Introduction.' In Linda Nicholson (ed.) *Feminism/Postmodernism.* London, New York: Routledge.

Nobes, G. and Smith, M. (1997) 'Physical punishment of children in two-parent families.' *Clinical Child Psychology and Psychiatry 2,* 2, 271–281.

Oakley, A. (1994) 'Women and children first and last: Parallels and differences between children's and women's studies.' In B. Mayall (ed.) *Children's Childhoods Observed and Experienced.* London: Falmer Press.

Okin, S. and Reich, R. (1999) 'Families and schools as compensating agents in moral development for a multicultural society.' *Journal of Moral Education 28,* 283–298.

Olson, D.S. and Bruner, J. (1996) 'Folk psychology and folk pedagogy.' In D. Olson and N. Torrance (eds) *Handbook of Education and Development: New Models of Learning, Teaching and Schooling.* Malden, MA: Blackwell.

O'Neill, J. (1973) 'Embodiment and child development: A phenomenological approach.' In H.P. Dreitzel (ed.) *Childhood and Socialisation: Recent Sociology Number 5.* New York: Macmillan.

Osman, N. (1999) *Primary Children's Views of Schools.* Honours thesis. Honours thesis. University of Western Sydney, Australia.

Osmotherly, J. (1998) 'Wangaratta district youth participation.' *Connect* August, 112.

Owen, D. (1996) 'Dilemmas and opportunities for the young active citizen.' *Youth Studies Australia 15,* 1, March, 20–23.

Owen, J. (1996) *Every Childhood Lasts a Lifetime.* Australia: Australian Association of Young People in Care.

Palincsar, A.S. (1998) 'Social constructivist perspectives on teaching and learning.' *Annual Review of Psychology 49,* 345–375.

Palmérus, K. (1999) 'Self-reported discipline among Swedish parents of preschool children.' *Infant and Child Development 8,* 155–171.

Parton, N., Thorpe, D. and Wattam, C. (1997) *Child Protection: Risk and the Moral Order.* London: Macmillan Press Ltd.

Patton, C. (1995) 'Between innocence and safety: Epidemiologic and popular constructions of young people's need for safe sex.' In J. Terry and J. Urla (eds) *Deviant Bodies: Critical Perspectives on Difference in Science and Popular Culture.* Bloomington: Indiana University Press.

Pearl, A. and Knight, T. (1999) *The Democratic Classroom: Theory to Practice Guide.* New Jersey: Hampton Press.

Pearl, A., Grant, D. and Wenk, E. (eds) (1978) *The Value of Youth.* California: Responsible Action, Davis.

Plummer, K. (1990) 'Understanding childhood sexualities.' *Journal of Homosexuality 20,* 1–2, 231–249.

Pomerantz, A. (1984) 'Agreeing and disagreeing with assessments: Some features of preferred/dispreferred turn shapes.' In J.M. Atkinson and J. Heritage (eds) *Structures of Social Action: Studies in Conversation Analysis.* Cambridge: Cambridge University Press.

Pomerantz, A. and Fehr, B.J. (1997) 'Conversation analysis: An approach to the study of social action as sense making practices.' In T.A. van Dijk (ed.) *Discourse as Social Action: Discourse Studies: A Multidisciplinary Introduction Volume 2.* London: Sage.

Postscript (1999) *Herald Sun.* 12 June.

Pringle, K. (1998) *Children and Social Welfare in Europe.* Buckingham and Philadelphia: Open University Press.

Prout, A. (2002) 'Researching children as social actors: An introduction to the Children 5–16 Programme.' *Children and Society 16,* 2, 67–76.

Prout, A. and James, A. (1990) 'A new paradigm for the sociology of childhood? Provenance, promise and problems.' In A. James and A. Prout (eds) *Constructing and Reconstructing Childhood: Contemporary Issues in the Sociological Study of Childhood.* London: Falmer Press.

Prout, A. and James, A. (1997) 'A new paradigm for the sociology of childhood? Provenance, promise and problems.' In A. James and A. Prout (eds) *Constructing and Reconstructing Childhood: Contemporary Issues in the Sociological Study of Childhood.* (2nd edn). London: Falmer Press.

Psathas, G. (1995) *Conversation Analysis: The Study of Talk-in-Interaction (Vol. 35).* Thousand Oaks, CA: Sage.

Putnam, R.D. (2000) *Bowling Alone: The Collapse and Revival of American Community.* New York: Simon and Schuster.

Putnam, R.D. (2001) 'Social capital: measurement and consequences.' *ISUMA – Canadian Journal of Policy Research* Spring, 41–51.

'Qld's foster care condemned.' *Sydney Morning Herald* (15 December) [online]. Available from: http://www.gaiaguys.net/vic.qldchlsdcaresmh16.12.0.htm

Qvortrup, J. (1985) 'Placing children in the division of labour.' In P. Close and R. Collins (eds) *Family and Economy in Modern Society.* London: Macmillan.

Qvortrup, J. (1990) 'Childhood as a social phenomenon – An introduction to a series of national reports.' *Eurosocial Report 36/1990.* Vienna: European Centre.

Qvortrup, J. (1993) 'Children at risk or childhood at risk: A plea for a politics of childhood.' In P. Heilio, E. Lauronen and M. Bardy *Politics of Childhood and Children at Risk.* Vienna: European Centre for Social Welfare Policy and Research.

Qvortrup, J. (1994) 'Introduction.' In J. Qvortrup, M. Bardy, G. Sgritta and H. Wintersberger (eds) *Childhood Matters: Social Theory, Practice and Politics.* Aldershot: Avebury.

Qvortrup, J., Bardy, M., Sgritta, G. and Wintersberger, E. (eds) (1994) *Childhood Matters, Social Theory, Practice and Politics.* Avebury: Aldershot.

Ramsland, J. (1986) *Children of the Backlanes. Destitute and Neglected Children in Colonial New South Wales.* New South Wales: New South Wales University Press.

Reed, P. (undated) *The Stolen Generations: The Removal of Aboriginal Children in NSW 1883 to 1969.* NSW Ministry of Aboriginal Affairs. New South Wales Family and Children's Services Agency.

Rees, S. and Rodley, G. (eds) (1995) *The Human Costs of Managerialism· Advocating the Recovery of Humanity.* Sydney: Pluto Press.

Rich, A. (1980) 'Compulsory heterosexuality and lesbian existence.' *Signs: Journal of Women in Culture and Society 5,* 4, 631–660.

Rimmerman, C. (2001) *The New Citizenship: Unconventional Politics, Activism and Service.* Boulder, CO: Westview Press.

Roberts, D. (1999) 'Poverty, race and new directions in child welfare policy.' *Journal of Law and Policy 1,* 63.

Robinson, K.H. (2002) 'Making the invisible visible: Gay and lesbian issues in early childhood education.' *Contemporary Issues in Early Childhood 3,* 3, 415–434.

Robinson, K.H. and Ferfolja, T. (2001) '"What are we doing this for?" Dealing with lesbian and gay issues in teacher education.' *British Journal of Sociology of Education 22,* 1, 121–134.

Robinson, K.H. and Jones-Diaz, C. (1999) 'Doing theory with early childhood educators: Understanding difference and diversity in personal and professional contexts.' *Australian Journal of Early Childhood 24,* 4, 33–39.

Robinson, K.H. and Jones-Diaz, C. (2000) *Diversity and Difference in Early Childhood: An Investigation into Centre Policies, Staff Attitudes and Practices. A Focus on Long Day Care and Preschool in the South West and Inner West Sydney Regions.* Newcastle: Roger A. Baxter, OAS Engineering Pty Ltd and The University of Newcastle Research Associates.

Roche, J. (1999) 'Children: Rights, participation and citizenship.' *Childhood 6,* 4, 475–493.

Rose, N. (1985) *The Psychological Complex: Psychology, Politics and Society in England 1869–1939.* London: Routledge and Kegan Paul.

Ross, N. (2002) 'Child-killing bully jailed for six years.' *Herald Sun.* 17 December.

Rudduck, J. and Flutter, J. (2000) 'Pupil participation and pupil perspective: "Carving a new order of experience".' *Cambridge Journal of Education 30,* 75–89.

Ryave, L. and Schenkein, J.N. (1974) 'Notes on the art of walking.' In R. Turner (ed.) *Ethno methodology: Selected Readings.* Harmondsworth: Penguin Education.

Sacks, H. (1974) 'On the analysability of stories by children.' In R. Turner (ed.) *Ethno methodology: Selected Readings*. Harmondsworth: Penguin.

Sacks, H. (1984) 'Notes on methodology.' In J.M. Atkinson and J. Heritage (eds) *Structures of Social Action: Studies in Conversation Analysis*. Cambridge: Cambridge University Press.

Sacks, H. (1992/95) Jefferson, G. (ed.) *Lectures on Conversation (Vol. I and II)*. Oxford UK: Blackwell.

Sanz, A. (1997) 'From Kundapur to Geneva. The international coordination of working Children.' *NATs Working Children and Adolescents International Review 3*, 3–4, 11–23.

Saunders, B.J. and Goddard, C.R. (1998) 'Why do we condone the "physical punishment" of children?' *Children Australia 23*, 3, 23–28.

Saunders, B.J. and Goddard, C.R. (1999a) *Why do we Condone the Physical Assault of Children by their Parents and Caregivers?* Melbourne, Monash University: Child Abuse and Family Violence Research Unit.

Saunders, B.J. and Goddard C. (1999b) 'Why is beating children condoned as physical discipline?' In *7th Australasian Conference on Child Abuse and Neglect, Proceedings – Volume 1*. Canning Bridge, Western Australia: Promaco Conventions.

Saunders, B.J. and Goddard C. (1999c) '"Physical discipline", child abuse and children's rights: A contribution to the debate.' In J. Mason and M. Wilkinson (eds) *Taking Children Seriously. Proceedings of a National Workshop*. Campelltown, University of Western Sydney: CYPRU.

Saunders, B.J. and Goddard, C.R. (2001) 'The textual abuse of childhood in the English-speaking world – The contribution of language to the denial of children's rights.' *Childhood: A Global Journal of Child Research 8*, 4, 443–462.

Saunders, B.J. and Goddard, C. (2003a) 'Parents' use of physical discipline: The thoughts, feelings and words of Australian children.' Paper presented at the *Ninth Australasian Conference on Child Abuse and Neglect*, 26 November, Sydney, Australia. Available from: www.nsw.gov.au/accan 2003

Saunders, B.J. and Goddard, C. (2003b) 'The role of mass media in facilitating community education and child abuse prevention strategies.' *Child Abuse Prevention Issues 16*, 1–22.

Saunders, B.J. (in preparation) *Parallel stories: Childhood reflected in parenthood and mirrored in the next generation – An exploratory study of intergenerational and professional views about parental discipline in the form of physical punishment*. Thesis (PhD). Monash University.

Save the Children (1995) *Towards a Children's Agenda: New Challenges for Social Development*. London: Save the Children.

Schneiderman, M., Connors, M., Fribourg, A., Gries, L. and Gonzales, M. (1998) 'Mental Health Services for children in out-of-home care.' *Child Welfare LXXVII*, 1, Jan/Feb.

Schnell, R.L. (1979) 'Childhood as ideology: A reinterpretation of the common school.' *British Journal of Educational Studies 27*, 1.

Schofield, G. and Thorburn, J. (1996) *Child Protection: The Voice of the Child in Decision Making*. London: IPPR Publications.

Scutt, N. (1995) 'Child Advocacy.' In C. Cloke and M. Davies (eds) *Participation and Empowerment in Child Protection*. Wiltshire: John Wiley and Sons.

Sedgwick, E. (1998) 'How to bring your kids up gay.' In H. Jenkins (ed.) *The Children's Culture Reader.* New York: New York University Press.

Semmens, R. and Stokes, H. (1997) 'Full service schooling for full citizenship: From theory to practice.' *Melbourne Studies in Education 38*, 2, November.

Sercombe, H. (1995) 'The face of the criminal is Aboriginal: Representations of Aboriginal young people in the West Australian newspaper.' In J. Bessant, K. Carrington and S. Cook *The Australian Experience. A special edition of the Journal of Australian Studies 43*, 76–94, 95.

Shemmings, D. (1996) 'Involving children in child protection conferences.' *Social Work Monographs* 152, UK: University of East Anglia.

Shields, M.K. and Behrman, R.E. (2000) 'Children and computer technology: Analysis and recommendations.' *The Future of Children 10*, 2, 4–30.

Silverman, D. (1994) 'Competing strategies for analysing the contexts of social interaction.' *Sociological Inquiry 64*, 179–198.

Silverman, D. (1998) *Harvey Sacks: Social Science and Conversation Analysis.* New York: Oxford University Press.

Silverman, D., Baker, C.D. and Keogh, J. (1998) 'The case of the silent child: Advice-giving and advice-reception in parent-teacher interviews.' In I. Hutchby and J. Moran-Ellis (eds) *Children and Social Competence: Arenas of Action.* London: Falmer Press.

Skawinski, S.F. and Thibodeau, S.J. (2002) 'A journey into portfolio assessment.' *Kappa Delta Pi*, Fall, *67*, 1, 81–91.

Smith, Dorothy E. (1988) *The Everyday World as Problematic. A Feminist Sociology.* Milton Keynes: Open University Press.

Smith, Dorothy E. (1989) 'Sociological theory: Methods of writing patriarchy.' In Ruth A. Wallace (ed.) *Feminism and Sociological Theory.* Newbury Park: SAGE.

Smith, Dorothy E. (1990a) *Texts, Facts and Femininity.* London – New York: Routledge.

Smith, Dorothy E. (1990b) *The Conceptual Practices of Power.* Boston: North Eastern University Press.

Smith, M. (1995) 'A community study of physical violence to children in the home and associated variables.' In F.C. Gulbenkian *Children and Violence: Report of the Gulbenkian Foundation.* London: Calouste Gulbenkian Foundation.

Sockett, H. and LePage, P. (2002) 'The missing language in the classroom.' *Teacher and Teacher Education 18*, 159–171.

Speier, M. (1976a) 'The adult ideological viewpoint in studies of childhood.' In A. Skolnick (ed.) *Rethinking Childhood: Perspectives on Development and Society.* Boston – Toronto: Little, Brown and Co.

Speier, M. (1976b) 'The child as conversationalist: Some culture contact features of conversational interactions between adults and children.' In M. Hammersley and P. Woods (eds) *The Process of Schooling: A Sociological Reader.* London: Routledge and Kegan Paul.

Speier, M. (1982) 'The everyday world of the child.' In C. Jenks (ed.) *The Sociology of Childhood: Essential Readings.* Aldershot: Gregg Revivals.

Stacey, M. (1981) 'The division of labour revisited, or overcoming the two Adams.' In P. Abrams *et al.* (eds) *Development and Diversity: British Sociology, 1950–1980*. London: George and Allen.

Stafford, A., Laybourn, A. and Hill, M. (2003) '"Having a Say": Children and young people talk about consultation.' Department of Social Policy and Social Work, University of Glasgow, Department of Applied Social Science, University of Stirling, *Children and Society* 17, 361–371.

Stafseng, O. (1993) 'A sociology of childhood and youth: The need of both?' In J. Qvortrup (ed.) *Childhood as a Social Phenomenon: Lessons from an International Project: Eurosocial Report 47/1993*. Vienna: European Centre.

Standing Committee on Law and Justice (2000) *Report on the inquiry into the Crimes Amendment (Child Protection – Excessive Punishment) Bill 2000*. New South Wales: Parliamentary Paper, No. 461, Report 15.

Stein, T. (1991) *Child Welfare and the Law*. New York: Longman.

Stokes, H. and Tyler, D. (1997) *Rethinking Interagency Collaboration and Young People*. Melbourne: Language Australia and the Youth Research Centre.

Straus, M. (1994) *Beating the Devil Out of Them*. New York: Lexton Books.

Subrahmanyam, K., Kraut, R.E., Greenfield, P.M. and Gross, E.F. (2000) 'The Impact of home computer use on children's activities and development.' *The Future of Children 10*, 2, 123–144.

Summary of the 404th meeting: Australia. 22 December 1997. CRC/C/SR.404. (Summary Record). Available from: http://www.unhchr.ch/

Sutherland, R., Facer, K., Furlong, R. and Furlong, J. (2000) 'A new environment for education? The computer in the home.' *Computers and Education 34*, 195–212.

Swift, A. (1999) *Working Children Get Organized. An Introduction to Working Children's Organizations*. London: International Save the Children Alliance.

Taipale, V. (1993) 'Preface.' In P. Heilio, E. Lauronen and M. Bardy *Politics of Childhood and Children at Risk*. Vienna: European Centre for Social Welfare Policy and Research.

Tate, T. (1992) 'The child pornography industry: International trade in child sexual abuse.' In I. Itzin (ed.) *Pornography: Women, Violence and Civil Liberties. A Radical New View*. New York: Oxford University Press.

Therborn, G. (1996) 'Child politics: Dimensions and perspectives.' *Childhood 3*, 1, 29–44.

Thomas, N. (2000) *Children, Family and the State: Decision-making and Child Participation*. UK: Macmillan Press.

Thomson, R. and Holland, J. (2002) 'Young people, social change and the negotiation of moral authority.' *Children and Society 16*, 2, 103–15.

Thorne, B. (1987) 'Re-visioning women and social change: Where are the children?' *Gender and Society 1*, 1, 85–109.

Thorne, B. (1993) *Gender Play: Girls and Boys in School*. Open University Press, Buckingham.

Thorpe, D. (1994) *Evaluating Child Protection*. Buckingham: Open University Press.

Titelius, R. and Dolan, S. (1999) 'JAIL for letting dogs die; FREE for bashing a child.' *Herald Sun*. 18 February.

Tolfree, D. (1998) *Old Enough To Work, Old Enough To Have A Say.* Stockholm: Rädda Barnen.

Torres, N. (1994) 'Working children, leading the struggle to obtain and defend their own Rights.' In E. Verhellen and F. Spiesschaert (eds) *Children's Rights: Monitoring Issues.* Gent: Mys and Breesch Publishers.

Treseder, P. (1997) 'Involving and empowering children and young people: Overcoming the barriers.' In C. Cloke and M. Davies (eds) *Participation and Empowerment in Child Protection.* Wiltshire: John Wiley and Sons.

Tucker, S. (1997) 'Youth working: Professional identities given, received or contested?' In J. Roche and S. Tucker *Youth in Society.* London: Sage Publications.

UN (1989) *Convention on the Rights of the Child,* UN Document A/44/25.

UN (1990) *Convention on the Rights of the Child.* New York: United Nations.

UNICEF (2002) 'UN Special Session on Children.' *Newsletter* 5, Oct. New York: UNICEF.

UNICEF (2004) 'United Nations Special Session on Children.' [online] Available from: http://www.unicef.org/specialsession/wffc/index.html

Van Beuren, G. (ed.) (1993) *International Documents on Children.* Dordecht: Martinus Nijhoff.

Van Dijk, T.A. (1987) *Communicating Racism. Ethnic Prejudice in Thought and Talk.* London: Sage Publications.

van Krieken, R. (1992) *Children and the State: Social Control and the Formation of Australian Child Welfare.* Sydney: Allen and Unwin.

Waksler, F.C. (1986) 'Studying children: Phenomenological insights.' *Human Studies 9,* 1.

Waksler, F.C. (1991a) *Studying The Social Worlds of Children: Sociological Readings.* London: Falmer Press.

Waksler, F.C. (1991b) 'Studying children: Phenomenological insights.' In F.C. Waksler (ed.) *Studying the Social Worlds of Children: Sociological Readings.* London: Falmer Press.

Waksler, F.C. (1996) *The Little Trials of Childhood and Children's Strategies for Dealing With Them.* London: Falmer Press.

Wallis, A. and VanEvery, J. (2000) 'Sexuality in the Primary School.' *Sexualities 3,* 4, 409–423.

Wartofsky, M. (1983) 'The child's construction of the world and the world's construction of the child: From historical epistemology to historical psychology.' In F.S. Kessel and A.W. Siegel (eds) *The Child and Other Cultural Inventions.* New York: Praeger.

Webber, R. (1998) 'Voices of authority: Press reports about "problematic young people".' *Just Policy,* 14, 32–40.

Weeks, J. (1986) *Sexuality.* London: Routledge.

West, A. (1997) 'Children and Political Participation.' In E. Verhellen (ed.) *Understanding Children's Rights. Ghent Papers on Children's Rights – No 2.* Ghent: Children's Rights Centre, University of Ghent.

Wilkinson, M. (1999) *From neglected to protected? Child welfare in New South Wales: 1945–1988.* Thesis (PhD). University of Sydney: unpublished.

Williamson, A. (1995) 'Students' perceptions of their empowerment at High School.' *Journal of the Australian College of Education 21,* 3, 51–63.

Willow, C. and Hyder, T. (1998) *It Hurts You Inside: Children Talking about Smacking.* London: National Children's Bureau Enterprises.

Wilson, K. and Bell, M. (2003) 'Ask the family.' *Community Care 27*, February, 5.

Wolfenstein, M. (1998) 'Fun morality: An analysis of recent American child-training literature.' In H. Jenkins (ed.) *The Children's Culture Reader.* New York: New York University Press.

Woodhead, M. (1998) *Children's Perspectives on Their Working Lives. A Participatory Study in Bangladesh, Ethiopia, the Philippines, Guatemala, El Salvador and Nicaragua.* Stockholm: Rädda Barnen.

Woodhead, M. (1999) 'Combatting child labour. Listen to what the children say.' *Childhood 6*, 1, 27–49.

Woodward, H. (1989) *An examination of the correlation between one school's stated policies in literacy teaching and evaluation and the teaching and evaluation practices in that school.* Honours dissertation. University of Wollongong, unpublished.

Woodward, H. (1993) *Negotiated Evaluation.* Newtown: Primary English Teaching Association.

Woodward, H. (1997) 'Developing observation skills through co-researching.' In *Australian Literacy in Education Association Conference*, July, Darwin.

Woodward, H. (2001) 'Time to assess: "Time to achieve".' *Classroom* Issue 3 2001. Mona Vale: Scholastic.

Woodward, H. and Munns, G. (2004) *Insiders' Voices: Self-assessment and Student Engagement.* Paper presented at Bergin EARLI Conference, June.

Woodward, H. and Munns, G. (forthcoming) 'Self assessment ways to become a classroom insider.' *Assessment in Education Policies and Practice* (special issue on assessment developments in the Asia-Pacific region).

Wyn, J. (1995) 'Youth and citizenship.' *Melbourne Studies in Education 36*, 2, 45–63.

Wyse D. (2001) 'Felt tip pens and school councils: Children's participation rights in four English schools.' Liverpool John Moores University: *Children and Society 15*, 209–218.

Yeatman, A. (1990) *Bureaucrats, Technocrats, Femocrats: Essays on the Contemporary Australian State.* Sydney: Allen and Unwin.

Zelizer, V.A. Rotman (1985) *Pricing the Priceless Child: The Changing Social Value of Children.* New York: Basic Books.

The Contributors

Leena Alanen is a sociologist and professor at the Department of Early Childhood Education, University of Jyväskylä, Finland. Leena was the Finnish representative on the international programme 'Childhood as a Social Phenomenon' (1987–92) and the foundation President to the Research Committee, Sociology of Childhood International Sociological Association. She has published research in Finnish, Swedish, German and English, including a recent English publication, co-edited with Berry Mayall *Conceptualizing Child–Adult Relations* (RoutledgeFalmer 2001).

Carolyn D. Baker, who died in 2003, was formerly an associate professor at the School of Education, University of Queensland. Carolyn's work drew on ethnomethodology to closely study social interaction, a special interest being adult–child talk.

Donna Berthelsen is a principal researcher in the Centre for Innovation in Education at Queensland University of Technology. Her research interests centre on the social inclusion of children in early-childhood education and care programmes and the epistemological beliefs of early-childhood teachers about their practices. She has taught in primary and special-education settings, and has extensive academic teaching experience in Australia and Singapore – with a teaching focus on child development in context and early educational practice that engages families and communities.

Natalie Bolzan is a Senior lecturer in the School of Applied Social and Human Sciences, University of Western Sydney, and a member of the Social Justice and Social Change Research Centre. Her research is concerned with exploring the ways in which marginalized groups (such as the young or those with mental illnesses) are able to resist or alter their marginalized status and achieve agency. She is particularly interested in methodologies that seek to engage young people in research that concerns them.

Susan Danby is Senior Lecturer in the School of Early Childhood at Queensland University of Technology. Her expertise is in using ethnomethodological approaches to investigate the everyday social and interactional practices of children and young people. Her most recent research projects investigate children's troubles talk on a national children's helpline and young children's governance in their everyday lives.

Toni Downes is the Head of School of Education and Early Childhood Studies at the University of Western Sydney. Her research projects and consultancies focus on quality leadership and technology, the investigation of the educational use of the Internet, young people's views about the use of computers in homes and schools, and the changing nature of literacies in new learning environments. Most recently, her focus has been on working at the national and international level in policy research in regard to teacher learning for the effective use of Information and Communication Technologies (ICTs) for teaching and learning in schools.

Toby Fattore is a researcher at the New South Wales Commission for Children and Young People. His research focuses on children's understandings of well-being, the paid and unpaid work of children and the political location of childhood in Australia. He has published in areas of child fatality and child-protection and managerial practice.

Chris Goddard is Professor and Head of Social Work in the Faculty of Medicine, Nursing and Health Sciences and Interim Director of the National Research Centre for the Prevention of Child Abuse at Monash University. He has published widely in the areas of child abuse, family violence and child protection, and writes regularly for the media on issues concerning children's rights. His most recent book (with Dr Janet Stanley) is *In the Firing Line: Violence and Power in Child Protection Work.* (Wiley 2002)

Roger Holdsworth is a senior research fellow at the Australian Youth Research Centre in the University of Melbourne. He has also been the editor and publisher of *Connect*, a journal supporting student participation, since late 1979; this is the focus of a strong and continuing interest in supporting curriculum and governance approaches in schools that enable students to have real roles of community value through their learning. (For full details of *Connect* refer to the references list).

Patricia Kiely is a clinical psychologist who has worked with families and children in the child-protection sector for over 30 years. She is currently the Manager of the Family Work Programme at Uniting Care Burnside in Sydney NSW Australia and has a private clinical practice. She has worked with Family Group Conferencing since 1996 and has undertaken a five-year longitudinal research project comparing the outcomes for families of family group conferencing with traditional case-planning processes.

Michele J. Leiminer is a doctoral candidate in the School of Education, University of Queensland. Her work draws on ethnography and ethnomethodological perspectives to explore the construction of stage of life and gender in child/youth–adult relationships in education and care settings.

Jan Mason is Professor of Social Work and Director of the Social Justice and Social Change Research Centre at the University of Western Sydney. She researches broadly in the area of social work as well as specifically in child welfare, having acquired in-depth knowledge of child welfare through involvement in practice, policy, and research in the area. She edited the book *Child Welfare Policy, Critical Australian Perspectives* (Hale and Iremonger 1993) and has been published in journals and edited books on child and family policy, childhood, child–adult relations and researching with children.

Berry Mayall is Professor of Childhood Studies at the Institute of Education, University of London. She has worked for over 30 years on empirical and theoretical studies of childhood and has contributed to the development of the sociology of childhood. Her most recent books are: *Towards a Sociology for Childhood: Thinking from Children's Lives* (Open University Press 2002); and *Childhood in Generational Perspective*, co-edited with Helga Zeiher (Institute of Education 2003).

Per Miljeteig is a psychologist and child rights consultant. He has been active in the international child rights discourse since 1984, working in various positions within government, in NGOs, within UNICEF and as Director of Childwatch International Research Network 1993–2001. He has lectured and published in several countries on issues related to the interpretation and implementation of the Convention on the Rights of the Child.

Neriman Osman completed a social work honours degree in 1999, then worked as a child protection officer for the NSW Department of Community Services. She is currently a project officer at the NSW Office of the Children's Guardian, which promotes the interests and rights of children and young people in out-of-home care. Her research interests are around the rights of children and young people in matters that affect them, and the facilitation of hearing their voices.

Kerry H. Robinson is a senior lecturer in the School of Education and Early Childhood Studies at the University of Western Sydney, where she teaches in sociology, cultural diversity and social-justice education. She has written and researched extensively on constructions of identity, especially in relation to gender and sexuality, with a particular focus on how these aspects of identity are constructed and played out in various educational contexts. Recently she co-edited a book titled *From Here to Diversity: The Social Impact of Lesbian and Gay Issues in Education in Australia and New Zealand* (Harrington Park Press 2002); and is currently co-authoring a book titled *Diversity and Difference in Early Childhood Education* to be published by the Open University Press.

Bernadette J. Saunders is a lecturer in social work at Monash University, and a researcher in the National Research Centre for the Prevention of Child Abuse. She has postgraduate qualifications in social work and education, and she has published on child-abuse risk assessment; language and children's rights; child abuse and the media; and the physical punishment of children. Her PhD research focuses on legally sanctioned physical punishment of children, children's rights, and the intergenerational transmission of family violence.

Chris Sidoti is Director of the International Service for Human Rights based in Geneva. He is also an adjunct professor at two Australian universities, the University of Western Sydney and Griffith University. He has been Australian Human Rights Commissioner (1995–2000) and Australian Law Reform Commissioner (1992–1995).

Nick Turnbull is a doctoral candidate in the School of Social Science and Policy at the University of New South Wales, Sydney, where he is investigating the philosophical foundations of policy theory. He has worked in the public sector and parliament, and published articles on public policy and rhetoric.

Marie Wilkinson, Bachelor of Social Work, Graduate Diploma of Education, Master of Social Work, Doctor of Philosophy, was for many years a child-protection worker with what is now the New South Wales Department of Community Services. For the last 11 years of her life she lectured in social policy and social work at the University of Sydney, where at the time of her death in 2003, she was Associate Dean of the Faculty of Arts. Her doctoral thesis entitled *From Neglected to Protected* (Wilkinson 1999) examined the political and administrative responses of the state of New South Wales to children in need of protection from 1945 to 1988.

Helen Woodward is an associate professor at the University of Western Sydney in the School of Education and Early Childhood Studies. The subject of assessment has been of both research and practical interest to her for some years. She has written one book on assessment, as well as having written articles and presented at conferences for national and international audiences. She has worked with educators across the world in establishing assessment programmes and strategies for students from primary school through to higher education.

Subject Index

Author Index